Business English in a Global Context

Best Practice

Intermediate

Bill Mascull and Jeremy Comfort

Coursebook

THOMSON

HEINLE

United Kingdom • United States • Australia • Canada • Mexico • Singapore • Spain

Contents

Best Practice is a business English series designed for both pre-work and in-work students. Its topic-based modules train students in the skills needed to communicate in the professional and personal sides of modern business life.

MODULE 1   PERFORMANCE

pages 4–25

This module looks at some of the factors that affect performance at work – job satisfaction, what motivates people, the incentives they receive, and how to get a balance between work and home life.

	Business Inputs	Language Work	Communication	Business across Cultures
1 Happiness at work	**Listening**: The happiest workers	**Grammar**: Comparisons	Talking about yourself	Understanding your own culture
2 Motivation	**Reading**: Theory X and Theory Y **Listening**: Employers' views on Theory X and Theory Y	**Expressions** to describe Theory X and Y work environments	Finding out about people	Understanding different types of culture
3 Incentives	**Reading**: SAS Institutes **Listening**: Discussing incentives and benefits	**Grammar**: First conditional	Building transparency in communication	Individuals and groups
4 Work and leisure	**Listening**: An interview with a 'work–life' balance expert	**Grammar**: Past simple and present perfect	Responding and developing communication	Women at work

Business Scenario 1   Improving morale

Review and Development 1–4

MODULE 2   INNOVATION

pages 26–47

This module deals with how companies and individuals create innovative products and try to enter new markets. It focuses on both the creative side of invention, and on the business challenges.

	Business Inputs	Language Work	Communication	Business across Cultures
5 Entrepreneurs	**Reading**: An article about entrepreneur Simon Woodroffe **Listening**: An interview about what makes a successful entrepreneur	**Expressions** to describe entrepreneurs	**Socialising 1**: Small Talk	Public and private space
6 Creativity	**Listening**: An interview with a trade consultant	**Grammar**: The future	**Socialising 2**: Positive Responses	The culture of organisations
7 Start-ups	**Listening**: A conversation about how to set up a business	**Grammar**: passives	**Meetings 1**: Running a meeting	Attitudes towards time
8 Inventions	**Listening**: An interview with the inventor, Mandy Haberman	**Grammar**: Past perfect and past simple	**Meetings 2**: Participating in meetings	Developing a culture of innovation

Business Scenario 2   Pitching for finance

Review and Development 5–8

1 Happiness at work

A **City & Guilds, an educational charity in the UK, gives these tips about being happy at work. Discuss them and add three more tips.**

- Start the day with a chat or gossip.
- Remember that every problem can be solved.
- Enrich your work environment with photos and flowers.
- Be positive.
- Have a laugh.

> The King of Bhutan says that the overall happiness of his people is more important than how rich they are.

🎧 1.1

A **Listen to the extracts and complete the table.**

Job	Speciality	What they like about the job
1 Lawyer	property law	meeting different clients
2 Fitness instructor		
3 Accountant		
4 Civil servant		

B **Listen again. Which speaker uses these adjectives?**

varied _3_   interesting ___   secure ___   well-paid ___

stressed ___   stimulating ___   rewarding ___   satisfying ___

C **With a partner, talk about what you like about your job or a job you would like to have.**

A **Look at the City & Guilds index of the happiest workers. Why do you think hairdressers are at the top and civil servants near the bottom?**

Position	Profession	%
1	Hairdressers	40
2	Clergy	24
3	_____	23
4	Beauticians	22
5	Plumbers	20
6	_____	20
7	Builders	20
8	Electricians	18
9	Florists	18
10	_____	18
11	Care assistants	18
12	Health care professionals	17
13	Media	16
14	Chartered engineers	15
15	Pharmacists	15

Position	Profession	%
16	Scientists/R&D scientists	15
17	Butchers	14
18	_____	13
19	Interior designers	9
20	Travel agents	9
21	Teachers	8
22	Bankers	8
23	_____	7
24	IT specialists	5
25	Lawyers	5
26	Secretaries/PAs	5
27	_____	4
28	Civil servants	3
29	Architects	2

B **Guess where these jobs go in the index, and say why. Then turn to page 128 to check your answers.**

mechanics   estate agents   fitness instructors   DJs   chefs / cooks   accountants

C **Can you see any patterns in the happiness index? For example, do the top five jobs and bottom five jobs have anything in common?**

Grammar

Comparisons

*Lawyers work **longer** hours **than** estate agents.*
*Hairdressers are **the happiest** workers.*

A **Complete the table.**

Type of adjective	Base form	Rule	Comparative	Superlative
One syllable	*long*	Add -er / est	longer	
Two syllables ending -y	*happy*	Change -y to -ier / iest		
Two or more syllables	*rewarding*	Put *more / the most* before the adjective		
Ending in -ed*	*stressed*	Add *more / the most*		
Irregular	*good* *bad*	~ ~		

*Adjectives ending in *-ed* refer to the people concerned, not to the work.

B **Complete the sentences using the words in the box. Use the comparative or superlative form.**

> noisy   long   fascinating   stressed   bad

1 Plumbers work _____longer_____ hours than DJs.
2 Lawyers are _____ than fitness instructors.
3 I worked in IT for three years but I hated it. It was _____ job I've ever had.
4 Builders have _____ working conditions than bankers.
5 I'm in R&D. I love developing new products. It's _____ work in the company.

C **Match the underlined phrases with their meanings (a–e).**

1 Hairdressers are <u>much</u> happier than teachers.   a equal to
2 Bankers are <u>as</u> happy <u>as</u> teachers.   b a little
3 DJs are <u>nearly</u> as happy as butchers.   c almost
4 Estate agents are <u>slightly</u> happier than civil servants. d not equal to
5 Pharmacists are <u>not as</u> happy <u>as</u> beauticians.   e a lot more

D **Using the happiness index, compare the jobs below. Use the patterns you practised in C.**

1 Beauticians / chefs   Beauticians are nearly as happy as chefs.
2 Scientists / pharmacists
3 Teachers / mechanics
4 IT specialists / estate agents
5 Hairdressers / civil servants

E **Now give possible reasons for some of the differences.**

Hairdressers are the happiest workers, perhaps because ...
A teacher's job is the most rewarding, but there are downsides, such as ...

F **With a partner, compare your own job, or a job you know, with another job.**

▶ Review and development page 22

▶ Grammar overview page 156

Communication

Talking about yourself

This section focuses on you as an individual. It helps you to develop your skills in introducing and talking about yourself.

🎧 1.2 **Ⓐ Listen to six people introducing themselves. What do they talk about? Match each speaker to one of the topics below.**

a job   b origins   c family   d interests

Ⓑ Work in pairs. Ask and answer questions to find out more about your partner. Use the Key language to help you.

Key language

	Question	Answer
Name	What's your name (first name / surname)?	My name's ... People call me / Everybody calls me ... (nickname / short name)
Job	What do you do? What's your job? What do you do for a living? Who do you work for? Where are you based? What business are you in?	I'm an engineer. I'm a teacher. I work in sales. I work for Digicom. I'm based in New York. I'm in IT / retail.
Origins	Where do you come from? Where were you born?	I come from Wisconsin / I'm from Ireland. I was born in Milwaukee. I was brought up in ...
Family	Are you married? Have you got any children?	I'm single / married / divorced / separated / widowed. No, but I live with my partner. Yes, I have four children.
Hobbies / Interests	What do you do outside work?	I play a lot of sport. I run a bit. I'm into vintage cars. My passion is ...

🎧 1.3 **Ⓒ In interviews, appraisals, and team-building sessions we often have to talk about ourselves. Listen to three people talk about their strengths and weaknesses. Match each speaker to one of the skills below.**

a people skills   b organisational skills   c communication skills

Ⓓ Work in small groups. Find out about each other's strengths and weaknesses. Use the Key language to help you.

Key language

	Strengths	Weaknesses
People skills	I usually get on well with my colleagues. I'm a team player.	I'm not so good at ... I'm rather bad at ... One of my weak points is ... I find it difficult to ...
Organisational skills	I'm well organised. I'm good at sorting things out. People tell me that I'm good at ...	
Communication skills	I'm a good listener. I think I communicate quite well.	

▶ Review and development page 25

▶ Communication page 150

Understanding your own culture

When working with people from different cultures, it is helpful to understand how they see your culture and what challenges they face when working with your culture. In the Communication section, we focused on you as an individual. In this section, we focus on the group, or culture, that you belong to.

Culture is like an iceberg. There are some aspects of culture which we can see easily above the surface, but there are many more below the surface.

A Brainstorm what culture means to you and put your ideas on the iceberg.

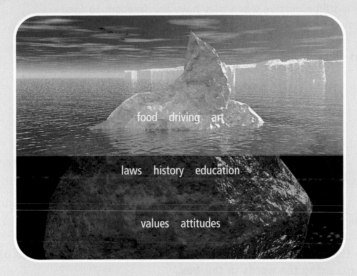

B Read what Sven Mansson, a Swedish manager, says about Sweden. He talks about five aspects of culture. Which of the following does he talk about?

| language | politics | food | music | geography |
| history | climate | industry | work | festivals |

Sweden is a big country – nearly 2,000 kilometres from north to south – and there are only nine million people in Sweden, so we have lots of space. Nobody needs to live close to each other. In winter, it's cold, especially in the north, where there is very little daylight. This makes us all worship the sun but it also seems to make us quite private people. We have learnt to be independent.

On the other hand, we have a long tradition of social democracy, and we believe in equality. This means that the differences between people in terms of their living standards are not very big. Of course, some people are richer than others, but our tax and social security system help to minimise the differences. Most people believe that the state should support all of us.

At the moment, we don't have very high unemployment. I would say that people in Sweden work hard, but we also value our free time. We like to leave work early in the summer and enjoy life outdoors. We have special days when we celebrate the light, like Midsummer and Santa Lucia.

C Write some notes about your country. Choose topics from B and add your own ideas.

▶ Business across cultures page 153

D Make comparisons between your country and another country you know or have visited. You could also compare regions within your country.

Checklist

✔ happiness at work: *satisfying, secure, stimulating ...* ✔ making comparisons: *more stressed than, the most rewarding ...* ✔ talking about yourself: *job, interests, strengths, weaknesses ...* ✔ understanding your own culture

2 Motivation

Start-up

A **Discuss these statements. Give reasons for your opinions.**

1 For the best results, managers should tell employees exactly what to do and how to do it.

2 Employees are more productive when they have the freedom to use their own ideas and make decisions.

> Companies spend millions every year trying to improve the motivation of their employees.

Reading and vocabulary

A **Match the nouns to their definitions.**

g 1 commitment   a when people decide what to do without being told

d 2 satisfaction   b the ability to think of good ideas

   3 responsibility   c when a manager tells an employee what to do and how to do it

f 4 initiative   d a good feeling you get when you have done something well

c 5 supervision   e when a manager tries to persuade an employee to do something

e 6 motivation   f the opportunity to make decisions

b 7 imagination   g the feeling of belonging to an organisation, causing you to work hard for it

a 8 encouragement   h the feeling of wanting or needing to do something

giving stimulus

B **Read about two theories proposed by Douglas McGregor in** *The Human Side of Enterprise.* **Complete the gaps using the words in the box.**

| satisfaction   commitment   supervision   initiative   responsibility |

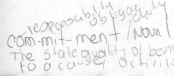

responsability obligaciuly
com-mit-ment /Noun/
The state quality of being dedicate.
to a cause/ activity etc.

THEORY X AND THEORY Y

Theory X says that people are lazy and need constant (1) <u>Supervision</u>. This means that managers have to monitor their employees closely to make sure that they work hard. According to Theory X, people don't want to make their own decisions so managers have to make them. Managers don't discuss decisions with employees – they just tell them what to do.

Theory Y says that people enjoy using their imagination and creativity to solve problems. This often means that they perform better and they get a lot of (2) _____ from working in this way. Employees are also given (3) _____ for their own projects. They use their own (4) <u>initiative</u> and don't have to consult their managers about everything they do. As a result, they feel a sense of (5) <u>respo</u>____ to the company and work harder. They feel that they are valued and that management appreciates the effort they make. All this contributes to a better sense of motivation among employees.

However, another theory, Theory W (not by McGregor), says that most work throughout human history has been done because people were forced to do it as slaves. (W stands for 'whiplash'.)

C **Form verbs from the nouns in A. Use a dictionary to help you, if necessary.**

commitment – to be committed to, to commit to

D **Go back to the answers you gave in the Start-up discussion. Have your ideas changed now that you have read about Theory X and Theory Y?**

Listening and speaking

2.1

A Listen to four managers and complete the table.

Which theory does each manager seem to prefer – Theory X or Theory Y?

	Organisation	Industry	Theory X or Theory Y?
1	Call centre		
2			
3			
4			

2.2 **B** Now listen to four employees. Which organisation in A do they work for?

C Listen to the employees again. Which speaker uses which expressions?

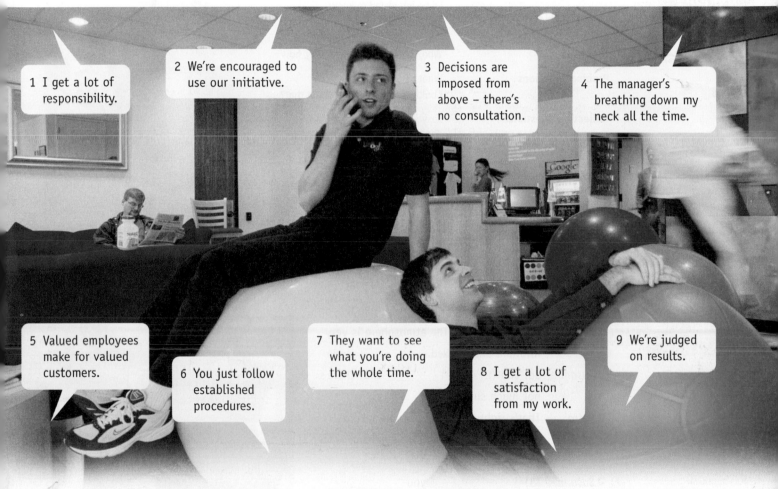

1 I get a lot of responsibility.

2 We're encouraged to use our initiative.

3 Decisions are imposed from above – there's no consultation.

4 The manager's breathing down my neck all the time.

5 Valued employees make for valued customers.

6 You just follow established procedures.

7 They want to see what you're doing the whole time.

8 I get a lot of satisfaction from my work.

9 We're judged on results.

D Look at the expressions in C. Which are more typical of Theory X organisations and which are more typical of Theory Y organisations?

E Work in pairs.

Student A: You are an employee who works under a manager who believes in Theory X.

Student B: You are an employee who works under a manager who believes in Theory Y.

Have a conversation about these topics in your respective organisations:

• working hours
• breaks
• initiative
• supervision
• working from home

▶ Review and development page 23

Communication

Finding out about people

Asking questions and responding to answers is the way that we find out about people. In business, we do this in many situations, including socialising and small talk.

 2.3

A **Listen to Michael talking to Susanne, a new employee in the company. As you listen, make notes about what he finds out about Susanne. Use the following headings to help you:**

place of birth   education   family   first job

B **Look at the Key language below. Then listen again and tick the types of questions and the comments that Michel uses.**

Key language

Open questions / comments	Could you tell me something about …? I'd love to hear about … I'd be interested to know …
Closed questions	Do / Did you …?
Wh- questions	Who, what, when, where, why, how
Probing questions	What / How exactly …? Could you tell me more about that?
Reflecting questions	So, you mean that …? If I understand you, you are saying …? I guess it's …?
Encouraging comments	That's interesting. Oh really?

C **Complete this conversation between Susanne and her new colleague, Petra.**

Susanne: So how long have you worked here?

Petra: Nearly two years now.

Susanne: And (1) ___how do___ you like it?

Petra: It's pretty good. The atmosphere is very informal and relaxed.

Susanne: So, you (2) ___do you think___ that there's not much supervision?

Petra: That's right. Of course, if you have a problem, you can talk to your team leader about it.

Susanne: (3) _____ you _____ me something about the flexitime system? I'm not sure I understand it.

Petra: Well, you have to be in the office between 11.00 and 3.00 but you can start and finish when you like.

Susanne: And (4) _____ you have to do an eight-hour day?

Petra: It varies. Nobody really counts.

Susanne: That (5) _____ great!

Petra: Yes, it is, especially if you have children.

Susanne: And what (6) _____ should I do to arrange my working hours?

Petra: HR will send you a form to fill out. It's pretty straightforward.

D **Work in pairs. Find out about your partner. Ask questions about and respond to comments about each other's life, work and interests.**

▶ Review and development page 25

▶ Communication page 150

MOTIVATION

Understanding different types of culture

There are different layers of culture, and these can have an impact on our behaviour. In this section, we will uncover some of these layers.

2.4 **A** Lin Ho is from Singapore. She used to work for a local company, Asian Finance, but now works for Finvest. She talks about her experiences in these two companies and how she sees the impact of culture. Listen and label the diagram for Finvest.

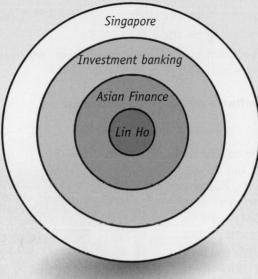

Singapore
Investment banking
Asian Finance
Lin Ho

Lin Ho

Asian Finance   Finvest

B Draw an onion diagram for the types of culture which surround you at work. Then explain it to a partner. Choose from these layers:

- country culture (e.g. British, Chinese, German)
- regional culture (e.g. north or south of the country, city or rural)
- company culture (name of your employer)
- functional culture (e.g. finance, sales, HR)
- sector culture (e.g. banking, retail, engineering)
- team culture (e.g. department or section)

2.5 **C** Lin Ho talks more about Finvest and the company culture. What aspects of culture does she talk about?

dress	body language	organisation	values
offices	management style	language	image
brands	communication	history	

D Draw an iceberg, like the one on page 7, of a company or organisational culture that you know. Use the aspects of culture listed in C above as a starting point.

▶ Business across cultures page 153

Checklist

✓ theory X and theory Y

✓ words to do with motivation: *initiative, encouragement, responsibility ...*

✓ finding out about people

✓ understanding different types of culture

PERFORMANCE

3 Incentives

Start-up

A **With a partner, put these benefits in order of importance to you.**

a in-company child care

b dance classes

c company restaurant

d financial advice for your children's education

e financial advice for retirement

f on-site clinic

g on-site gym

h on-site shops: travel agent, dry cleaners, etc.

> Mid-size companies in the USA spend an average of $19,991 per employee per year on benefits.

Reading and speaking

A **Read the article about the US software company, SAS Institutes.**

What is truly unusual about SAS is not the software it creates but the way in which it does business. Employees describe the company's work environment as easy-going. SAS treats its employees very well – there is no limit on how many sick days they can take; they can even stay home to care for sick family members.

SAS has the largest on-site day-care operation in North Carolina. To encourage families to eat lunch together, the SAS cafeteria has baby seats and high chairs. To encourage families to eat dinner together, the company has adopted a seven-hour workday. Most people at SAS leave the office by 5 p.m. SAS has 3,000 square metres of gym space

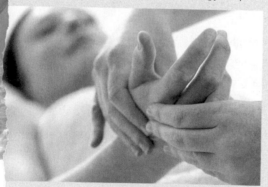

and a ten-lane swimming pool. Massages are available several times a week, and classes are offered in golf, African dance and tennis. If you're worried about finding a retirement home for your ageing mother, the company's coordinator for the care of elderly relatives will assist you. If you need to see a doctor, you'll be able to see one on-site, at the SAS health clinic.

A group at the company meets monthly to discuss proposed new benefits, evaluating them in the context of a three-part test: Will the benefit fit into SAS's culture? Will it serve a significant number of employees? Will it be cost-effective: that is, will its value to employees be at least as high as its cost? Every benefit has to pass all three tests. Coming soon: advice on financial planning for college and retirement.

B **Look again at the benefits listed in Start-up above. Which of them are mentioned in the article? Which of them does SAS already provide?**

C **True or false?**

1 SAS's work environment is relaxed.

2 The company's policy on sickness only covers employees.

3 SAS encourages people to work late.

4 Employees can take family members to the company restaurant.

5 Possible new employee benefits are analysed according to two criteria.

ocabulary and listening

A **Match these benefits to their definitions.**

1	incentives	a	all the advantages available to employees such as healthcare, free gym membership, etc.
2	benefits package	b	a general word for advantages designed to make people work harder and perform better
3	perks	c	extra money earned for reaching a particular target etc.
4	performance bonus	d	time off given to a female employee who will have / has had a child
5	maternity leave	e	time off given to a male employee who will have / has had a child
6	paternity leave	f	a savings fund for retirement
7	company pension	g	an informal word for benefits

B **What other possible benefits do you know of (perhaps ones offered by your organisation or one you would like to join)? Which benefits are the most attractive for you personally?**

🎧 3.1   **C** **Listen to a job candidate discussing incentives and benefits with an interviewer. Make a list of the benefits mentioned.**

Grammar

First conditional

To form the first conditional, you use the present simple in the *if* clause. In the main clause, you use *will* + infinitive.

You use the first conditional to talk about a possible future situation.

If you reach 110 per cent of your target, you'll get a performance bonus of €1000.

Our financial advisor will advise you if you need help with financial planning.

Unless means the same as *if not*

You won't get a bonus unless you reach the target.

A **Complete the sentences using the first conditional.**

1 What _____ the benefits package _____ (contain) if I _____ (join) the company?

2 We _____ (pay) all the bills, if you _____ (need) hospital treatment.

3 If you _____ (become) seriously ill, the company _____ (give) you up to four months' sick leave on full pay.

4 If you _____ (need) to have your clothes cleaned, our on-site laundry service _____ (take care) of it.

5 You _____ (get fired) if you _____ (call in) sick six Mondays in a row!

B **Rewrite the sentences using *unless*.**

1 If employees do not inform us first, their families cannot use the restaurant.
   Unless employees inform us first, their families cannot use the restaurant.

2 You can't go to dance classes if you don't finish your work first.

3 Employees will not get the end-of-year bonus if they do not arrive on time in the mornings.

4 You can't take more than three days off sick if you do not phone your manager.

5 If you do not tell your boss about your summer holiday dates by 31 January, you will not get the dates you want.

▶ Review and development page 23

▶ Grammar overview page 157

Communication

Building transparency

Business often breaks down because of a lack of understanding. Business colleagues and partners need to check, clarify, and confirm their understanding to make sure that communication is effective.

 3.2 **A** **Nikos Mathios is discussing business with a new supplier, Phil Vickery, in the UK. He needs to be sure he understands the deal. Listen to their conversation and complete the notes.**

> Annual contract
>
> Monthly deliveries: date: (1)………. quantity: (2) ………. price: (3)…………
>
> Quantity adjustments: to be confirmed by (4)……………. of previous month
>
> Price adjustment: charge at list price if order decreases by more than (5)……. %.
>
> Qualify for a further (6)….% discount if orders exceed planned quantity by more than (7)…..%

B **Listen again and tick the expressions in the Key language box that you hear.**

Key language

Confirming	Could we go through that again? — together repeat
	Let me just repeat that … — my self
	Could I go over that again? — focus on me
Clarifying	Could you clarify that? explain in another time refresh
	So this means that …?
	Are you saying that …? —
	I mean that … ≠
	What do you mean by …?
Showing that you understand	I understand that.
	That's OK / right / correct.
	That's clear.
	Right.
Showing that you don't understand	Sorry, I'm not with you. mentally
	I'm sorry, that's not clear.

C **Work in pairs. Student A looks at this page. Student B looks at page 102.**

Student A You are travelling with Student B to a trade fair. Your information may be incorrect. Clarify and confirm the correct information by talking to Student B.

> **MEMO**
>
> **MAJESTIC TRADE FAIR**
> **Dates:** 16 – …. February?
> **Cost:** $200 per delegate per day (individual rate)
> **Accommodation:** booked into the Adelphi hotel for three nights?
> **Travel:** return flights from Hamburg to Chicago
> **Depart:** 15 February, 19:15? Flight number LH 25768
> Transfer from airport to hotel? Cost?

▶ Review and development page 25

▶ Communication page 150

Individuals and groups

A key question when working with a new culture is how much the culture expects of the individual as opposed to the group. In this section, we explore the impact these differences have when doing business.

3.3 **A** Listen to project leader A giving feedback to team members, Peter, Marta, and Miguel. What is the feedback?

3.4 **B** Listen to project leader B giving feedback. What is the feedback? How is it different from the feedback given by project leader A?

C Which type of feedback do you prefer – A or B? Give reasons for your answer.

D Read about the differences between individualist and collectivist cultures. Use the checklist below to decide whether your culture (country or company) is more individualistic or collectivist.

Individualism versus collectivism

Individualistic cultures focus on what the individual can do. Individuals are encouraged to stand out and emphasise their independence. They are encouraged to stand on their own. **Collectivist cultures** focus on what the group can do. Groups are encouraged to work together. They are encouraged to look to the group for support and protection.

Individualistic behaviour	Collectivist behaviour
• Reward the best individuals.	• Reward the team or group.
• Rank people in order of their performance.	• Do not pick out individuals.
• Give feedback to individuals.	• Give positive feedback to the group.
• Push individuals to get the best out of them.	• Expect the group to push itself.
• Support personal development.	• Focus on the development of the group and community.
• Value free time for the individual.	• Value time spent socially with the group.

E Read about the situation below and discuss your attitudes towards work, family life, and individual independence.

CULTURE CLASH

WHEN KEITH SUMMERS worked in his home town, he used to leave work at around 6 p.m. and then return home to be with his family. He occasionally met his colleagues after work, but most of the time he kept his work and home life separate. Two years ago, he moved with his family to Japan. For the first year he found his life very difficult. In his old job, he tended to work on his own to achieve his targets. Now he found he needed to wait for his Japanese colleagues to get involved. They worked very long hours, didn't take much time off and frequently went out together after work. He felt very stressed about not seeing his family in the evenings. He has got used to it now, but he still does not accept that this is the right way to live.

▶ Business across cultures page 153

 Checklist

| ✓ words to do with incentives: *perks, bonus, benefits ...* | ✓ first conditional: *If you reach your target, you'll get a bonus.* | ✓ building transparency in communication | ✓ individuals and groups |

4 Work and leisure

What do you understand by the term 'work–life balance'?

In the 1960s experts foresaw the beginning of the 21st century as a time of declining work hours and increasing leisure.

A **Listen to the interview with Professor Stevens, an expert on work–life balance and answer the questions.**

4.1

1 What definition does Jack Stevens give of 'work–life balance'?

2 In the EU what is the maximum number of hours that people can work per week?

3 What effects can long working hours have?

4 What European country does Jack Stevens mention? How many hours a week do people there work?

5 Which historical period does he mention? How many hours a day did some people work at that time?

4.2 **B** **Listen to the rest of the interview and complete the graph.**

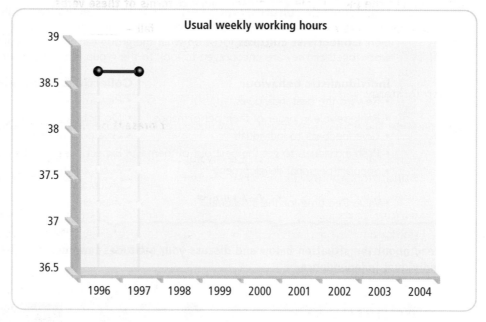

Usual weekly working hours

Y-axis: 39, 38.5, 38, 37.5, 37, 36.5
X-axis: 1996 1997 1998 1999 2000 2001 2002 2003 2004

C **Discuss these questions.**

1 Should work be (a) more important, (b) just as important, (c) less important than family or leisure time?

2 What do you do to keep a good balance between work and leisure?

3 How many hours a week do you work? Has this changed much over the years?

Grammar

Past simple and present perfect

A Look at these sentences from the interview with Professor Stevens. Can you identify which tense is used in the sentences below – the past simple or the present perfect?

*In 2001 people **worked** 38 hours a week on average.*

*Since 1996 the number of working hours **has decreased** from 38.7 per cent to 37.3 per cent.*

B Now complete the rule.

You use the _____ tense to talk about actions and events that happened at a specific time in the past.

> *Between 1994 and 1996, I worked for a large investment bank.*

You use the _____ tense to talk about actions and events that happened in the past and continue in the present. You often use it with *for* and *since* to describe the duration up to the present.

> *I've worked in London for three years.*
> *I've worked in the oil industry since 2001.*

C Complete the past simple and present perfect forms of these verbs.

rise – rose – risen   fall – _____ – _____

go up – _____ – _____   go down – _____ – _____

increase – _____ – _____   decrease – _____ – _____

remain steady – _____ – _____

D Complete the news story with the past simple or present perfect form of the verbs in brackets.

A recent survey shows that the average British worker is working less and spending more. Since 1996, the average number of working hours (1) _____ (fell) from 38.7 per cent to 37.4 per cent. But fewer hours don't mean less money. Between 1990 and 2000, the average salary (2) _____ (go up) by 12 per cent. This means more disposable income. And do we like to spend it! Over the last ten years, the amount of money spent on holidays abroad (3) _____ (increase) by 18 per cent. Since 2003 the average number of meals eaten in restaurants (4) _____ (rise) by 18 per cent. The impact on TV and the cinema, however, is different. Over the last seven years, the amount of time we spend in front of the TV (5) _____ (go down) from 25 to 19 hours a week. Between 1993 and 2003, the number of cinemas (6) _____ (remain) steady at around 5,500.

Speaking

A Discuss the following questions:

1 Are the leisure activities mentioned in D popular in your country?

2 What are the trends for leisure activities and the leisure industry in your country?

▶ Review and development page 24

▶ Grammar overview page 158

Communication

Responding and developing communication

We keep the channels for communication open by showing we are listening and interested in what people are saying. This section focuses on ways of responding and developing communication.

🔊 4.3 **A** Dieter Paul is talking to a new client, Frank Brown of Southern Security Systems. Frank is talking about his business and Dieter shows his interest and develops the dialogue. As you listen, make notes about the business.

SOUTHERN SECURITY SYSTEMS

Founded: .... years ago

First big client: ....

Ratio of private to public sector business: ....

New target markets: ....

Key to breaking into these markets: ....

B Listen again and tick the expressions in the Key language box that you hear.

Drawing conclusions	That must be / have been … (+ adjective) That can't be / have been … (+ adjective)
Expressing interest / surprise	That's interesting. Really? I don't believe it. I didn't know that.
Expressing sympathy	What a pity! What a shame. I'm sorry to hear that.
Congratulating	Well done! Congratulations!
Expressing enthusiasm	That sounds great / exciting.
Expressing doubt	I don't suppose so. I doubt it.

C Work in pairs. Student A looks at this page. Student B looks at page 102.

Student A

1 Listen to Student B telling you about his / her work–life balance. Respond and develop the conversation by making comments and asking questions.

2 Tell Student B about your work–life balance. Talk about:

working hours   holidays   time with family   leisure time

▶ Review and development page 25

▶ Communication page 150

BUSINESS ACROSS CULTURES

Women at work

A major area of cultural difference around the world is the role women play in society and at work. This section explores these differences.

A Read about four countries. Which of the following topics are mentioned in the texts?

a time off for children ~~oft time~~

b time off for leisure or sickness

c flexible hours

d women in senior positions

e women's pay

f women's management style ✓

g working in industry

h working in the service sector

i working in agriculture — faim

j time off for caring for the elderly ✓ olol

1 Norway has a large percentage of women in the labour market and this is supported by policies such as 'daddy month' leave – an extra four weeks' paternity leave taken in the child's early years. Norway's 'feminine' culture has been supported by state policies in areas like child care and flexible working.

2 The Netherlands is traditionally a single breadwinner culture. There is limited concern about women in top jobs. However, there is support for a more 'feminine' style of leadership and legislation which supports shared parenting.

3 Japan has an ageing population and to combat this, policies have been introduced to encourage workers to take time off to care for the elderly, although it is still assumed that women will do this. There is a significant gender gap in pay. The working environment is very intensive and traditionally very little time is taken off work.

4 In India most people still work on the land although there is a vibrant and growing industrial and commercial sector in which both women and men are employed. Gender politics and the work–life balance are seen as luxuries by most; the majority consider economic development as a priority.

B Build up a profile of your culture's attitudes and behaviour towards women. Use the topics in A to help you.

C Read the text below. What do you think is happening in the team? What advice would you give to Patrick?

CULTURE CLASH

PATRICK WAS BORN and brought up in France. His background is in marketing and sales. He has worked in Africa and South America. His company has now sent him to the UK to be in charge of a project team which has to design and implement a new sales training programme. Five out of six members of the team are women. Four of them have a background in human resources and training. He likes to compliment women on their appearance and has always found this is much appreciated. But he has the impression that his remarks are not appreciated by his new team. He is focused on results and found the first project meeting very slow and polite – too much listening and not enough action. He has started to feel unsure about his team. He is not used to this and it makes him feel uncomfortable.

▶ Business across cultures page 153

| **Checklist** | ✓ work–life balance | ✓ past simple and present perfect | ✓ responding and developing communication | ✓ women at work |

Improving morale

Background

Province Advertising is based in Australia's second city, Melbourne. It employs around 120 people, designing and selling advertising for TV, local newspapers, and street hoardings. Morale in the company is low. The CEO, Roxanne Simon, has commissioned a human resources consultant, James Murdo, to find out why.

[handwritten: company]

[handwritten: hoarding:]

Speaking

The problems

Roxanne Simon has received the faxed report below from James Murdo but some of the information is unclear. She phones him to obtain it.

Student A: You are Roxanne Simon. Look at this page.

Student B: You are James Murdo. Look at page 103.

Student A

FAX

	Agree	Disagree
Management understands our problems.	15%	85%
The work is well ░░░░░ by managers.	░░░	░░░
Working hours are ░░░░░.	36%	64%
The company is ░░░░░.	░░░	░░░
The company building is in a ░░░░░.	49%	51%
Our offices are ░░░░░.	░░░	░░░

The company also has these problems:

High staff ░░░░░: About ░ people leave the company every year, and have to be replaced. Many of those leaving go to work in ░░░░░ for a higher salary.

Days off for ░░░░. About ░ per cent of working days are lost because of it. (The national average is 2 per cent.)

Grammar

Talking about figures

<u>Only</u> a quarter of employees think that the company is well managed.

<u>Just over</u> a <u>third</u> think that working hours are reasonable.

<u>Nearly</u> two-thirds think that working hours are not reasonable.

<u>More than half</u> think the company is not family-friendly.

<u>The vast majority</u> think that the offices are unattractive.

Those who think working hours are reasonable are <u>in the minority</u>.

Use the underlined expressions to talk about these figures from James Murdo's report.

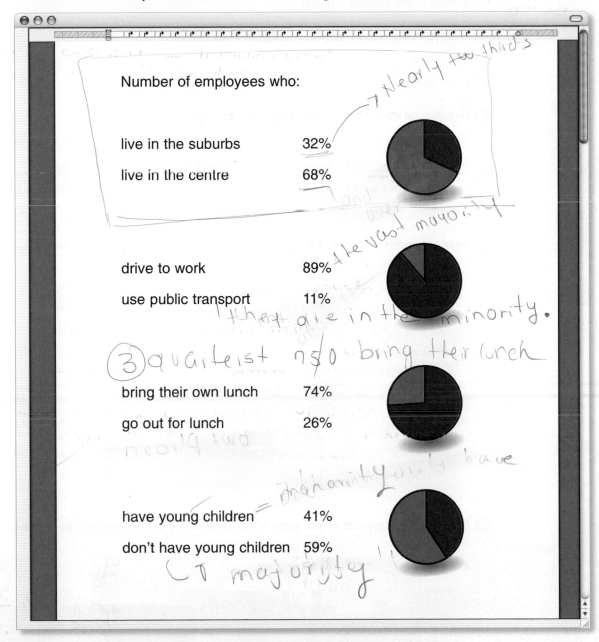

Number of employees who:	
live in the suburbs	32%
live in the centre	68%
drive to work	89%
use public transport	11%
bring their own lunch	74%
go out for lunch	26%
have young children	41%
don't have young children	59%

Role play

Work in groups of three. You are in a meeting to discuss the findings of the report on employee morale.

Student A: You are the CEO. Turn to page 103.

Student B: You are the General Manager. Turn to page 108.

Student C: You are the Human Resources Manager. Turn to page 110.

Writing

Write a short report on the discussion at the meeting from the point of view of the person whose role you played. Say what was decided and why.

REVIEW & DEVELOPMENT

1–4

Grammar

Comparisons

A Look again at the rules and examples on page 5. Then put these adjectives into the correct category, and make the comparative form.

a thick – *one syllable* – *thicker*
b efficient — more efficient — the most efficient
c pretty — prettier — prettiest
d powerful — more powerful — the most powerful
e relaxed — more relaxed – the most relaxed.

[handwritten margin note: Ausét 132]

B Use comparative forms of the adjectives above to complete the text.

The Mango communications device is only slightly (1) _thicker_ (thick) than a credit card. It's (2) _prettier_ (pretty) and (3) _more powerful_ (powerful) than other communications devices. It will make you a (4) _more efficient_ (efficient) worker and leave you feeling (5) _____ (relaxed) at the end of the day.

C Read this review from a computer magazine. Choose the correct word to fill each gap.

Mango is (1) _much_ easier to use than other similar devices. You have a full QWERTY keyboard, so the device is (2) _as_ easy to use (3) _as_ a personal computer: the keys on Mango are (4) _nearly_ as big as keys on a PC keyboard. The letters on the screen are only (5) _slighter_ smaller than the letters on a PC screen. The only problem is that the Mango is (6) _not_ as fast as some of its competitors!

1 a more	b much	c lot
2 a as	b just	c than
3 a that	b than	c as
4 a next	b near	c nearly
5 a more	b slightly	c almost
6 a not	b much	c most

[handwritten margin note: Slig pag 132]

D Compare two products of the same kind. Choose one of the products below or use your own ideas.

mobile phone   digital camera   cars

Vocabulary

Motivation

A Look again at the words and expressions to do with motivation on page 8. Then complete these sentences with the correct form of the word in brackets.

[handwritten: pg 132 has the answers]

[handwritten top right: Homework vocab]

1 I have no problem with _motivation_ (motivate). I leave home at 6.30 a.m. and I'm at my desk by 7 a.m.

2 When people disagree with a proposal, it's often because they haven't been _consulted_. (consult).

3 Our employees are self-starters: they produce results without constant _supervision_ (supervise).

4 We are _commitmented_ *[handwritten: passive voice]* (commit) to equal opportunities for men and women in our organisation.

5 Employees don't need much _encouragement_ (encourage) to leave early on Fridays.

6 _Discussion_ (discuss) is fine, but there comes a point where you have to make a _decision_. (decide). *[handwritten: tive]*

7 The project was _initia_ *[handwritten: tive]* (initiate) in our Boston office, but managed by our people in London.

B Work in pairs. Have a conversation between someone who believes in Theory X and someone who believes in Theory Y.

A: We don't consult our employees. We just tell them what to do.

B: We always consult our employees before we take any major decisions that will affect them.

Grammar

First conditional

A Look again at the examples and rules on page 13. Then make complete sentences using the prompts below. (Be careful with the order of the clauses.)

1 increase your salary by 10 per cent each year / reach your annual targets
We'll increase your salary by 10 per cent each year if you reach your annual targets.

2 complete the first year successfully / send you to our Paris office
If you complete the first year successfully, we will send you to our Paris office.

3 promote you quickly / have management potential

4 improve your communication skills / put you in charge of a team of engineers

5 increase your budget / win the contract

6 exceed sales targets / give you a top-of-the-range BMW

7 go far / produce results

B Now rephrase the sentences above using *unless*.

1 We won't increase your salary each year unless you reach your annual targets.

C You are talking to employees in your organisation. Make sentences like those in A and B.

We'll give you a bonus if you reach your sales targets.

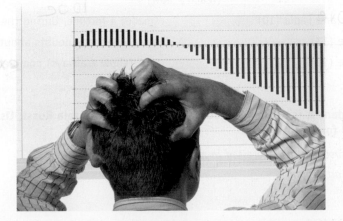

▶ Grammar overview
page 157

Vocabulary

Company incentives

A Look again at the vocabulary on page 13. Then replace the underlined words in sentences 1–6 with one of the expressions (a–g). Add an article (*a, the*) where necessary.

a performance bonus   c benefits package   e perks
b maternity leave   d paternity leave   f company pension

Paternity leave

1 It's great. When my wife goes back to work after six months off, I can take off another three months to look after the baby. *The paternity leave is great.*

benefits package

2 It's very generous: there's six weeks' holiday a year, a company car, a good pension, and lots of other things.

company pension

3 It's amazing: the company pays twice as much as I do. I'll be able to retire at 55 on three-quarters of my final salary.

bonus

4 They're unusually good for an airline: they include free travel for all employees' relatives up to five times a year.

5 At this call centre, you get <u>one</u> if you've dealt with more than 50 calls a day on average throughout the year.

6 The company guarantees that women can have their job back when they come back after <u>it</u>.
(→ maternity leave)

Grammar

Past simple and present perfect

A Look again at the examples and rules on page 17. Then look at the position of the underlined words in the sentences below.

I <u>first</u> became interested in engineering when I was about five years old. I've <u>always</u> wanted to be an engineer.

I've <u>recently</u> opened a shop in Chelsea.

Have you <u>ever</u> considered starting your own company? – No, I've <u>never</u> thought about it.

B Complete the text with the past simple or present perfect forms of the verbs in brackets. (Where there is more than one word, make sure they are in the correct order.)

Paola Rossi (1) _____ (become / first) interested in making jewellery when she (2) _____ (be) at art school. She's a born entrepreneur: she (3) _____ (not finish) the course because she (4) _____ (leave) in order to set up her own business making silver jewellery. Over the years, Paola (5) _____ (raise) €200,000 to develop her business. At the start, her family (6) _____ (invest) €100,000, and a bank (7) _____ (lend) her another €50,000. But since then, she (8) _____ (need) another €50,000 to move to bigger premises and buy more equipment. Sales (9) _____ (reach / now) €1 million per year and Paola (10) _____ (made) a fortune. During the 10 years of the company's existence (11) _____ (have / ever) any doubts about her ability to succeed? Never! She (12) _____ (show / always) complete confidence in herself!

C Work in pairs. Student A is a business journalist. Student B is Paola Rossi. Use the information above as the basis for an interview.

A: *When did you first become interested in making jewellery?*

B: *When I was at art school.*

▶ Grammar overview
page 158

Communication

Look again at the communication skills pages in Units 1–4. Then complete these exercises.

A Match the phrase (1–12) with its purpose (a–l).

Phrase

1 I was brought up in Bangalore. *i*
2 I live with my partner and our two children. C
3 I'm into computer games. *e*
4 Could you tell me more about that? K
5 That sounds fun. *h*
6 I'd be interested to know something about your time in India. L
7 Could we go through that again? *f*
8 Sorry, I'm not with you. *a*
9 Are you saying that you have no experience of IT? *g*
10 I'm sorry to hear that. *J*
11 I don't suppose so. *b*
12 That must have been very difficult. *d*

Purpose

a Show you don't understand.
b Express doubt.
c Talk about your family.
d Draw a conclusion.
e Talk about your interests.
f Ask for confirmation.
g Ask for clarification.
h Express enthusiasm.
i Talk about your origins.
j Express sympathy.
k Ask a probing question.
l Ask an open question.

B Complete the extract from an interview between Siri and Ahmed with the words in the box.

based	born	brought up	worked	tell	mean	sounds	move

Siri: So your early life was spent in Jordan?

Ahmed: Well, I was (1) __born__ in Amman, but then I went to Cairo where I was (2) __brought up__ by my aunt and uncle.

Siri: Did you go to university there?

Ahmed: That's right, and then I got my first job as an engineer. I (3) __worked__ for an energy company.

Siri: Were you (4) __move__ in Cairo?

Ahmed: Yes, but I travelled around – mainly in the Arab world.

Siri: That (5) __sounds__ interesting. Could you (6) __tell__ me more about the type of work?

Ahmed: Of course. It was mainly maintenance of power plants. It was a good job and I enjoyed it, but I decided to (7) __move__ to Europe.

Siri: I see. So you (8) _____ you wanted to broaden your experience?

Ahmed: That's right. I got a job with RCW in Germany in their Engineering department.

Siri: That must have been a real challenge – a new language and culture?

Ahmed: Yes, it was. The first year was very difficult, but then my wife joined me.

C 1 Prepare some notes about yourself. Include some information about your origins, family, education, job, interests, strengths, and weaknesses.

2 Pass the notes to your partner. Take it in turns to interview each other. The interviewer should ask questions, clarify, and also respond and react to the answers.

▶ Writing resource 17
page 92

5 Entrepreneurs

Start-up

A Discuss these questions.

1 What are the characteristics of a successful entrepreneur?

2 Are entrepreneurs born or is it possible to learn entrepreneurship?

Reading and speaking

A Read this article about a successful entrepreneur.

Simon Woodroffe is no ordinary businessman, even if he is a very rich one. The son of an army officer, he says he and his brother were from an 'upper middle-class family but with no money.' He worked as a record producer with rock bands, in theatre stage design and in TV programme distribution before setting up Yo! Sushi, the business that made his name and fortune. A Japanese friend suggested the idea of selling sushi on conveyor belts like restaurants in Japan and told him to staff the café with girls in short PVC skirts. He dropped the uniform but kept the conveyor belts and the result was queues along Poland Street in London's Soho. Woodroffe opened his first Yo! Sushi in 1997. The chain grew to 13 restaurants and three bars in Britain and a branch in Dubai before Woodroffe sold his majority stake in 2004. He made £10 million.

He reinvested the proceeds in a number of new projects, for example Yotel, another Japanese-style concept – tiny but beautifully designed luxury hotel rooms that will utilise 'space that nobody else wants' – basements underneath central London car parks, for example. Woodroffe had the idea for Yotel when he was flying first class on British Airways – he saw the way comfort can be created in a very small space. At Yotel, the bed is also a sofa, the bathrooms take up a quarter of the 10 square metre units, and the mood lighting and wi-fi facilities are aimed at professionals who want to work, play and then sleep in luxury that is affordable (£75 a night).

Woodroffe's creed, and he makes a living preaching it to more mainstream businessmen, is decentralisation, not anarchy. He makes a prediction: 'Entrepreneurs will replace celebrity pop stars and footballers as idols for young people. They will look at how you can make money if you have a passion for an idea and you make it work and they will want some of this themselves.'

B Answer the questions.

1 What did Simon Woodroffe do before he became an entrepreneur?

2 When did he set up Yo! Sushi?

3 What two innovations did he consider introducing? Which did he finally introduce?

4 How many restaurants and bars were there in the chain when he sold it?

5 How much did he sell his stake for?

6 What does 'concept' mean?

7 Where did Simon Woodroffe get his idea for Yotel?

8 What are the rooms like?

9 Who are Yotel's potential customers?

10 What is your opinion of Simon Woodroffe's prediction that entrepreneurs will replace pop stars and footballers as idols for young people?

Vocabulary and listening

A These adjectives (1–9) can be used to describe entrepreneurs. Match them to their meanings (a–i).

1 independent
2 innovative
3 self-confident
4 inquisitive
5 persistent
6 reliable
7 strong
8 bold
9 competitive

a powerful and not easily hurt
b want to be more successful than others
c try to do things even when they are difficult
d able to work on your own
e confident and brave
f think up new and original ideas
g do what you say you will
h interested in finding out about things
i believe in yourself

[handwritten annotations: i, F, i, H (curious), C, e, a, g, b]

B Look again at the text on page 26. Which of the adjectives in A would you use to describe Simon Woodroffe? *[handwritten: Independent, strong, innovative, inquisitive, bold]*

5.1 **C** Listen to the interview with Gabbie Kung, founder and CEO of Europe Wings, and answer the questions.

1 Which of the adjectives in A does she mention as characteristics of entrepreneurs?
2 What adjectives does she use to describe entrepreneurs who fail?
3 How many reasons does she give for the failure of new businesses? What are they?
4 Why do so many new business ideas come from entrepreneurs, rather than organisations?

D Look at the examples and then complete the table below.

People usually think of entrepreneurs as <u>self-confident</u> individuals. (adjective)

That's right, you need a lot of <u>self-confidence</u>. (noun)

Adjective	Noun
independent	independence
innovative	*innovation*
self-confident	*self-confidence*
inquisitive	*inquisitiveness*
persistent	*persistence*
bold	*boldness*
reliable	*reliability*
strong	*strength?*
competitive	*competitiveness*

[handwritten margin notes: brave, no weak]

E Use the correct adjective or noun from D to complete this advice to entrepreneurs.

1 You need to find out as much information as possible about your customers, the market, and your competitors. You really need to be _____*inquisitive*_____ to succeed as an entrepreneur.

2 Entrepreneurs have to be very _____*independent*_____. They need to be able to work by themselves and not rely on the support of a big team.

3 _____*Innovation*_____ is the key to success – there's no point in offering something that's been done before.

4 One of the most important characteristics is to be _____*persistent*_____. A lot of people might not like your idea, but you can't give up if you want to succeed.

5 If people ask you to do something, you need to do it. Entrepreneurs who can't offer _____*reliability*_____ won't last long in the business.

► Review and development page 44

► Grammar overview page 159

Communication

Socialising 1: *Small talk*

Getting to know someone depends on finding topics to talk about. This section focuses on developing your socialising skills around a range of topics.

🔊 5.2

A Listen to these extracts from eight conversations. Match each one to the topics (a–h).

a jobs   e entertainment
b family and relationships   f business environment
c home   g health and lifestyle
d sport   h holidays

B What other topics could you talk about in a social situation?

C Complete the texts using the words in the box.

applied	build	buy	commute	diet	divorced	exercise	fit	had	joined	look
lose	married	move	partner	promoted	redundant	see	shape	share	work

Talking about jobs

The first job I (1) _applied_ for was in a bank. After that I (2) _joined_ a financial services company and worked there for 10 years. They made me (3) _redundant_ last year and I had to (4) _look_ for a new job. Now I'm in insurance. It's going well – I've just been (5) _promoted_ to General Manager.

Talking about the family

We got (6) _married_ when I was just 23 and we (7) _had_ two children. Unfortunately, things didn't (8) _worked_ out and we got (9) _divorced_ two years ago. I now live with my new (10) _partner_, but I (11) _see_ my children every weekend.

Talking about home

I (12) _share_ a flat with a friend. Ideally, I'd like to (13) _buy_ some land and (14) _build_ a house of my own. But land is expensive here. I'd have to (15) _move_ out of the city. Dayton is a possibility, but it's a long (16) _commute_ to work.

Talking about health and lifestyle

I used to be very (17) _fit_ but I'm not in such good (18) _shape_ now. I need to (19) _lose_ some weight. I was thinking of starting a (20) _diet_ and I should take more (21) _exercise_.

D Work in pairs. Chose two or three of the topics in A and talk to your partner about them.

▶ Review and development page 47

▶ Communication page 151

BUSINESS ACROSS CULTURES

Public and private space

There are big cultural differences in how we view our private and public space. This section focuses on how we build relationships both at work and outside work.

5.3 **A** **Listen and match the remark (1–6) to the purpose (a–f).**

Remark	Purpose
1	a to invite you to their house
2	b to find out about your private life
3	c to find out your opinion
4	d to pay you a compliment
5	e to comment on your appearance
6	f to invite you to share a drink after work

B **Listen again and decide if you feel comfortable with the remarks.**

C **Read this text about relationship building.**

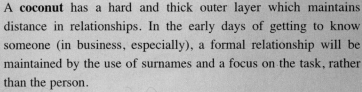

The peach/coconut image provides a simple way of thinking about cultural differences in relationship building.

A **peach** has a soft outer layer into which people are quickly invited. Personal details are shared and generally there is an emphasis on sharing your private space.

A **coconut** has a hard and thick outer layer which maintains distance in relationships. In the early days of getting to know someone (in business, especially), a formal relationship will be maintained by the use of surnames and a focus on the task, rather than the person.

D **Are you a peach or a coconut? Work in pairs. Use the questions below to interview each other about your style in relationship building.**

1 Do you keep your business life separate from your personal life? For example:
  • Do you invite business partners to your house?
  • Do you mix socially after work with your colleagues?
  • Do you expect to build personal friendships with your colleagues at work?

2 Do you maintain a physical distance between people? For example:
  • How close do you stand to people?
  • How much physical contact do you have with people?

3 Do you use language to maintain a distance between people? For example:
  • Do you use first names or surnames?
  • Do you have a formal form of 'you' in your language?

E **Prepare to brief someone coming to work and live in your country. Make notes under the following headings and then advise your visitor how to build successful business relationships in your country.**

▶ Business across
cultures page 153

meetings   socialising   business relationships   emotions   other

Checklist

✓ being an entrepreneur

✓ adjectives describing entrepreneurs: *innovative, self-confident, competitive ...*

✓ small talk: *family, health, lifestyle ...*

✓ public and private space

INNOVATION

6 Creativity

Start-up

A What is creativity? What do you think of the statement on the right?

> Creativity can't be taught. You either have it or you don't.

B In which of these company departments is creativity most important? Why?

Accounts   Marketing   Human Resources   Research and Development

Listening and speaking

 6.1

A Listen to this interview with Jackie Lang, a consultant in international trade, and answer the questions.

1 What examples of creativity does Jackie Lang give?
2 Who came up with the idea of the shipping container?
3 When did this happen?
4 What advantage did these shipping containers have over boxes?
5 What prediction was made in 1968 about trade between Britain and the United States?
6 Did anyone foresee the expansion of trade caused by containerisation?
7 Why did this happen?
8 What prediction did trade experts *not* make in the 1950s?
9 What are the implications of this for creativity in general?

B Discuss some of the consequences, foreseen and unforeseen, of these innovations.

supermarkets
People drive to the supermarket to do their weekly shopping, rather than shop locally, leading to more traffic.

low-cost air travel

downloading music from the internet

wireless connections for computers

old and new cinema films on DVD

Grammar

The future

Going to and *will* can both be used to make predictions based on present evidence or the present situation. Both can be used to talk about what the speaker considers to be certainties about the future.

Five container ships will be enough for all the trade between Britain and the United States.

Containers are going to change the world.

A Make affirmative and negative predictions about the year 2050 using *going to* and *will / shall*. Use contractions for the negative forms.

1 Space tourism / be / popular
Space tourism is going to be popular. / Space tourism isn't going to be popular.
Space tourism will be popular. / Space tourism won't be popular.

2 We / have / most successful product on the market

3 Scientists / find / new sources of energy

4 People / live to be 100

5 Company employees / have / more leisure time

When the future reference is based on decisions, plans or intentions, *going to* is used.

Birgitta's going to change jobs. She's going to move to Berlin.

B Computer Services (CS) have just won a big contract with the government's Department of Work (DW) to supply and run its computer system. Make sentences about the changes at CS, using the prompts and *going to*.

1 CS can't stay in their present offices.
They / move to / bigger offices
They're going to move to bigger offices.

2 CS's boss doesn't know much about working with the government.
He / do / a lot of research

3 DW is worried about CS employees seeing confidential information.
CS employees / sign / a confidentiality agreement

4 Some of DW's employees are leaving the department.
They / work / directly for CS

5 DW have ensured that CS will produce the results that they promised.
CS / pay / a big penalty / if not reach their targets

Will can also be used to make requests or promises, and to offer help.

Will you help me with this report? (request)

I won't be late again. (promise)

I'll do the presentation on Friday, if you like. (offer)

C What would you say in these situations?

1 A customer phones to tell you that an order hasn't been delivered.

2 A client phones and wants to speak to your colleague, Jim.

3 A member of the public complains about the dangerous driving of one of your company's drivers.

4 Your boss asks for some information. You can't find it immediately.

▶ Review and development page 45

▶ Grammar overview page 160

Communication

Socialising 2: *Positive responses*

We express our feelings partly through our body language (smiles, gestures and eye contact) and partly through the language we use. This section focuses on developing language to express positive responses.

A Work in pairs. Practise using the Key language below.

Key language

	Question / Statement	Response
Offering	Would you like to come to dinner?	I'd love to. I'd love to, but I'm afraid I can't.
Requesting	Would you mind giving me a lift? Could you call me later?	No problem. Of course.
Asking permission	May I call you later?	Please do / Of course / Certainly.
Suggesting	Why don't we meet for dinner?	Great idea!
Thanking	Thank you for all your help.	It was a pleasure. You're welcome.
Apologising	I'm very sorry.	Don't worry. It doesn't matter. Never mind.
Gift-giving	I've brought you a small present.	You shouldn't have. That's very kind of you. Thank you.
Agreeing	I thought it was an excellent presentation. I hope the weather improves.	So did I. So do I.
Saying goodbye	It was a lovely evening. Have a good weekend. I look forward to our next meeting.	I'm glad you enjoyed it. You, too. Me, too.

6.2 **B** Listen to the comments and questions. In each case, choose an appropriate response from the Key language box.

C Work in pairs. Student A looks at this page. Student B looks at page 104.

Student A

1 Get the right response from Student B in these situations:
 a Invite Student B to visit your house for dinner.
 b Thank Student B for his / her help.
 c Say goodbye to Student B and wish him / her a safe journey home.
 d Apologise to Student B for arriving late for a meeting.
 e Ask Student B's permission to leave the office early.

2 Now respond to Student B.

D Work in groups. Group 1 looks at this page. Group 2 looks at page 104.

Group 1

One of your colleagues is leaving for a new job. Prepare a short farewell speech. Use these notes to help you.

- Thank your colleague for his / her hard work.
- Apologise for not meeting more often after work.
- Suggest meeting one evening next month.
- Say goodbye – you hope to stay in contact in future.

▶ Review and development page 47

▶ Communication page 151

The culture of organisations

Attitudes towards power – who has it and how they deal with it – vary from company to company. This section focuses on how company cultures deal with power.

6.3 **A** Listen to four people talking about the structure of their organisations. Place each one on the scale below.

National Health Service   Thorntons   TLC Ltd   The Metal Cooperative

Flat

hierarchical

B What type of organisation do these words and phrases describe? Place them on the left or the right of the scale above. Use a dictionary to help you.

belonging to

to incline or bend

hierarchical   flat   transparent   complex   top-heavy   climb the ladder   top-down
bureaucratic   lean   democratic   network   bottom-up   many-layered   slow

C Read this text about high and low power distance cultures.

distance   power go

Cultures vary in terms of the distance between layers in society and organisations.

High power distance cultures are characterised by big gaps between one layer and the next. In business, the gaps are emphasised by status symbols such as cars, large offices and secretaries. Hierarchy is respected and important for the effective running of society – everybody knows his or her 'place'. Distance is also maintained by the use of more formal language and an attitude which does not encourage close relationships across the layers.

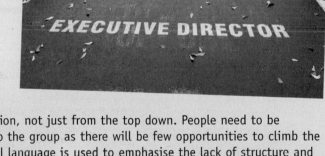

EXECUTIVE DIRECTOR

Low power distance cultures are characterised by small, if any, gaps in society. In business, organisations have few layers and channels of communication are open in every direction, not just from the top down. People need to be motivated by membership and loyalty to the group as there will be few opportunities to climb the ladder of promotion. The use of informal language is used to emphasise the lack of structure and there is no sense of people being superior or inferior.

D What are the advantages and disadvantages of flat and hierarchical organisations? What kind of organisation would you prefer to work for?

▶ Business across
cultures page 154

| Checklist | ✓consequences of innovations | ✓future: *going to* / *will* | ✓positive responses: asking permission, apologising | ✓the culture of organisations |

33

7 Start-ups

Start-up

A Would you consider investing money in these opportunities? Why / why not? What further information would you require before you made your decision?

1 A relative with no business experience is going to open a restaurant and asks you to invest in it.

2 The national lottery in your country announces a special prize of $5 million in the next draw.

3 Someone with a background of successful business ventures asks you to invest in a new company, promising a 30 per cent return on investment.

4 Shares in a high-tech company are made available for the first time on the stock market. Financial journalists write about a possible return on investment of 20 per cent in the first year.

5 Your bank offers a new type of savings account with a fixed annual interest rate of 5 per cent.

Listening and vocabulary

🎧 7.1

A Listen to the conversation and answer the questions.

1 Who are the two speakers and what are they talking about?

2 What does a venture capitalist do?

3 Why do venture capitalists put money into companies knowing that some of them will fail?

4 What does a business angel do?

5 Do business angels always want to be involved in running a company that they invest in?

6 What is the secret of a good pitch?

7 What can happen if a business wants to raise a lot of investment for expansion?

B Listen again and complete the sentences below.

1 The company _____ _____ on the stock exchange in an IPO.

2 IPO stands for _____ _____ _____.

3 Then the company _____ _____ on the stock market.

4 Shares in the company _____ _____ and _____ by investors on the stock market.

Grammar

Passives

- The passive is formed with the verb *to be* in the appropriate tense + the past participle of the verb.
- You use the passive when you are not interested in or do not need to know who performed an action.
- If you want to mention who performs the action, you can use *by*.
- The passive is often used to describe processes and procedures.

The electronic components <u>are made</u> in China.
The new product <u>was developed</u> in 2006.
Your business plan <u>will be examined</u> by our team.
You <u>could be asked</u> to demonstrate the product during your pitch.

A Match the two parts of the sentences.

1 Novo software products were
2 The software was not
3 Novo was
4 Half the money for investment was
5 Later, shares in Novo were

a considered to be central to the company's strategy.
b provided by GX; the other half was raised from a venture capital company.
c sold in an IPO to finance further expansion.
d spun off from GX as a new company.
e written by a team of programmers at GX.

B Change the sentences from the active to the passive.

1 An entrepreneur founds the company.
2 A mechanical engineer develops the new product.
3 A business angel invested $75,000 in the company.
4 In the future, the company will need more investment.
5 The founders will float the company on the stock exchange.
6 They could raise more money on the stock market.

C Write the sentences in the passive.

1 New projects for investment / very carefully. (should / choose)
   New projects for investment should be chosen very carefully.
2 Large amounts of money / in this market in the next 10 years. (could / make)
3 Forecasts of future sales / in our business plan. (can / find)
4 Our profits / by changes in the tax laws. (could / affect)
5 The company / by a stronger competitor. (might / take over)

▶ Review and development page 46

▶ Grammar overview page 161

Communication

Meetings 1: *Running a meeting*

A lot of business is done in meetings. Making your meetings effective can make a big difference to your working life. This section focuses on the main elements of running a meeting.

7.2 **A** Listen to four extracts from meetings. Identify which stage of the meeting (a–d) they come from.

a before the meeting
b at the start of the meeting
c at the end of the meeting
d after the meeting

B Complete these sentences with words from the extracts. Listen again and check your answers.

a There are three _____ on the agenda.
b Could we _____ a meeting for tomorrow?
c I'm sorry. I won't be able to _____ the meeting.
d Peter has agreed to _____ the minutes.
e Let's _____ down to business.
f Sarah, how far have we got with the _____ from the meeting?
g We're going to _____ the meeting in the boardroom.

Key language

Before the meeting	Could we fix the next meeting? Peter, could you prepare the agenda? Is everybody available?
At the start of the meeting	Welcome. Nice to see you all. Does everybody know each other? Let's get started / down to business. Have you all seen the agenda? Could we aim to finish by 11 a.m.?
Managing the purpose	Our objective today is to … By the end of this meeting, I'd like to …
Managing the process	So, the first item is … Peter, could you start? Let's turn to the second item … That brings us to the end.
Managing the people	Peter, could you take the minutes? Sally, would you like to add anything? John, could you let Sally finish?
After the meeting	Did you get the minutes? There are some actions to follow up.

C Work in groups. Prepare the objectives, agenda and timing for the following meeting:

You have noticed increased levels of stress in the workplace. Your objective is to try to improve the situation. This is the first of a series of regular meetings to identify the causes of stress and work out ways to reduce stress levels.

D Now hold your meeting. Make sure you manage the purpose, the process and the people. Use the Key language to help you. Make a note of any actions.

▶ Review and development page 47

▶ Communication page 151

Attitudes towards time

Attitudes towards time differ from culture to culture. In some cultures, time is always being measured, in others it is more fluid. This section explores how these different attitudes to time have an impact on business.

A Read these three scenarios and choose a or b.

1 You have a business meeting at 15.00. The time is 14.58. As you walk towards the meeting room, you meet a colleague you haven't seen for a long time.
   a Do you greet them and then excuse yourself so that you are on time for the meeting?
   b Do you start a conversation and, as a result, arrive 10 minutes late for your meeting?

2 You are in a business meeting. It was scheduled to finish at 15.00. The time is now 15.30. The meeting started late and you have spent a long time discussing options for business development, but without reaching any conclusions.
   a Do you feel frustrated and impatient?
   b Do you feel that it is good to have the chance to talk through some ideas?

3 You are having a very busy day. You are expecting a business partner to arrive for a meeting at 15.00. It is already 15.15. They haven't phoned to explain why they are late.
   a Do you feel this is rude and unprofessional?
   b Do you feel this is normal and that he / she will arrive as soon as he / she can?

> ### Analysis
>
> If you chose **a**, you probably come from a **monochronic** culture, where time is tightly controlled. In these cultures, time is seen as a line with clear start and finish times and it is important to measure time. Punctuality is a virtue.
>
> If you chose **b**, you probably come from a **polychronic** culture, where time is seen more flexibly. In these cultures, time is not so tightly controlled. It is more important to finish your conversations, rather than to finish on time. Meetings are usually less structured and you tolerate more things happening during any time period.

B Read these profiles of monochronic and polychronic styles. Decide which is closest to your culture. Then compare it to another culture you know.

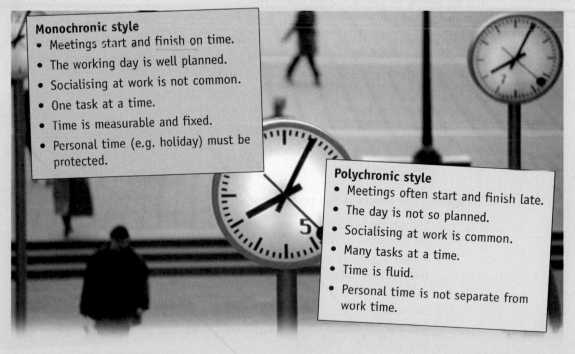

Monochronic style
- Meetings start and finish on time.
- The working day is well planned.
- Socialising at work is not common.
- One task at a time.
- Time is measurable and fixed.
- Personal time (e.g. holiday) must be protected.

Polychronic style
- Meetings often start and finish late.
- The day is not so planned.
- Socialising at work is common.
- Many tasks at a time.
- Time is fluid.
- Personal time is not separate from work time.

▶ Business across cultures page 154

Checklist

✓ words to do with start-ups: *venture capitalist, backer, business plan ...*

✓ passives: *this product was developed by a small software company*

✓ running a meeting

✓ time: monochronic and polychronic styles

8 Inventions

Thomas Edison (1847–1931) said that invention is 99 per cent perspiration and 1 per cent inspiration.

Start-up

Ⓐ Do you agree with what Thomas Edison said about invention? Why / why not?

Ⓑ What other qualities do inventors need?

Ⓒ Discuss some common inventions. Which do you think are the most useful and which are the least useful?

Vocabulary and listening

Ⓐ Match the two parts of these statements related to inventions.

If you ...

1 want to see if your idea works in practice,
2 make a big improvement,
3 want to protect your idea so that others cannot copy it,
4 want to show your product to possible buyers,
5 want someone to invest in your product.
6 allow others to make and sell a product based on your idea,
7 want to sell your product yourself,
8 make large quantities of products for customers,

a you **apply for a patent**.
b you **manufacture** them **on an industrial scale**.
c you **make a breakthrough**.
d you **license your product** to them: you **sign a licensing agreement**.
e you could **exhibit at trade shows**.
f you **make a series of prototypes**.
g you **look for a financial backer**.
h you need to **set up your own company**.

🎧 8.1 Ⓑ Listen to the interview with Mandy Haberman, inventor of a non-spill cup for children. Which of the expressions in bold in A do you hear?

Ⓒ Listen to the interview again and answer the questions.

1 What gave Mandy Haberman the idea for a non-spill cup?
2 What area did she have experience in?
3 Did she want to manufacture the cups herself at the beginning?
4 What did she do to market the cups?
5 How did she persuade Tesco to sell the product?

Ⓓ Put the events in the correct order.

a She set up her own company to make the non-spill cups.
b Mandy Haberman had the idea for a non-spill cup when she saw a girl spilling a drink. 1
c She looked for companies to make and sell her product.
d She applied for a patent.
e She made a series of prototypes.
f Tesco, the supermarket chain, agreed to sell her product.
g She demonstrated her product at trade shows.

Grammar

Past perfect and past simple

- Look at these examples. Underline the past simple and past perfect in each sentence.

When Mandy developed the non-spill cup, she had worked with plastics before.

She didn't go to see companies until she had made a finished product.

Had Mandy applied for a patent when she went to see companies about her product?

A Look at the first two sentences above again. Which happened first in each one, a or b?

1 a Mandy developed the cup   b Mandy worked with plastics.

2 a She made a finished product.   b She went to see companies.

B Match each tense (1–2) to its use (a–b).

1 Past simple   a You use this to refer to an event in the past

2 Past perfect   b You use this to refer to an event that happened before another event in the past.

C Complete the rule.

The past perfect is formed using _____ + the _____ _____ of the verb.

D Complete the sentences using the past perfect or the past simple.

1 Before Mandy _____ (go) to see the company, she _____ (already make) a finished product.
Before Mandy went to see the company, she had already made a finished product.

2 She _____ (not apply) for a patent until she _____ (make) a series of prototypes.

3 She _____ (make) a series of prototypes after she _____ (see) a child spilling a drink.

4 Before manufacturing _____ (start), Mandy _____ (already set up) her own company.

5 Mandy _____ (send) the package after she _____ (contact) the Tesco buyer.

6 When she _____ (start) work on the project, _____ she _____ (already meet) the company CEOs?

E Make sentences about Tamsin Bart using the past perfect.

She had already studied French before she moved to Geneva.

She had completed her MBA when she joined Credit Suisse.

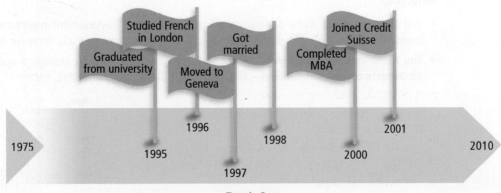

Tamsin Bart

▶ Review and development page 46

▶ Grammar overview page 162

F Draw a timeline showing events in your own life and career. With a partner, talk about events on your timeline.

Communication

Meetings 2: *Participating in meetings*

When we participate in meetings, we have different roles – we may be expected to present something or help to make decisions or plan action. In many meetings, it is important to come up with new ideas. Brainstorming is a way of getting as many ideas as quickly as possible. In all types of meetings, it is important to be clear about what is expected of the participants.

8.2 **A** **Listen to the openings of three meetings (1–3). What does the chairperson expect of the participants?**

a to update and inform each other

b to innovate and create new ideas

c to consider options to solve a problem

B **Do you go to these types of meetings? Do you go to any other types of meetings?**

8.3 **C** **Listen to an extract from a brainstorming session. The participants are discussing ways to improve their exhibition stand at a trade fair. Make a note of their ideas.**

D **Listen again and tick the expressions in the Key language box that you hear.**

Key language

Check understanding of the task	Is that clear? Where do we want to be at the end of the meeting?
Ask for opinions / ideas	What do you think? What's your opinion? What do you feel about ...? Do you have you anything to add?
Give opinions	I think ... In my opinion, we should ... As I see it, ...
Clarify opinions / ideas	Do you mean ...? If I understand you correctly, you are saying ...? In other words, you think ...
Interrupt	Excuse me, ... May I interrupt? ...
Summarise	Let me summarise, ... Before we move on, let's see what we've got so far ...

E **Choose one of the topics below and hold a brainstorming session. Use the Key language to help you.**

- You all work in the same open-plan office. The working environment hasn't changed for years – it looks the same; feels the same, and sounds the same. How can you improve it?
- You never celebrate with your colleagues. This year you want to arrange a special party. Explore all aspects of this celebration – the best time, place, type of event, etc.

▶ Review and development page 47

▶ Communication page 151

Developing a culture of innovation

Management writer Peter Drucker thought that 'business has two and only these two basic functions: marketing and innovation.' There is no doubt that encouraging innovation at work is critical for business success. This section explores how companies can develop a culture of innovation.

A **What do you think of these ideas for encouraging innovation at work? Can you add any other ideas?**

–reward employees who come up with new ideas

–make sure the R&D boss is on the board

–paint the offices yellow

–reduce the number of layers in a company

–hold meetings standing up

–recruit creative people

–don't punish mistakes

–increase the R&D budget

B **Read about Google and how it tries to encourage innovation. Which of the ideas in A are mentioned in the text? Are there any additional ideas?**

What's it like inside Google? It's a collection of really smart people who think they are creating something that's the best in the world, according to Peter Norvig, a Google engineering director.

Google hires two sorts of engineers. First it looks for young risk-takers – people who have no fear of going outside the limits of what they know. But it also hires stars, the top brains from the industry – people who know enough to shoot holes in ideas before they go too far.

The challenge is negotiating between risk and caution. Google used to have management in engineering and the structure was telling people "you can't do that". So Google got rid of the managers. Now most engineers work in teams of three, with project leadership rotating among team members. Wayne Rosing, who heads Google's engineers, says "It works because the teams know what they have to do. They understand that they are the boss. They don't wait to be managed."

Its talent allows Google flexibility – the ability to experiment and try many things at once. Their website includes at least ten technologies in development. It wants feedback and ideas. People understand that not everything Google puts on view will work perfectly. Google has said: "We're going to try things and some aren't going to work". Failure is good.

Google doesn't market in a traditional sense. Instead, it observes and it listens. Ten full-time employees do nothing but read emails from users. The result is that Google has a unique understanding of its users. Most companies would sooner let temporary workers into their executive washroom than let customers anywhere near their core technology but Google takes advantage of engaged customers.

Google has no strategic planning department. The CEO Eric Schmidt does not say which technologies should be developed or which products should be launched. The more popular an idea, the more support it wins, the better its chances.

▶ Business across cultures page 154

C **Brainstorm how you would make your company / organisation more innovative.**

Checklist

✔ developing new products: *make a breakthrough, apply for a patent, look for a financial backer …*

✔ past perfect: *before she went to the company, she had developed the finished product*

✔ participating in meetings

✔ developing a culture of innovation

Pitching for finance

Background

Tiger Venture Capital (TVC) is based in Amsterdam. Every month it invests €110 million in new projects. This month three teams of entrepreneurs are pitching for financial backing. They want to raise capital to finance a new product or service.

Work in four teams: TVC and three teams of entrepreneurs, A, B, and C. Read all the instructions on this page before you begin.

Procedure

Make your pitch

Each team of entrepreneurs makes a pitch about its product or service to the TVC team. (The notes in the box provide some ideas to help you get started.)

The other teams listen to each pitch.

The TVC team asks questions to find out more about the product / service.

TVC team: Look at the instructions on page 43.

Team A: Turn to page 104.

Team B: Turn to page 111.

Team C: Turn to page 112.

Making a pitch

Be ready to talk about:

- the details of your product and / or service
- the competition, and how your product / service is different / better etc
- your management team
- the company's operations
- the financial aspects
- the chances of success

Discussion

The whole class discusses the viability of each project.

Decision time

TVC decides to back one or two projects this month. It decides which project(s) to back and gives its reasons.

TVC team

You will listen to each team make their pitch and then ask questions to find out more information about each product or service. Challenge what the presenters say, if necessary.

Team A wants financial backing for a helicopter service for business people.

Team B wants financial backing for a vending machine which sells flowers.

Team C wants financial backing to develop a range of designer jewellery.

Below are some possible ways of starting questions. Prepare more questions of your own.

Can you tell us something / more about ...?

Can you go into more detail about ...?

How would you describe ...?

Could you explain in more detail ...?

Writing

In groups, write an email from TVC to the team of entrepreneurs whose project has been rejected.

- Thank them for coming to your offices in Amsterdam.
- Thank them for their pitch and say that you have decided not to invest in their project. Give your reasons.
- Close suitably.

43

| Vocabulary | **Personal characteristics** |

A Look again at the vocabulary in Unit 5. What do these statements reveal about the people who made them? Match the characteristics (a–g) with the statements (1–7).

a self-confident   c risk-taking   e inflexible   g over-cautious

b creative   d flexible   f unimaginative

1 I've got my own ways of working, and I don't like adapting to other people's ways.

2 When my manager asked me to think of a slogan for our new product, my mind was a complete blank.

3 When I left university, I set up my own company, but unfortunately it failed after a year. I knew it would be tough, but I was willing to take the chance.

4 I don't mind changing the way I do things to fit with other members of my team.

5 I like standing up in front of a large audience to give a presentation. I know they're going to be impressed!

6 In my last job, I had a budget of €200,000 for a new product launch. I only used €30,000 because I didn't want to spend too much. Sadly, the launch failed.

7 When someone asks me to write advertisements, I'm never short of ideas.

B Work in pairs. You are at a job interview. Take turns to be the interviewer and the candidate. Ask and answer questions about the characteristics (a–d) above. For example:

A: *Would you say that you're self-confident?*

B: *Yes, in my last job I managed ten research scientists – they're very independent people. You have to be self-confident to do that!*

▶ Grammar overview
page 159

C Look again at the vocabulary in Unit 5. In some of the sentences below, one or more of the word endings are wrong. Tick (✓) the correct sentences and correct the incorrect words.

1 Entrepreneurs need two kinds of strongness – mental, and physical – to be able to work 16 hours a day.

2 Innovement is the key to success for new companies.

3 In the long run, businesses must be competitiveness to survive and grow.

4 Reliability is essential if you want your customers to trust you.

5 Persistment means being able to accept 100 negative replies before you get a positive one.

6 Inquisitiveness is a key quality for any future entrepreneur.

7 Self-confidentiality is fine, but be careful it doesn't turn into arrogance!

Grammar

Will and going to

A Look again at the rules and examples on page 31. Then match each sentence (1–3) with its use (a-c).

1 She is going to look for a new job.

2 I won't use this company again. Your service is terrible!

3 With so much competition these days, it'll be really difficult to increase sales.

a a prediction based on present evidence

b a promise about the future

c a future plan or intention

B Complete the sentences using the correct form of the verbs in the box. (Sometimes there is more than one possibility.)

| promote   recruit   recover   increase   finish   ~~be~~   lose   go up   cut |

1 The company _____won't be_____ successful as it hasn't adapted to the changing environment.

2 They _____ their advertising budget next year to save money.

3 Employees who arrive late for work every morning _____ their jobs.

4 The reputation of the company _____ because they found bacteria in its products.

5 Because of the increase in inflation, prices _____ .

6 If employees work hard now, the company _____ them.

7 They _____ the best engineers to work on the new model.

8 I _____ this report by Monday morning.

9 She has worked really hard this year. We _____ her salary by ten per cent.

C Now match each sentence in B, with its correct use from A. The first one has been done for you as an example.

1 The company *won't be* successful as it hasn't adapted to the changing environment.   a

▶ Grammar overview
page 160

Grammar

Passives

A Look again at the examples and rules on page 35. Make a present passive sentence about each of these steps in a company's recruitment process.

1 Request from department manager for new staff member
A new staff member is requested by a department manager
2 Place advertisement on appropriate websites
3 Sort and analyse candidates' applications
4 Draw up shortlist
5 Interview shortlisted candidates
6 Check references
7 Notify successful candidate

B Now use the passive to talk about the recruitment process in your organisation, or one you have applied to work for.

C Complete this article with the correct passive forms of the words in brackets.

The island of Doluba was discovered in 1498. The forests on the island (1) _____ (log) for many years. Now nearly all the trees (2) _____ (cut down). At this point, there are a number of possibilities. The president suggests that new trees (3) _____ (might / plant). But opponents say that it's better for agriculture to (4) _____ (develop). And others say that investment (5) _____ (should / pour) into tourism. A decision (6) _____ (make) soon.

▶ Grammar overview page 161

Grammar

Past perfect

A Look at the rules and examples on page 39. Complete the sentences using the past perfect form of the verb in brackets.

1 Did James Watt invent the steam engine? No, Denis Papin _____ already _____ (invent) the steam engine. Watt improved it.

2 Was Marconi the first to work on radio technology? No, Heinrich Hertz _____ _____ (work) in this area ten years earlier.

3 Did John Logie Baird invent television? Yes, but there _____ already _____ (be) a lot of research in the United States.

4 Was the computer invented by a commercial company after the Second World War? No, Alan Turing _____ _____ (build) the first computer in the UK during the war.

5 Did Tim Berners-Lee invent the Internet? No, the American military _____ _____ (develop) it during the 1980s. Berners-Lee wrote the computer language that allowed computers to talk to each other on the World Wide Web.

▶ Grammar overview page 162

ommunication Look again at the communication skills pages in Units 5–8. Then complete these exercises.

A Complete the following verb phrases.

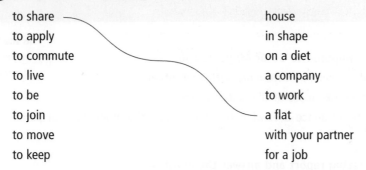

to share	house
to apply	in shape
to commute	on a diet
to live	a company
to be	to work
to join	a flat
to move	with your partner
to keep	for a job

B Work in pairs. Ask and answer questions using the phrases in A.

C Match each question or comment to an appropriate response.

Questions / Comments	Response
1 Would you like to meet for a drink?	a No, that's fine.
2 May I call you John?	b It was a pleasure.
3 I'm really sorry. I didn't mean to.	c I'd love to.
4 Would you mind calling later?	d So did I.
5 Here you are. It's just something small.	e Please do.
6 I look forward to seeing you again.	f That's very kind. You shouldn't have.
7 I really enjoyed the film.	g So do I.
8 Thanks for all your support.	h Never mind.

D Complete this advice about meetings using the words in the box.

items	taking	circulate	attend	actions	copy
fixed	follow up	agenda	hold	get down	

Before you (1) _____ a meeting, it is important to prepare the (2) _____ _____ and ask participants to propose (3) _____ they want to discuss. You also need to make sure that the participants can (4) _____ the meeting and ask them to prepare any special contributions. Once you have (5) _____ the time of the meeting, it's a good idea to circulate a (6) _____ of the agenda.

At the start of the meeting, you may want to (7) _____ to business quickly. Try to keep an eye on the main purpose and direction of the meeting. It's easy to spend too much time on some items and then have to rush the meeting at the end. Make sure that somebody is (8) _____ the minutes and recording any (9) _____ which need to be taken. Soon after the meeting, (10) _____ the minutes and (11) _____ on any actions.

E In pairs, practise asking for, giving, and clarifying an opinion.

Example
A: *What do you feel about meetings?*
B: *I think they are a waste of time.*
A: *Do you mean all meetings?*
B: *Well, maybe there are one or two which you need to have.*

Talk about these topics:

• making meetings more effective   • socialising after work   • developing creativity at work

▶ Writing resource 18
page 94

9 Kids as consumers

Start-up

Do you think that compared to 30 or 40 years ago:

- parents and children communicate more with each other?
- parents and children like more of the same music?
- children have more influence over what the family eats, the products their parents buy, where they go on holiday, etc.?

> In the USA, children see an average of 30,000 TV commercials every year.

Reading

A Read this marketing report and answer the questions.

USING "PESTER-POWER" IS NO WAY TO BUILD A BRAND
Today's Families Operate Under Team Decision-Making Dynamic

For years, marketers have used phrases like "pester-power" and the "nag-factor" to describe the way children talk their parents into making purchases. According to marketing consultancy Yankelovich, Inc., these phrases miss several key, emerging trends among parents and kids.

John Page, Youth Insights Manager at Yankelovich says, 'From cookies to cars, video games to video cameras and snack foods to stores, kids and parents are making decisions together about what to buy, do and enjoy.' The "nag-factor" is a thing of the past because parents often find enjoyment in the very same things their children do. In fact, 74 per cent of parents say 'my child and I have a lot in common when it comes to things we like to do and buy,' according to the Yankelovich study. Examples in the marketplace include:

- the latest electronic gadgets
- blockbuster film hits
- the continuing popularity of "evergreen" brands in the food and drink category.

The study also found half of parents say they 'really enjoy a lot of today's pop culture, such as music, fashion, the popular shows and celebrities, and things like that.'

So marketers have tremendous opportunities in this area. They can tap into the "team decision-making" dynamic by understanding that the pre-shopping, actual purchase and usage of many products and offerings are family experiences. 90 per cent of parents say they 'talk about more things with my child than my parents talked about with me.' Children have plenty of influence in the decision-making process.

---

1 What are 'pester-power' and the 'nag-factor'?

2 Why are they less relevant now than before?

3 For what types of products do parents have the same tastes as their children?

4 Give examples of two or three 'evergreen' brands in your country.

5 Why do you think parents and children often share the same taste in music, fashion and TV programmes?

6 What does all this mean for marketers?

Information exchange

Grammar

Exchange more information about the way parents and children make decisions about their purchases. Student A looks at page 105. Student B looks at page 109.

Count and uncount nouns

* Some nouns can have a plural form. These are count nouns.

New trends are emerging in the decisions that families make about their purchases.

* Some nouns do not have a plural form. You cannot use them with *a / an*. These are uncount nouns.

Parents often find enjoyment in the very same things their children do.

* Some nouns can be count or uncount.

America is the land of opportunity.

Marketers have tremendous opportunities in this area.

* You can use *some*, *a lot of*, *lots of*, and *plenty of* with both count and uncount nouns.

Some children refuse to take 'no' for an answer.

Parents often find a lot of enjoyment in the very same things their children do.

Children have plenty of influence in the decision-making process.

* You use *much* with uncount nouns and *many* with count nouns.

How much influence do children have?

There aren't many products that parents choose without consulting their children.

Ⓐ Which of these nouns are count nouns, which are uncount, and which can be both?

influence	enjoyment	power	popularity	decision
purchase	factor	gadget	advertising	information

Ⓑ Underline the correct answers.

1 Husbands and wives make (much / lots of) their important buying decisions together.
2 There aren't (much / many) trends that marketers are unaware of.
3 'Evergreen' products have benefited from (many / a lot of) popularity over the years.
4 Advertising has (a lot of / many) power, but it shouldn't be overestimated.
5 Consumer choice is affected by (plenty of / much) different influences, including word of mouth.
6 Consumers don't make (much / many) big purchases in January.
7 Some people don't get (many / much) enjoyment from the products they buy.

▶ Review and development page 66

▶ Grammar overview page 163

Communication

Telephoning 1: *Opening and responding*

The opening step in communication is always critical. This is particularly true on the telephone when you need to make contact with your business partner from a distance.

9.1 **A** Listen to the opening of five calls. Match the caller to the purpose.

Caller	Purpose
1 Patrick	a to chase a delivery
2 Gerard Manley	b to pass on some news
3 Helen	c to get payment
4 Morgan Benton	d to make a request
5 Susan Freeman	e to talk about tax

B Listen again and tick the phrases in the Key language box that you hear.

Key language

	Opening a call	Responding
Identifying yourself	This is … My name is … … speaking It's … here.	Good morning, Customer Service. What can I do for you? Who's calling? Can I take your name? How can I help you? I'm sorry. I didn't catch your name. I thought I recognised your voice.
Asking for connection	Could I speak to …? Could you put me through to …?	I'll see if I can connect you. I'm afraid the line's engaged / he's out / not answering his phone. Can I get him to call you back? Could you call back later? Can I take a message?
Reason for calling	I'm calling about … The reason I'm calling is …	Could you tell me what it's about? What's it in connection with?

C Work in pairs. Student A looks at this page. Student B looks at page 105. Practise telephoning Student B. Just practise the opening of these calls.

Student A

1 You want to speak to Susan Barker. You want to arrange a meeting with her.

2 You want to speak to Greg Sayer. He is a client and you want to discuss a new project with him.

3 Call the company Filtons. You want to speak to someone in Accounts about an unpaid invoice.

Now practise responding to Student B's calls.

4 Student B calls to speak to Max Clifton. Max is away on holiday. Find out the purpose of the call.

5 Student B calls your company: Milligans. He / she wants to speak to someone in the order despatch department. Make sure you get the name of the caller and the purpose of the call before you connect him / her.

6 Student B calls to speak to Dan Peters. You are Dan Peters and you are in charge of Purchasing. Student B is a supplier. He / she wants to discuss your new purchasing contract. This is not a good time to speak. Arrange to call back.

▶ Review and development page 69

▶ Communication page 151

Understanding corporate culture

As we saw in Unit 2, there are different layers of culture. In business, sometimes company culture is more significant than the local country culture. This section focuses on the culture of one company and aims to develop your understanding of corporate culture in general.

A Read the article about Semco, an unusual company based in Brazil.

The company was founded in 1952 by Antonio Semler and specialised in manufacturing marine pumps. When his son Ricardo took over in 1980, one of his first actions was to dismiss 75 per cent of the senior executives. Semco has no job titles, no organisation charts, and no headquarters. If you need an office, you go online and reserve space at one of the few satellite offices scattered around São Paulo.

Many workers, including factory workers, set their own schedules and choose their own salaries. What prevents them from taking advantage of this freedom? First, all the company's financial information is public, so everyone knows what everybody else makes. Second, associates must reapply for their jobs every six months. Pay yourself unfairly and you could soon be looking for a new job. Finally, employee compensation[1] is tied directly to the company's profits so there is enormous peer pressure to keep budgets in line.

Workers choose their managers and evaluate them twice a year. The results are publicly posted. Meetings are voluntary; if no one shows up, it means that the topics must be untimely or unimportant. Semco has no receptionists, secretaries, or personal assistants. All employees, including Semler, greet their own guests, get their own coffee, write and send their own correspondence, and make their own photocopies.

If all this sounds like a recipe for chaos and anarchy, consider this – Semco's products are so good and its customer service so efficient that 80 per cent of its turnover comes from repeat business. Over the last decade, the company's sales increased by 600 per cent and profitability by 500 per cent. With a current backlog of more than 2,000 job applications, Semco has had less than 1 per cent turnover among its 3,000 employees in the last six years.

[1]Compensation = salary and benefits

B Discuss the questions.

1 What is the impact on company culture of making all financial information public?
2 What is the impact on employee motivation of allowing workers to decide their own schedules and salaries?
3 What do you think about evaluating managers twice a year?
4 Do you agree with getting rid of receptionists, secretaries, and personal assistants?
5 Would you like to work for a company like Semco?

C Draw an iceberg (see Unit 1, page 7) of a company or organisational culture that you know. Use these ideas to get you started.

Above the surface

- what you observe when you enter the company or walk around the factory / offices
- how people are dressed

Below the surface

- history of the company
- management style
- relationships between owners and employees
- compensation scheme
- values of the organisation

▶ Business across cultures page 154

Checklist

✓ marketing to parents and children

✓ count and uncount nouns: *influence, enjoyment, trend, power*

✓ opening and responding to a telephone call

✓ understanding corporate culture

51

10 Selling yourself

A What do you think are the secrets of success at work? Use these ideas to help you.

qualifications   experience   personal qualities   connections

> The US personal coaching industry – where coaches help people to sell themselves – is now worth $100 million a year.

 10.1

A Listen to an interview with Rebecca Sands, a human resources specialist. In what order does she mention the advice below? Which item does she *not* mention?

a writing a personal mission statement
b updating your skills through training so that you remain marketable
c seeking the services of a coach
d reading professional magazines
e keeping a work diary
f doing psychometric tests
g developing self-awareness

B Listen again and make notes about each topic in A that Rebecca mentions.

10.2 **C** Listen to four people talking about the advice in A. In each speech, which of the items (a–g) does the word *it* refer to?

D Discuss these questions with a partner.

1 What do you think of the advice in A above? Have you ever followed any of it?

2 Are you good at selling yourself? What could you do to improve?

Vocabulary and speaking

A Complete the first two columns of the table and then match the adjectives with their definitions.

Noun	Adjective	Adjective definition
		Someone who …
1 self-awareness	self-aware	a puts a lot of work and effort into doing things
2	numerate	b is able to change their methods, approach etc. easily
3 motivation		c uses their imagination to produce new ideas
4 flexibility		d understands and can use numbers
5	creative	e works hard on something and does not abandon it
6 energy		f is willing to do things without being told to
7	committed	g works well with others
8 cooperation		h knows and understands their own character and personality

B Complete these sentences with appropriate forms from the table.

1 I seem to have a lot of _____. I start each day with a 30-minute run, I work 14 hours a day, and I never get tired.

2 People tell me that I'm quite _____ – I'm good at coming up with new approaches to problems.

3 I stayed with my last employer for 15 years. Though I say it myself, I was very _____ to the company.

4 In my last job I prepared some pretty complicated budgets. I think I have a reasonable level of _____.

5 I consider that I'm a self-starter. In my last job, I saw what needed to be done and just did it without being told to by my managers. I was very _____.

6 I think it's important not to be rigid. If I see that one approach isn't working, I change it. _____ is key.

7 People tell me I'm very _____ and that I work well with others.

C Read the explanation, then make other sentences about Tom with the adjectives below.

To form negatives, you sometimes use prefixes like -un, -in etc.
Sometimes you use *not very*.
motivated → Tom's *unmotivated*. / He's *not very motivated*.
self-aware → Tom's *not very self-aware*.

1 flexible
2 creative
3 energetic
4 committed
5 cooperative
6 numerate

D Work in pairs. Say five things about yourself using appropriate forms.

I'm self-aware – I know what my strengths and weaknesses are.

▶ Review and development page 67

▶ Grammar overview page 164

Communication

Telephoning 2: *Leaving and taking messages*

We leave messages on answerphones, voiceboxes, and with colleagues. We also take messages, write them down and pass them on to colleagues. This section focuses on leaving and taking clear messages.

🔊 10.3 **A** Listen to three messages and complete the notes below.

Name of caller: . . . .
Message: . . . .
Action: . . . .
Contact number: . . . .

Name of caller: . . . .
Message: . . . .
Action: . . . .
Contact number: . . . .

Name of caller: . . . .
Message: . . . .
Action: . . . .
Contact number: . . . .

Key language

	Taking a message	Leaving a message
Offering / requesting help	Can I take a message? Would you like to leave a message?	I'd like to leave a message for …
Names	Could I take your name, please? Could you spell that, please?	It's Gifford. Shall I spell that for you? It's G - I - double F - O - R - D.
Numbers	Could I have your number? Has he / she got your number?	Let me give you my mobile number. It's 07801 200 087. He's got my number.
Requesting action	Let me get a pen. OK. Go ahead.	Could you tell him / her that …? Could you ask him / her to …? Could you / he / she call me back? Please tell him / her I'll call back later.
Checking details	Could you say that again, please? Let me just repeat that.	Of course. That's right.
Confirming action	I'll make sure she gets the message. I'll tell him you called. I'll get him to call you as soon as he gets back.	Thanks. Thanks for your help.

B **Work in pairs. Use the Key language above to help you. Student A looks at this page. Student B looks at page 105.**

Student A

1 Practise leaving the following messages with Student B.

   a You'd like to speak to Patrick Sullivan about a meeting next week. Please ask him to call back. Leave your mobile number.

   b You want to speak to Garfield Tober. He called you this morning and you are returning the call. You are going out but will be in the office tomorrow morning.

2 Practise taking Student B's messages.

   a Kate O'Brien is not available. Take a message.

   b Pretend to be the voicebox of Pascal Durand. Say 'I am out of the office. Please leave your name, number, and message and I'll get back to you as soon as possible.'

▶ Review and development page 69

▶ Communication page 151

Customer service culture

Customer service has become key for companies who want to remain competitive. This section focuses on what it means to put the customer at the centre of your business.

A Read about the mission of Carphone Warehouse, Europe's most successful mobile phone retailer.

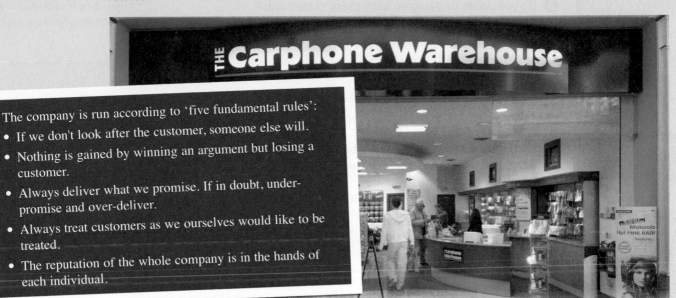

The company is run according to 'five fundamental rules':

- If we don't look after the customer, someone else will.
- Nothing is gained by winning an argument but losing a customer.
- Always deliver what we promise. If in doubt, under-promise and over-deliver.
- Always treat customers as we ourselves would like to be treated.
- The reputation of the whole company is in the hands of each individual.

B Which of these statements does *not* fit with the five fundamental rules in A?

a The customer is always right.

b One bad employee can damage a company.

c Look after your employees.

d Deliver what the customer wants.

e Competitors will steal your customers if you don't pay them enough attention.

C What are the opposites of these words and phrases? (Some of the answers are in the text in A.)

to look after a customer
to gain a new customer
to over-promise
to treat a customer well

to be competitive
to be helpful
to smile
to be polite

D Discuss your own experiences of good and bad customer service. Think of examples from these areas:

public sector (e.g. schools, tax authority)
retail (a shop or chain of shops)
utility companies (e.g. energy, telecoms)
transport (e.g. airlines, trains)

E How would you get employees to care about customers? Brainstorm some ideas, for example:

> Business across cultures
> page 154

training   incentive schemes   profit sharing

Checklist

✓ selling yourself: *qualifications, skills, experience ...*

✓ adjectives to do with personal qualities: *self-awareness, flexibility, energy ...*

✓ leaving and taking telephone messages

✓ customer service culture

11 Think global, act local

Start-up

A Do you agree or disagree with these statements? Give your reasons.

1 Industrialised countries are becoming more and more similar:
around the world, people are increasingly buying the same clothes, eating the same foods and buying the same products.

2 The remaining differences between countries will eventually disappear.

3 People in this global market respond to advertisements in the same way.

Listening and vocabulary

A Listen to the first part of an interview with Jane Williams, an expert on global advertising. Which company does she mention? Which countries does she mention?

11.1 **B** Listen again and complete the information about the first advertising campaign.

Slogan: _____

Brand idea: _____

Outcome: _____

What the ad consisted of: _____

Strapline: _____

11.2 **C** Listen to the second part of the interview and complete the information about the second campaign.

Brand idea: _____

Media: _____

What the ad consisted of: _____

Example from website: _____

D Listen again to both parts of the interview and identify six expressions beginning with *global*. Then match the expressions to their meanings.

1 ___advertising___

2 _____

global 3 _____

4 _____

5 _____

6 _____

a when people all over the world know about something

b coordinated advertising that is seen all over the world

c a product or company name known all over the world

d a means of communication received all over the world

e when a company has operations all over the world

f TV stations seen all over the world

Grammar

Infinitives and *-ing* forms

Some verbs are followed by the infinitive form, and some verbs are followed by the *-ing* form. There is no special reason why some verbs take one form and some verbs take the other.

1 Verbs followed by the infinitive form:

agree   decide   fail   guarantee   offer   plan   promise   tend

Technology companies tend to rely on a single global campaign.

They decided to change their brand image.

2 Verbs followed by the *-ing* form:

admit   consider   delay   imagine   involve   mention   risk   suggest

Globobank considered making all their advertisements in English.

He suggested using a new advertising company to launch the product.

Some common phrasal verbs followed the *-ing* form:

carry on (= continue)   put off (= delay)

give up (= stop)   set about (= begin)

3 Sometimes both the infinitive and the *-ing* form are possible and there is no difference in meaning.

Does HSBC intend to continue with ads like this?

Yes, HSBC intends continuing with campaigns of this kind.

Other verbs that can be followed by either the infinitive or the *-ing* form:

attempt   begin   continue   hate   like   prefer   start

Ⓐ Match the two parts of the sentences.

1 Megaco put	a to rebrand its existing product range.
2 The company set	b up advertising on TV.
3 SDF gave	c changing the company logo.
4 They considered	d about attacking the Asian market for the first time.
5 Sonotral Inc. carried	e on filming all its ads in English.
6 ABT planned	f off launching its campaign for six months.

Ⓑ Complete the text by putting the verbs in brackets in the correct form. (Sometimes there is more than one possibility.)

Carla had intended (1) _____ (run) a global campaign, but George persuaded her not to.

He suggested (2) _____ (produce) a number of different local campaigns. George

mentioned (3) _____ (work) on other big campaigns of this kind in the past. He said

he planned (4) _____ (do) something different for Megabank. He had considered

(5) _____ (produce) all the ads in English, but in the end, decided (6) _____

(make) the ads in different local languages. George offered (7) _____ (conduct) more

market research before he started (8) _____ (design) the campaign. Carla agreed

(9) _____ (wait) for the results of this research.

▶ Review and development page 68

▶ Grammar overview page 165

Communication

Telephoning 3: *Structuring a call*

Making an effective telephone call depends on preparation, a clear purpose, an effective process and staying in tune with the person you are calling. This section focuses on the process.

 11.3 **A** Listen to this telephone conversation between Mike Brent and his colleague in Hong Kong, Lucy Chen. Put the points they discuss in the right order.

___ delivery date of headsets   ___ logistics   ___ reason for call: new product launch

___ point-of-sale material   ___ promotion

Key language

Stating the purpose	I'm phoning about … The reason I'm calling is … I'd like to discuss …
Structuring the call	I'd like to cover two main points. Firstly / Secondly / Thirdly / Finally … Now, on the promotion side … Another thing is … I'd like to have a word with you about …
Checking	Is that OK with you? Is this a good time to talk about this?
Deflecting	Can we deal with that another time? I'll get back to you about that.
Taking further action	Could you send me an email to confirm that? Would you inform Peter?
Making a final check	Is there anything else? Is that everything?
Deciding	So we've decided to … Right. Then I'll … I'll leave that to you. Shall I deal with the logistics?

B Listen again and identify the phrases in the Key language box that Mike uses to:

a introduce the purpose of the call

b structure the call into two subjects

c check with Lucy for her agreement

d introduce the first subject

e introduce the second subject

f check for any final points

g deflect a point he doesn't want to deal with now

C Work in pairs. Student A looks at this page. Student B looks at page 106.

Student A

1 You are responsible for organising an important meeting next week. Student B is taking care of the arrangements. Call him / her to confirm the arrangements:

 • Timing: start and finish times, lunch arrangements?

 • Agenda: this needs to be circulated to all the participants – you will email it to Student B after the call

 • Dinner arrangements?

2 Student B will call you about a project you are responsible for. You are writing a progress report and can complete it today. You haven't prepared an update on the budget yet. You also want to talk about a promotion you have been promised.

▶ Review and development page 69

▶ Communication page 152

BUSINESS ACROSS CULTURES

Work and play

Do you like to mix your working life and your social life? Do you socialise with your colleagues after work? This section focuses on key moments in working and playing internationally.

11.4 **A** **Match the conversations (1–5) to the situations (a–e).**

Conversation	Situation
1	a giving a gift
2	b paying for a meal
3	c telling a joke
4	d playing golf
5	e sharing a drink

B **Where can you expect to find this behaviour? Choose your answers from the countries in the box.**

| Poland | France | Australia | China | Brazil | Egypt | Japan | Greece | USA |

a In a pub, it is vital to remember that each person pays for a round of drinks. Missing your turn to 'shout for a round' is a sure way to make a bad impression.

b Sometimes a compass can be a good gift. It enables you to always know where Mecca is. Make sure you give or receive gifts with both hands or your right hand, not with the left hand.

c You can expect up to fifteen courses to be served at a meal. Your host will keep filling your bowl with food whenever you empty it. Finishing all your food might insult your host since it could mean you did not get enough to eat.

d When entering your host's home, take off your shoes at the door. You will wear one pair of slippers from the door to the living room, where you will remove them. You will put them on again to walk to the bathroom, where you will change them for 'toilet slippers.'

e Dinner could take place any time from 19.00 to 22.00. Dinner parties can easily continue until 2.00 a.m. or even later.

f Always bring a gift when visiting. Flowers are the most common gift. Give the flowers, unwrapped, to your hostess. Always bring an odd number of flowers, and avoid red roses (used for courting) and chrysanthemums (used at funerals).

C **Read this advice about humour. Do you agree?**

> It is rarely a good idea to tell jokes, especially political ones. Humour does not easily cross cultural boundaries and what you find amusing will often seem totally unfunny to your guests. You may remember the cartoon where the interpreter listens to the joke the American ambassador is telling, then as a translation announces, "The foreigner just told a joke, everybody laugh!"

D **Prepare some advice to foreigners visiting your country.**

▶ Business across cultures page 154

Checklist

- ✔ the global market: *global campaign, global advertising ...*
- ✔ infinitives and *-ing* forms: *he agreed to make an offer; he considered making an offer ...*
- ✔ structuring a telephone call
- ✔ work and play

PROMOTION

12 The grey market

Start-up

A **Do you agree or disagree with these statements? Give your reasons.**

People over 50 are becoming more similar to younger people in:

the clothes they wear   their musical tastes   the cars they drive

their leisure activities   their choice of holidays   their outlook on life

> **35 million people in the USA are over 65. By 2050, the number will more than double to over 90 million.**

Reading and speaking

A **Read these extracts from an article about advertising in the UK. Answer the questions below.**

By James Arnold BBC News business reporter

… Every creative director knows that the over-50s – currently 20 million strong, and growing fast – hold 80 per cent of the nation's wealth. Trouble is, no one wants to do anything about it: according to a recent survey, two-thirds of elderly consumers felt advertising portrays them negatively, and three-quarters simply didn't relate to it at all

… It doesn't have to be this way … In fact, a few simple rules would suffice:

Don't just entertain – inform.

… Having often more time and more patience than the young, older shoppers will research their purchases in far greater detail, says Reg Starkey, a veteran ad man and creative consultant at agency Millennium Direct. An effective advert, therefore, has to contribute to that research, rather than simply trying to push the emotional or cultural buttons that turn on the young.

Remember: old people are different. Or are they?

… The great debate in the industry is over whether it's worth advertising to older people at all. One camp argues that elderly consumers form their tastes early in life, and barely budge after 40 – and almost never in response to advertising. The other camp insists that the old are just as changeable as the young – they just need special handling.

The second camp seems to be winning out. "Everyone has misconceptions about being old until they are old themselves," says John O'Sullivan, chairman of MWO Advertising. "Anyone who thinks we stop taking in fresh information about products when we're over 50 must be mad." …

1 How many people in the UK are over 50? Is this number increasing?

2 How much of the country's wealth do they own?

3 According to the survey, what proportion of older people relate to advertising?

4 How do older people differ from younger people in what they expect of advertising?

5 In your own words, summarise the two opposing views on older people and advertising. Which view is gaining support?

6 What is your opinion of these two opposing views?

B **Prepare outlines for two different advertisements for one of the products / services below. The first ad should 'push the emotional buttons' for a young audience, and the second should 'contribute to the research' of the older audience.**

cruise ship holiday   skincare cream   motorcycle

mobile phone banking   loft apartment   jeans

Grammar

Present perfect simple and continuous

You form the present perfect simple with *has / have* + the past participle of the verb.

You form the present perfect continuous with *has / have* + *been* + *-ing* form of the verb.

When you want to talk about an action which started in the past and continues up to the present, or is connected with the present in some way, you can often use either the present perfect simple or the present perfect continuous with little difference in meaning.

Life expectancy has increased / has been increasing since the Second World War.

You use the present perfect simple to focus on an action that is now completed and there is a 'result'.

I've written a report on advertising for the over 50s. (The report is now finished.)

You use the present perfect continuous to talk about an action, which may or may not be completed, when you want to want to focus on the action and not the result.

I've been writing the report all morning but I still have to check some facts. (Focus on the continuous action.)

Some common verbs do not usually take a continuous form:

know   like   remember   understand   want

A Complete the sentences. Put one verb in each sentence in the present perfect simple, and the other in the present perfect continuous.

1 We _____ (study) the grey market for some time and we

_____ (decide) to adopt a new strategy for this sector.

2 AXT _____ (run) a successful advertising campaign on TV using retired sports

celebrities. Sales among consumers over the age of 55 _____ (increase) by

8 per cent.

3 Our company _____ (sell) car insurance for five years. This year we

_____ (invest) in a new range of products for older drivers.

4 Until now our commercials _____ (portray) older consumers in a negative light

but _____ (consider) ways to make them appeal to a broader age range.

B Three of the sentences below are not possible. Tick (✓) the ones that are possible. Put a cross (✗) next to the ones that are not possible.

1 For the past ten years, TV advertising has been declining in importance.

2 The Marketing Department has been spending $3 million on the new campaign.

3 Sales have risen dramatically since the new campaign was launched.

4 I'm not sure I've been understanding the results of this market survey.

5 Recent studies have shown that young people are using the Internet more and more.

6 We've been knowing that our product is in difficulty for some time.

7 She's been doing a lot of research on the current state of the market.

▶ Review and development page 68

▶ Grammar overview page 166

Communication

Telephoning 4: *Closing a call*

Bringing a telephone call to an end can be difficult. Some calls are too long, others are too short. You need to listen for closing signals and be able to use these signals appropriately yourself.

🎧 12.1 **A** **Listen to two telephone calls. What are the actions as a result of the calls?**

1 _____ 2 _____

B **Look at the Key language below. Then listen again and identify the expressions used.**

Call 1	Call 2
Signal closing: _____	Confirm action: _____
Confirm action: _____	Promise action: _____
Promise action: _____	Signal closing: _____
Close positively: _____	Close positively: _____

Key language

Signal closing	Anyway / Right / OK … Shall we leave it there? It's been good to talk to you. Is there anything else? I'm sorry I have to go.
Confirming action	Can I just confirm that …? Let me just go over that. Would you like me to put that in writing? Could you confirm that by email?
Promising action	I'll get on with it straight away I'll get back to you as soon as possible. I'll do that.
Thanking	Thanks again. Thanks for your support / help.
Closing positively	Nice to speak to you. Have a good trip / weekend. See you on Monday. I hope you catch your train.

C **Work in pairs. Student A looks at this page. Student B looks at page 106.**

Student A

1 You have been talking to Student B, who will join your team next month. You called to discuss the arrangements for his / her first day. You have arranged to meet him / her for lunch on Tuesday. Close the call and finish positively.

2 Student B is your boss. He / she has called you to ask for a report to be finished as soon as possible. Respond to Student B appropriately.

▶ Review and development page 69

▶ Communication page 152

(handwritten at top: ≠ Reportments.)

Working in cross-functional teams

Inside organisations, there is often a 'silo mentality', that is, a breakdown of communication and understanding between different departments. For example, Finance doesn't understand Marketing or Human Resources has little experience of the concerns of Logistics. One way to stop the silo mentality is to encourage people to work in cross-functional teams.

(diagram of departments: R&D, Marketing, Production, Logistics, Human Resources, Finance — with handwritten notes: "Research on Development / Create new products", "silo", "hire people", "money - more y")

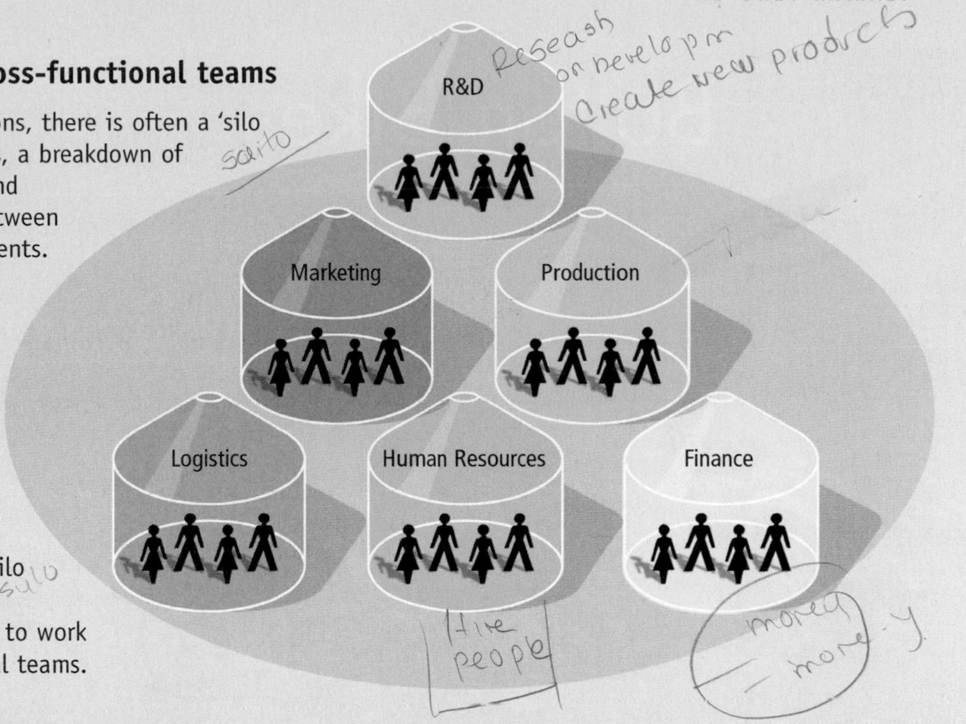

A Match the department to its role.

Department		Role
1	R&D	a to manage the flow from raw material to customer delivery
2	Marketing	b to control and plan the use of resources to cover costs and investment
3	Production	c to equip the organisation with the right people
4	Logistics	d to match the company's products and services to the needs of consumers
5	Human Resources	e to guarantee a pipeline of new products and innovations
6	Finance	f to maintain the supply of top quality products

(handwritten: equip, Pipe/information)

🎧 12.2 **B** Listen to four people talking about their concerns. Which of the departments in A do they come from?

C We often have stereotypes about people who work in different departments. Decide which of these adjectives describe which department, and then add a few of your own.

dynamic   innovative   thorough   steady   boring   vague
detailed   supportive   thoughtful   exciting   caring   slow

(handwritten annotations surrounding the adjectives: Logistics, R&D, Finance, R&D HR, marketing, Production logistic, Human resource, undecided, etc.)

D Discuss the role of different departments in the success of a business. Which department is the most important?

E Work in cross-functional teams. In your team, choose one of the roles on page 106 and discuss the problem below.

Your company produces personal security products. You have recently launched a new product called Protector XP, which combines an alarm with a mild form of pepper spray. Sales have been very good. Women like this product, which they can use to protect themselves. However, you have just been informed of a case in which a criminal used the pepper spray to attack a woman and steal her money. This news will reach the press in the next hour. What are you going to do?

▶ Business across cultures page 155

Checklist

✓ selling products and services to the grey market

✓ present perfect simple and continuous

✓ closing a telephone call

✓ breaking down the silo mentality

Bolton Bikes

Background

Bolton Bikes is a Canadian company founded in Vancouver 20 years ago by former cycling champion, Tessa Bolton. The bike's revolutionary design has made it a big success among leisure users and commuters alike. Increasing costs mean that the company is transferring all its production to China.

The right qualities

A Look at this job advertisement.

BOLTON **BIKES**

PRODUCTION MANAGER

Based in China

As part of our strategic development plan, we are transferring manufacturing to our own plant in Shanghai, China. We are looking for a Production Manager to help us get this exciting project off the ground.

The position involves:
- overseeing installation of new machinery and opening of plant.
- recruiting 300 local workers in conjunction with a local agency.
- ensuring good working conditions and efficiency.
- reaching production targets set by management in Vancouver.

This is a challenging role for an experienced person. Ability to speak Cantonese desirable but not essential (local interpreters available).

Duration of contract: 18 months non-renewable. Attractive package (salary + benefits)

B Managers on international assignments need the following skills / qualities:

language skills	openness	drive	patience
communication skills	flexibility	emotional strength	sensitivity
cultural understanding	autonomy	physical stamina	

Look at the job advertisement again. Which of these qualities will the Production Manager need?

roup interview

SaS company

Tessa Bolton has asked an outside consultant, Tim Lombard, to help with the recruitment of the new Production Manager for the Shanghai plant. She has asked him not to look at CVs, but to have an informal group discussion with the three candidates, Susie Chang, Jim Kolowski (both of whom work at Bolton Bikes) and Lee Kong (an external candidate).

Work in groups of four:

Student A: You are Tim Lombard. Look at this page.

Student B: You are Susie Chang. Look at page 107.

Student C: You are Jim Kolowski. Look at page 109.

Student D: You are Lee Kong. Look at page 113.

Student A

You are Tim Lombard, the outside consultant employed by Tessa Bolton to help with the recruitment of the new Production Manager for the Shanghai plant. You will have an informal group discussion with the three candidates.

Use the notes below to help you prepare questions and add some questions of your own.

- Ask candidates to introduce themselves briefly and say something about their backgrounds.
- Ask them to say more about their personal skills and qualities.
- Ask them what specifically makes them suitable for this job, in relation to their:
  background   education   personal qualities and skills   recent achievements
- Ask them what they think the toughest challenges will be.

Writing

Write an email from Tim Lombard to Tessa Bolton, saying which candidate you think is the most suitable and why.

Grammar

Count and uncount nouns

A Look again at the rules and examples on page 49. Then decide which of these nouns are uncount only, and which can be both count and uncount.

influence   experience   employment   progress   information   behaviour

B Use the correct forms of the nouns above to complete these sentences.

1 In this part of the country, there is full _____ and no one is unemployed for long.

2 Marketers are very interested in consumer _____ and it's also a popular subject in business schools.

3 Children are exposed to many different _____, not only from advertising, but also from their family and friends.

4 There's always plenty of _____ when you want to buy a computer: the problem is to make sense of it all!

5 We're looking for people with a lot of _____ in managing salespeople: at least five years.

6 Some _____ has been made in understanding how the human mind works, but the

C Work in pairs. Using combinations from the table, ask and answer questions about your own organisation, or one you would like to work for.

some	travel
much / many	advice
a lot of / lots of	experience
plenty of	employees
	opportunities for promotion
	different products and services

Example:

A: *Is there much travel in your job?*

B: *Not much. About one trip every three months, to a trade fair.*

Vocabulary

Personal qualities

A Look again at the vocabulary on page 53. Then rephrase sentences 1–6, replacing each underlined expression with one of these nouns in the box.

| capability   commitment   honesty   literacy   maturity   responsibility |

1 Diana shows very high levels of <u>willingness to work hard and make sure that things are done as well as possible</u>.
2 Senior managers have high levels of <u>duty to make sure that things go as planned, and will get blamed if things go wrong</u>.
3 School leavers have lower levels of <u>ability in reading and writing</u> than 20 years ago.
4 People working for Astrup are known for their <u>high moral standards and the fact that they never cheat or lie</u>.
5 Paul shows <u>very good judgment and behaves in a very sensible way</u> for someone so young.
6 Does Rachel have the <u>talent and skill</u> to manage a team?

B Now form adjectives related to the six nouns above.

C Look at these prefixes used to form opposites, and the examples of adjectives containing them. Match each adjective to its meaning.

dis-	il-	im-	in-	ir-	un-
disloyal	illogical	impatient	inflexible	irreplaceable	uncreative

Someone...
1 who cannot change the way they do things is ...
2 who cannot wait for something to happen is ...
3 who does not easily get new ideas is ...
4 who does not think in a sensible way is ...
5 who does or says things that do not help their organisation is ...
6 whose job could not be done by anyone else is ...

D Form the opposites of the adjectives in B above and put each one in the correct place in the table above. (Each prefix is used once.)

E Make sentences using the adjectives in B and C. They could be about people you have known or heard about, or you could invent people. For example:

A salesman who left our company to work for a competitor took all his clients with him. That was really disloyal.

▶ Grammar overview page 164

Grammar

Infinitives and *-ing* forms

A Look again at the rules and examples on page 57.

B Choose the correct word to complete the email.

```
  ● ● ●                                                                          ⊖

    1 message
    From                          Subject                    ▲  Date & Time

    Antonio,

    I am very concerned. Our joint venture together has completely failed (1) _____.

    You guaranteed (2) _____ results very quickly, but we have just lost more and more

    money. You promised (3) _____ me the results each month, but I haven't received

    anything for three months.

    I hate (4) _____ projects, but I can't risk (5) _____ any more money

    into this joint venture. I am afraid to tell you that I think the next step involves

    (6) _____ my lawyers. I have started (7) _____ to them about how we

    can end this agreement. I cannot delay (8) _____ this action any longer.

    Best wishes

    James
```

1	a taking off	b take off	c to take off
2	a got	b getting	c to get
3	a sent	b to send	c sending
4	a abandoning	b to abandon	c abandonment
5	a to put	b putting	c put
6	a bringing in	b to bring in	c brought in
7	a talks	b talked	c talking
8	a take	b to take	c taking

▶ Grammar overview page 165

Grammar

Present perfect simple and present perfect continuous

A Look again at the rules and examples on page 61. Choose the correct option in italics to complete the sentences.

1 The city transport authorities *have finished / have been finishing* their study of rush-hour traffic congestion.

2 I'm very tired – I *have worked / have been working* overtime three days this week.

3 Jason *has had / has been having* some bad news – he's been made redundant.

4 I *have been learning / have learnt* Japanese for three years but I still can't hold a simple conversation.

5 We *have talked / have been talking* about this project for weeks but we *haven't decided / haven't been deciding* anything yet.

6 I *have known / have been knowing* Emma Jackson for 10 years – she's an excellent manager.

B Work with a partner. Talk about events in your life and work using the present perfect simple and the present perfect continuous. Use the prompts below to help you.

business activities   leisure and hobbies   family

▶ Grammar overview page 166

mmunication

Look again at the communication skills pages in Units 9–12. Then complete these exercises.

A Peter Menzies of Galton Appliances is calling a supplier, Crystal Lighting. He wants to change an order. He gets through to the receptionist at Crystal Lighting and is then put through to Jim Brown in the sales department. The text of the telephone call has been mixed up. Put it in the correct order.

Jim: Sales, how can I help you?

Jim: Do you have the reference number?

Jim: Oh yes, that's one of Maggie's. I'm afraid she's out of the office at the moment. Can I get her to call you back?

Peter: Yes it's 456/IND/MC.

Peter: It's Peter Menzies from Galtons.

Peter: This is Peter Menzies from Galtons Appliances. I'm calling about an order I placed last week.

Peter: Goodbye.

Receptionist: Of course. Who's calling, please?

Receptionist: Good morning, Crystal Lighting. How can I help you?

Peter: I'm sure she has, but just in case – it's 0355 634 4577.

Jim: OK. I'll make sure she gets the message. Goodbye.

Jim: I'm sorry to hear that. I'll get her to call you as soon as she gets back. Has she got your number?

Peter: Could I speak to someone in Sales?

Receptionist: Just a moment, Mr Menzies. I'll put you through.

Peter: Yes, please. Could you tell her that we were expecting a delivery this morning and nothing has arrived.

B Work in pairs. Student A looks at this page. Student B looks at page 107.

Student A

Practise making two telephone calls. Use the information below, and add your own ideas.

1 You are the Export Manager for Biltons, a specialist air-conditioning business. You are trying to find an agent to represent your company in Malaysia. You have been recommended to contact
Ms / Mr Chu at AC Services in Kuala Lumpur. Call him / her and arrange to meet on your trip to Malaysia next month.

2 You are the HR Manager for Kenton International in Dubai. You use Maisey and Cooper, a recruitment agency in London, to find staff for your business in the Middle East. Call your contact, Ms Cooper, about two positions in Marketing that you need to fill in Dubai.

▶ Writing resource 19
page 96

13 The industry of industries

Start-up

A **Discuss these questions.**

1 What are the most popular cars in your country? Where are they produced?

2 Who typically buys these kinds of cars?

saloon cars   sports cars   4x4s   people carriers

Reading

A **Match the statements to the cars.**

1 "It goes very fast – 0 to 60 miles per hour in 8 seconds! It corners so fast. What I'm most interested in is performance."

2 "I use it to drive my kids to and from school. I don't allow them to walk to school – it's not safe. My main criterion when I'm buying a car is space – it has to have space for as many children as possible!"

3 "It's so handy – good for driving around town, manoeuvrable and very easy to park. It's the manoeuvrability that I really like."

4 "It's good to be able to sit so high and get such a good view of the traffic. Unlike a lot of users, I drive it off-road when I go to my home in the country. That's the main reason I bought it – I need a vehicle that I can use off-road."

5 "It's what they call a saloon in Europe. I like to drive in comfort! Fuel consumption isn't an issue – if you can afford $100,000 for a car, it doesn't matter if fuel costs $1 or even $2 per gallon – that's 25 or 50 cents a litre!"

a

b

c

d

e

B **Underline the main reason that each person above bought their car. Which of these reasons is most important for you when buying a car?**

C **Discuss these questions about your country.**

1 Are cars produced in your country? Where are the main centres of production? Which companies are involved?

2 What is your government's policy on cutting traffic pollution and congestion?

Listening and speaking

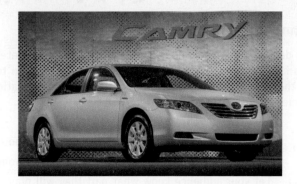

A Match these words about production to their definitions.

1	plant	a	money used to develop an activity
2	capacity	b	factory
3	demand	c	the number of things actually produced
4	output	d	the number of products that are sold or that could be sold
5	investment	e	the maximum number of products that it is possible to make in a plant

13.1 **B** Listen to this interview with James Evans, an expert on the car industry. According to him, are these statements true or false?

1 Car manufacturing is the industry of industries only because cars are desirable consumer products.

2 Making cars is important in advanced and developing countries.

3 There are not enough car plants around the world to satisfy demand.

4 Some car companies are cutting back on investment and closing plants.

13.2 **C** Listen to the rest of the interview and answer the questions.

1 What past and future oil prices does James Evans mention?

2 What future situation are people beginning to think about?

3 Why are electric cars not the answer?

4 What is a hybrid car?

5 How much more expensive is a hybrid car than the ordinary model?

6 Which company is making hybrid cars in the US?

7 Is the complete car made in the US?

D Discuss these questions. Give reasons for your answers.

1 Do you think of cars as status symbols or just a means of getting from A to B?

2 Would you consider paying a congestion charge to drive into the city centre?

3 Would you buy a hybrid car if it was (a) more expensive than an ordinary car, (b) the same price as an ordinary car?

4 Would you consider using public transport one or two days a week instead of your car?

Vocabulary

A Match these words typically combined with *investment* with their meanings below.

1 direct
2 indirect
3 foreign / inward   } investment
4 long-term
5 massive / major / substantial

a an organisation invests by building a plant or opening a business, rather than buying shares in another company

b money goes into a country for investment

c money is invested over many years, rather than for a short time

d the amount of investment is very large

e an organisation invests by buying shares in or lending money to another company

▶ Review and development page 88

71

Communication

Presentations 1: Opening

Making a good presentation depends on your understanding of the needs and interests of the audience and your ability to meet these needs. The opening is always critical in telling the audience how you are going to meet their needs. Your objective when starting a presentation should be to cover the following five elements.

1 Introduce yourself:	Let your audience know who you are
2 Topic:	Tell your audience what you're going to talk about
3 Objective(s):	Tell your audience what benefit they will get from your presentation
4 Role of the audience:	Let your audience know what part they will play
5 Timing:	Tell the audience how long your presentation will be

 13.3 **A** **Listen to two presentation openings. Do they include these five elements?**

B **What other element, not listed above, do both of these openings include?**

C **Listen again and tick the phrases in the Key language box that you hear.**

Key language

Introducing yourself	Let me introduce myself … My name's … I'm in charge of / responsible for … I've been here for … years.
Introducing your topic	I'd like to tell you about … I plan to present … I want to give you an overview / idea of … I'll cover two main areas …
Objective(s)	I aim / want to … My purpose is to … By the end of this presentation, I hope …
Role of the audience	Just sit back and relax. If you've got any questions, please ask. I'd be happy to answer any questions.
Timing	I'm going to speak for about … minutes. This will take about ten minutes. Don't worry, this won't take long!

D **Practise opening a presentation. Choose one of the topics below and use the table to help you.**

- Present your region to a group of visitors.
- Present your company / organisation to a group of new employees.

Content	Language
Introduce yourself:	*I'd like to introduce myself.*
Topic:	
Objective(s):	
Role of the audience:	
Timing:	

▶ Review and development page 91

▶ Communication page 152

Body language

We communicate as much with our eyes, hands, and the rest of our bodies as we do with spoken language. In all cultures, body language is used to communicate information, emotions and attitudes. However, different signals are used in different cultures.

A Match the body language to the country and the meaning.

Body Language	Country	Meaning
Smile	Japan	Shows trust.
Tip head back, suck air in	Korea	I'm pleased.
Bow very low	All countries	That's difficult.
Males stand close and make contact	UK	Come to me.
Males go though door first, ahead of women	USA	I'm interested.
Palm facing in, index finger moving	China	Shows great respect.
Constant eye contact in one-to-one communication	Saudi Arabia	Shows males are dominant.

B What do the examples of body language in A mean in your country? How would you react to this body language?

C Develop a body language checklist for people visiting your country. Use the ideas below to help you.

hand / arm gestures   physical distance between people   posture

greetings   physical contact   facial expressions

🔊 13.4 **D** Listen to some advice about body language when giving a presentation to an international audience. Make notes about what you hear.

E Give a short presentation. Other students should observe and give feedback on your body language.

▶ Business across cultures
page 155

Checklist

✓ the car industry: *hybrid cars, investment, congestion charges ...*

✓ words to do with investment: *substantial, indirect, foreign ...*

✓ opening a presentation

✓ body language

14 Something for nothing?

A **Discuss these questions.**

1 What are the leading newspapers in your country? How are they positioned in relation to one another?

2 Are there any free newspapers? If so, what are they?

> America's five leading newspapers have lost more than 7 per cent of their circulation in the past ten years.

A **Read the article and answer the questions.**

PELLE THE CONQUEROR

THERE IS NOW A METRO NEWSPAPER IN VIRTUALLY EVERY MAJOR CITY IN THE WORLD. COSIMA MARRINER MEETS THE MAN BEHIND THE GLOBAL FREESHEET REVOLUTION.

Pelle Tornberg of Kinnevik Media has been with Metro International since the beginning. *Metro* started with just one free newspaper in Stockholm in 1995. Today it publishes 59 editions in 83 cities. You can pick up a copy of *Metro* in New York, Hong Kong, Rome, St Petersburg and Santiago.

Under Tornberg, *Metro* has successfully adapted its freesheet formula to suit different cultures. Its continued growth in readership and advertising revenues has raised questions about the future of paid-for titles. Boasting more than 15 million readers around the world today, *Metro* is the most-read newspaper outside of Japan. Its titles have a combined circulation of 5.1m in Europe, much more than the 3.7m copies Germany's *Bild* sells, and the 3.2m sold by *The Sun* in the UK. Targeting the young urban professionals so valued by advertisers, *Metro* has seen its revenues soar from $9.6m in 1995 to $302m last year.

Tornberg attributes the success of *Metro* to its strict editorial formula and its 'scientific' approach to distribution. The standardised editorial style and design of the papers provides advertisers with a consistent product. "*Metro* has the same editorial line

and layout around the world but every *Metro* is perceived as being a local newspaper," he says. The company modifies its distribution system to best reach commuters in each market. Less than 30 per cent of *Metro* copies are distributed on public transport: the papers can be found in any "high commuter traffic zone," including shopping malls, offices, universities, libraries and Italian coffee bars. It is a huge operation: 7m copies are printed each night at 53 plants and then delivered by 500 trucks to 3,200 hand distributors and 22,000 racks.

International expansion has not been without its teething problems. In the Czech Republic, *Metro* was forced to employ guards to give out the paper in train stations, after it discovered old women were taking 100 copies at a time back to their villages to sell. "We created a lot of entrepreneurs," Tornberg says.

1 How many editions of *Metro* are produced? In how many cities?

2 How many copies does it sell in Europe?

3 By how much have revenues increased between 1995 and last year?

4 What kind of readers does *Metro* target?

5 What two factors account for its success?

6 Where and how is it distributed?

7 Has the launch in all countries been entirely trouble-free?

B **Discuss the question below in pairs.**

Metro has had difficulties in other countries. What do you think these difficulties might be?

Now check your answers. Student A looks at page 108, Student B looks at page 110. Exchange the following information:

Which countries are mentioned?

What is the situation in each country?

Listening and speaking

🎧 14.1

A Listen to these people talking. Complete each beep with one of the items (a–f).

a radio   c newspapers   e freesheet
b PDA   d internet   f 24-hour news channels

B Discuss these questions with a partner.

How do you access the news?

What are the most important factors that influence your choice? (e.g. cost, editorial line, quality of writing)

Vocabulary

A Look at these compounds from the article on page 74.

Type 1 Adjective + noun

Metro started with just one <u>free newspaper</u> in Stockholm in 1995.

Type 2 Noun + noun

Metro has successfully adapted its <u>freesheet formula</u> to suit different cultures.

Type 3 -ed adjective + noun

Its <u>continued growth</u> in readership ...

Type 4 -ing noun + noun

... and <u>advertising revenues</u> has raised questions ...

Type 5 Adjective + adjective + noun

Targeting the <u>young urban professionals</u> so valued by advertisers ...

B Find other compounds in the article of the same types as those above, with the meanings shown.

Type 1
– a newspaper for a particular place or region (para 3)
– buses, trains etc. for use by everyone (para 3)
– a very large activity (para 3)
– growth in different countries (para 4)

Type 2
– the arrangements for making a product available to people (para 3)

Type 3
– the total of all the copies distributed in different markets (para 2)

Type 4
– buildings or covered areas where you can buy things from different retailers (para 3)
– difficulties when a new activity starts (para 4)

C Now find a compound of the type adjective + noun + noun + noun in paragraph 3 of the article.

D Work in pairs. Replace the underlined words with compounds from A and B above, and take turns asking and answering the questions about your own organisation or one you know well.

1 Is it a <u>very large activity</u>?
   – Is it a huge operation?
   – Yes, we operate 25 plants in 12 countries.
2 Do you expect continued <u>growth in different countries</u>?
3 What are <u>the arrangements for making products / services available</u>?
4 Were there any <u>problems when you started operating</u>?
5 Are <u>young people in professional jobs living in cities</u> among your customers?

▶ Review and development page 89

▶ Grammar overview page 167

75

Communication

Presentations 2: *Developing the message*

Once you have made a good start to your presentation, you need to deliver the objectives you have promised.

 14.2 **A** **Maggie Peters is giving a presentation about her company. Listen to these extracts from her presentation and makes notes on the main points of each part.**

Objective(s): _____

Part 1: _____

Part 2: _____

Part 3: _____

Summary: _____

B **Listen again and tick the phrases in the Key language box that you hear.**

Key language

Objective(s)	I aim to give you an overview of ... I want to convince you ... By the end of this presentation, you will be able to ...
Labelling the focus	Firstly / Secondly / Thirdly we'll look at ... That brings me to ... Let's move on to ...
Balancing the talk	One option is to ... Another option is to ... On the one hand ... On the other hand ... Alternatively, you could ...
Referring back	As I mentioned earlier ... As I said in my introduction ... You may remember, I promised to ...
Referring forward	Before I come to the final part of my presentation, I'd like to ... I'll come back to that later.
Summarising	So, where have we got to? Let's take a look at where we are. Let me just summarise.

C **Prepare a presentation on a topic of your own choice. It should include at least two parts. Use the table below to help you.**

Content	Language
Objective:	*I aim to convince you ...*
Part 1:	
Part 2:	
Summary:	

D **Give your presentation. Get feedback from other students on whether you have delivered your objectives.**

▶ Review and development page 91

▶ Communication page 152

Communication style

Our culture influences our communication style. In some cultures, people believe it's better to get to the point quickly. In others, this style would be considered rude. This section focuses on communication styles in speaking and writing.

A Look at the two emails. What differences do you notice?

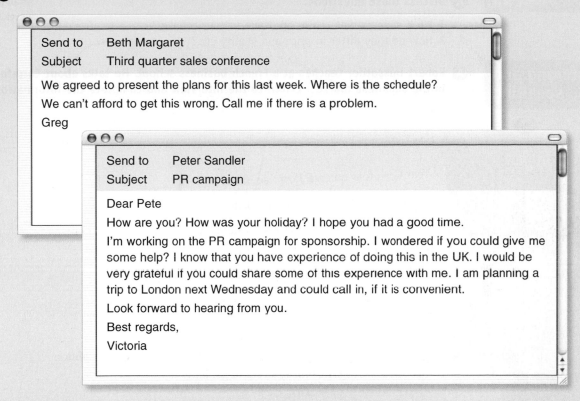

Send to   Beth Margaret
Subject   Third quarter sales conference

We agreed to present the plans for this last week. Where is the schedule?
We can't afford to get this wrong. Call me if there is a problem.
Greg

Send to   Peter Sandler
Subject   PR campaign

Dear Pete
How are you? How was your holiday? I hope you had a good time.
I'm working on the PR campaign for sponsorship. I wondered if you could give me some help? I know that you have experience of doing this in the UK. I would be very grateful if you could share some of this experience with me. I am planning a trip to London next Wednesday and could call in, if it is convenient.
Look forward to hearing from you.
Best regards,
Victoria

B Read about two types of culture and decide which you belong to.

> In **low-context** cultures, language is more direct. It is important to say what you mean. Directness is appreciated. Indirectness is seen as unhelpful.
>
> In **high-context** cultures, language is more indirect. It is important to show respect when you speak, in order to maintain harmony and avoid confrontation. Directness can be seen as rude.

C Decide whether the following are typical of low or high-context cultures.

saying 'no'	saying 'yes'	getting to the point quickly
being very polite	criticising	reading between the lines
pleasing everybody	disagreement	packaging the message with a nice beginning and end

D Rewrite the first email in A and make it more indirect.

Rewrite the second email and make it more direct. Compare your versions with the key.

E Write emails for the following situations:

a Write to a colleague asking him / her to send you some documents you need.
b Write to your boss asking for a meeting to discuss your salary.
c Write to a customer to arrange a visit so that you can present your latest product.

▶ Business across cultures
page 155

Checklist

✓ news media: *free newspapers, TV news channels, internet ...*

✓ compound nouns: *continued growth, advertising revenue, young urban professional*

✓ developing the message in a presentation

✓ communication style

INVESTMENT
15 In search of new markets

Start-up

A Discuss these questions.

1 What supermarket chains are there in your country?
2 How do they differ in price and quality etc.?

Listening and speaking

🎧 15.1

A Robert Dussollier teaches at a French business school. He talks about Carrefour's experiences in the Japanese market. Listen to the interview and complete the information.

Year Carrefour entered Japanese market: _____

Year Carrefour withdrew from Japan: _____

Price paid by Aeon for Carrefour's stores: ¥_____ / €_____

Company whose success Carrefour wanted to copy: _____

Reasons for Carrefour's failure in relation to customers: _____

Number of shops per 100,000 people in Japan: _____

Number of shops per 100,000 people in U.S.: _____

Reasons for Carrefour's failure in relation to Japanese business culture: _____

Market that Carrefour is now trying to get into: _____

Carrefour 家乐福

B Work in pairs. Student A is the interviewer. Student B is Robert Dussollier. Use the notes above to reconstruct the conversation.

C Robert Dussollier commented on Carrefour's experience in Japan. Listen again and complete the sentences.

1 They _____ _____ _____ the market more carefully.
2 They _____ _____ _____ that the car industry and the retail industry were the same.
3 They _____ _____ _____ more research into the Japanese retail market.
4 They _____ _____ _____ more attention to product quality.
5 They _____ _____ _____ to wait longer for a return on investment.

Speaking

A An international supermarket chain is opening stores in your country. Give them advice on how to succeed. Talk about (a) business factors and (b) cultural factors in relation to food.

B Which is the most important factor of those you mentioned in A?

C Now give similar advice to:

- a distributor of domestic appliances (washing machines etc.)
- a chain of fast food restaurants
- a chain of DIY (do-it-yourself) stores

(Perhaps you will advise them not to try to get into your market! If so, give your reasons.)

Grammar

Speculating about the past: *should / shouldn't have, could have*

You use *should have* + past participle to talk about past events which did not happen.

You use *shouldn't have* + past participle to talk about unwanted things that happened in the past.

You can use them to offer advice or opinions or to express criticism.

They should have done more market research.

They shouldn't have assumed the car industry and the retail industry were the same.

You use *could have* + past participle to talk about 'missed opportunities' – possible actions in the past that did not happen. It can also be used to offer advice or opinions or to express criticism.

They could have paid more attention to consumer demands.

A Look at these statements about business mistakes. Say what the companies should or shouldn't have done.

1 IBM allowed other companies to make PCs using its operating system and lost the chance to dominate this area.
   IBM should have made all the PCs itself.
   IBM shouldn't have allowed other companies to make PCs using its operating system.

2 Coca-Cola dropped its traditional formula in 1985 but consumers didn't like it and sales fell sharply.

3 British Leyland used two brand names – Austin and Morris – for the same car, causing confusion in consumers' minds.

4 Elf expanded abroad rapidly. This caused a lot of difficulties within the organisation.

5 Siemens entered the mobile phone market alone. This wasn't very successful as they didn't know the market well.

6 Gerald Ratner damaged his jewellery business when he said in a speech that the jewellery he sold in his shops was rubbish.

B Think about some of your own mistakes in the past – if any! Say what you should have done to avoid them.

Before I started using the product, I should have read the instructions.

I shouldn't have turned down an opportunity to work in the USA.

C The Acme company tried to get into a new market but failed. Use the correct form of the verbs in brackets to say what they should or could have done.

1 (find out) more about the market
   They could have found out more about the market.

2 (use) a market research company

3 (talk) to people who know the market

4 (work) with a local partner

5 (advertise) in the local press

6 (listen) to what people were telling them

▶ Review and development page 90

▶ Grammar overview page 168

Communication

Presentations 3: *Using visuals*

Many people respond better to pictures than to words. This section focuses on how you can use visuals (charts, mind maps, pictures, etc.) to get your message across.

A Match the words to the correct visuals.

1 pie chart
2 graph
3 organisation chart
4 flow chart

5 bar chart
6 picture
7 mind map

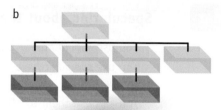

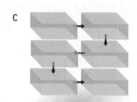

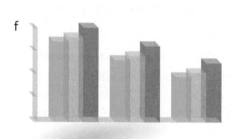

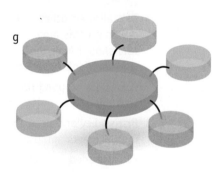

15.2 **B** Listen to extracts from two presentations. Which visuals are they talking about?

Key language

Introducing a visual
Let's look at this ...
Here you can see ...
I've prepared this chart to show / illustrate ...

Focusing on details
Can I draw your attention to ...?
I'd like you to notice the ...
If you look here, you can see ...

Useful terms for different charts
- pie chart: *segment, slice*
- graph: *vertical / horizontal axis / axes, solid / dotted / broken lines, scale*
- organisation chart: *box, matrix, report to*
- bar chart: *narrow / thick, high / low*

Useful verbs
- *rise / increase / grow, reach a peak*
- *fall / decrease / go down / decline, reach a low-point*
- *level off / remain stable / stagnant, reach a plateau*

▶ Review and development page 91

▶ Communication page 152

C Give a short presentation on a topic of your choice, using one or more visuals. Use the visuals and the Key language above to help you.

Leadership

Business leaders can have very different styles. Some are 'top dog' and like to be in charge; others are more democratic and prefer to be 'one of the people'. Leadership styles also vary across countries and companies. This section explores different aspects of leadership.

A **Complete the questionnaire and then compare your answers in pairs.**

	Agree	Disagree	Not sure
1 Leaders are born, not made.			
2 Leaders must lead by example.			
3 Leaders must be physically fit.			
4 Leaders must be decisive.			
5 Leaders must have a vision.			
6 Leaders must be good listeners.			
7 Leaders should be highly paid.			
8 Leaders need to take risks.			
9 Being a leader is a lonely job.			

Score
agree: 2 points
disagree: 0 points
not sure: 1 point

Analysis
13–18 points: You like strong, charismatic, and individualistic leaders.
8–12 points: You like strong leaders in some situations.
0–7 points: You are sceptical about strong leaders.

15.3 **B** **Listen to three leaders talk about leadership. Which of the points in A do they mention and which additional points do they mention?**

C **Brainstorm words and phrases to describe leaders. Then use them to describe some leaders in your country and / or company.**

Example
charismatic   strong   a good communicator   able to motivate people

D **Prepare a profile of the sort of leader you would like to be.**

▶ Business across cultures
page 155

Checklist

✔ investing in the food retail business: Carrefour in Japan

✔ should / shouldn't have, could: *I should have read the report; they could have done more research*

✔ using visuals in a presentation

✔ leadership

16 Bollywood goes global

Start-up

A Think of a recent successful film in your country. What were the reasons for its success?

Global cinema ticket sales are more than $20 billion per year.

Vocabulary

A Match these words connected with films and film-making to their definitions.

1 producer
2 director
3 good / bad box office
4 gross
5 blockbuster
6 location
7 scriptwriter
8 screenplay

a money taken in ticket sales, before the costs of making the film are deducted

b used to talk about the financial success / failure

c the person who co-ordinates all the activities of a film, finds the finance to make it, etc.

d the person who manages the actual making of a film

e the place where scenes are filmed, not in a studio

f a very successful film

g a film's story and dialogues

h the person who writes the film's story and dialogues

Listening and speaking

 16.1

A A film journalist, Ruby Bennett, talks to Bharat Mistry, an Indian film producer, about Bollywood. Are the statements below true or false?

1 International audiences are interested in Bollywood films.
2 Films made for overseas markets are exactly the same as those made for India.
3 The finance for Bollywood films is always provided through family partnerships.
4 A typical Bollywood film for the overseas market has to make between $25 and $30 million in sales in order to make a profit.
5 The film training school at Film City will cost $3 million.
6 Scriptwriters have traditionally been very important in India.
7 The training school will only teach scriptwriting.

Grammar

Second conditional

You use *if* + past simple in one clause, and *would* + infinitive in the other clause.

You use the second conditional to talk about imaginary or hypothetical events in the future.

If we made a film for overseas markets, we would make two versions – one in English and one in Hindi.

A **Complete these sentences using the correct form of the verbs in brackets.**

1 Who _____ (cast) in the lead role? We _____ (use) Sienna Miller if she _____ (be) available.

2 Where _____ (shoot) the film? We _____ (go) on location to Italy and England if it _____ (not cost) too much.

3 Who _____ (choose) as a scriptwriter? We _____ (ask) Woody Allen to write the script if he _____ (accept) a lower fee than usual.

4 How much _____ (pay) the director? We _____ (give) them $5 million.

5 When _____ (begin) making the film? We _____ _____ (start) as soon as possible.

B **What actions would you take to encourage film-making in your country?**

I would open a Film Studies school.
I would charge lower rates of tax on the film industry.

Speaking

A **Work in pairs or small groups. You are film financiers. Think of a book or a story you would like to make into a film. Brainstorm your ideas on the following issues.**

title and story   cast   director   budget   locations   scriptwriter   marketing

B **Now describe your film project.**

Our film would be called ... It would be about ... First, we would hire the best scriptwriter we could find ...

▶ Review and development page 90

▶ Grammar overview page 169

Communication

Presentations 4: Closing

The end of a presentation is as important as the beginning. There are five important objectives to remember when closing a presentation:

1 Signal to the audience that you have reached the end.
2 Tell them your main conclusions / recommendations.
3 Tell them what the next steps are.
4 Encourage them to ask questions.
5 Tell them that you appreciate their attention.

 16.2 **A** Listen to the closing of three presentations. Do they achieve these objectives?

B Listen again and tick the phrases in the Key Language box that you hear.

Key language

Signalling the end	That brings me to the end of my presentation. That's all I have to say … That covers everything I wanted to say.
Summarising	To sum up, … In brief, … Before I finish, let me go over …
Concluding	I said at the start that I wanted to … I hope that gives you a good overview / understanding of … In conclusion, …
Recommending	I think you / we should … I would recommend that you / we …
Inviting questions	Are there any questions? I'd be happy to answer any questions.
Following up	I've prepared a folder with more information about … There are some handouts which I will pass round. If you would like to know more, please contact me.
Thanking	You've been a very attentive audience. Thank you for your attention.

C Work in groups. Practise closing the following presentations. Take turns to speak, using the prompts (1–5) to guide you.

Presentation 1

You have just presented a quarterly sales report.

1 Signal the end.
2 Sum up the main message: sales increase in last quarter but difficult period ahead.
3 Handout of sales figures.
4 Thank the audience.
5 Invite questions.

Presentation 2

You have just presented a plan for entering a new market

1 Signal the end.
2 Recommend the setting up of a subsidiary in this new market.
3 Pass around print-outs of the slides you have presented.
4 Thank the audience.
5 Invite questions.

▶ Review and development page 91

▶ Communication page 152

 16.3 **D** Listen to the opening of three presentations. Prepare a suitable closing for each one.

Decision-making

The way we make decisions is influenced by our personality and the country and company culture we work in. Some people make decisions in groups, some people make decisions alone; some people decide quickly, others decide more slowly; some only trust a decision when it is written down, while for others a handshake will be enough.

A **Read the situation below and answer the question.**

> You are a Department Manager. Your company has recently upgraded its IT network so that all employees now have permanent access to the Internet. You have noticed that employees are often on the Internet, and are not always on work-related sites. Sometimes they seem to be making personal arrangements or just surfing the Web for fun. You feel they should not be doing this at work. You could investigate which sites they are accessing and also record how long they spend on these sites.

How would you decide what to do next? Would you make your decision:

a by yourself, and then inform the staff of your decision.

b after discussing it with management colleagues.

c after discussing it with your staff.

d together with your staff.

B **Read the situation below and answer the questions.**

> In your company, you employ a large office staff. Some of the staff work very long hours and are very dedicated. Your company is considering offering the option of allowing employees to work from home one day a week. This would be some compensation for those employees who work longer hours than they have to. It would also enable employees to work on projects without the usual office distractions.

1 In my culture, decisions like this are generally made:
   a before announcing it to the staff.
   b during a meeting with the staff.
   c after a meeting with the staff.

2 In my culture, decisions like this are taken:
   a quickly.
   b slowly and with much thought.
   c with many delays and are sometimes never finalised.

3 In my culture, we would communicate a decision like this:
   a verbally.   b in writing.   c orally and then follow it up in writing.

C **Read the text and discuss why the Swedes did not win the contract. What advice would you give them?**

> Mats Petersson arrived in Venezuela with his team of negotiators from Sweden. They were confident that they would win a contract to supply telecoms systems to a large operator in Caracas. They flew in the night before and went into the negotiation the next day. They knew they had the right product at the right price and on the right delivery terms. They had sent the offer in advance and expected the decision to be made during the negotiation. To their surprise, the Venezuelan customers listened and asked some questions and then said they would be in touch. The next day the Swedish team flew home. Several weeks later they heard indirectly that they had not won the contract.

▶ Business across cultures
page 155

Checklist

✓ investing in the film industry: *blockbuster, gross, scriptwriter, screenplay*

✓ second conditional: *I would charge lower rates of tax; I would use the best actors*

✓ closing a presentation

✓ decision-making

Seniorservices

Background   Read this information about Seniorservices, a company targeting consumers over the age of 60.

seniorservices

Contact:
Seniorservices
412 Flinders Street, Brisbane 4000
(07) 8259 1900
info@seniorservices.au

Holidays for **active seniors** in our own resorts

Stamp Here

Join us at one of our fabulous resorts. Come with your friends, come alone and make new friends, relax and enjoy life – you deserve it!

www.seniorservices.au

Brisbane-based Seniorservices has reported pre-tax profits of A$1.2 million. Chief executive Janet Townsend said, 'Since I founded the company five years ago, growth has been excellent. Our four resorts have been growing at 30 per cent a year in terms of sales, and now we are looking at new areas for expansion.'

The grey market

The population of Australia is about 19 million. About 25 per cent of these are over 60. This percentage is set to rise, and in 10 years' time about 27 per cent of the population will be over 60. These are the baby boomers – people born in the years after the Second World War. In this group there is a significant segment of healthy, affluent people with money to spend. They have a high disposable income of about A$40,000 a year on average, set to rise to A$45,000 over the next 10 years.

xpanding the business

Janet Townsend, the CEO of Seniorservices, and her management team are considering some ideas for expanding the business. Three small teams – A, B, and C – each consider a potential opportunity and then present it for discussion by the whole team.

During the discussion consider the pros and cons of each idea.

Following the discussion, everyone votes for the project they think is most likely to be profitable.

Student A: You are Janet Townsend, the CEO of Seniorservices. You lead the discussion. Look at this page.

Team A: Look at page 108.
Team B: Look at page 110.
Team C: Look at page 113.

Student A

While teams A, B, and C are preparing their presentations, think about what kind of information you will need to make your decision and prepare some questions. Use these ideas to get you started:

details of the idea   costs   return on investment   pros   cons

Writing

Write an email to a colleague who was not at the meeting. Explain which project was chosen, and why.

Vocabulary

A Complete this crossword using words from Unit 13.

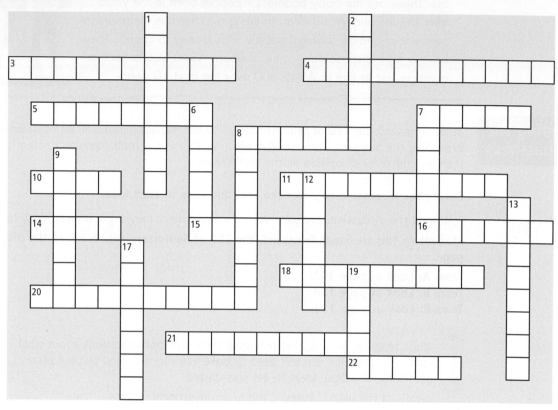

Across

3, 5 Car production is important in _____ countries as well as _____ ones (10, 8)

4 Another word for major (11)

7 Car buyers with large families are interested in this (5)

8 This word describes investment into a country (6)

10, 14 Over a number of years, rather than a short period (4, 4)

11 When there's a lot of traffic (10)

15 _____ investment is when a company puts money into its own factories and business activities, rather than into other companies (6)

16 See 7 down

18 New businesses in a region or country often brings work for local _____ (9)

20 Money put into an activity with the aim of making more money (10)

21 When air or water is dirty (9)

22 If a product starts to be very successful, it _____ off (5)

Down

1 The amount a factory can produce (8)

2 _____ cars can run on petrol or batteries (6)

6 The amount sold, or that could be sold (6)

7 A product you buy to impress other people (6, 6)

8 Opposite of direct (8)

9 _____ investment is when money come into a country from abroad (7)

12 The number of things produced (6)

13 A _____ buys products for his / her own use, not for resale (8)

17 Very large (7)

19 Factory (5)

B Match items from each box below to form two-word compounds that mean:

1 when a company grows in its own country, rather than abroad
2 when a company gets bigger more slowly than before
3 vehicles like people's cars, rather than taxis, buses, trains etc.
4 the sales of two or more products added together
5 prices paid to advertise
6 lists of things available to buy
7 difficulties that continue
8 an activity that is complicated to organise and manage
9 all the things that make up the way a product is made available and sold
10 a type of publication sold all over the country
11 a number of places where you can eat or drink, owned by the same person or company

advertising	newspaper
catalogues	ongoing
combined	operation
expansion	private
complex	problems
chain	reduced
distribution	rates
growth	restaurant
domestic	sales
network	shopping
national	transport

C Work in pairs to make sentences using the compounds in B.

Example

Advertising rates have increased 10 per cent this year.

The design of our new shopping catalogue is excellent.

Grammar

should / shouldn't have, could have

A Look again at the rules and examples on page 79. Choose the correct word to fill each gap in the text.

IBM made a strategic mistake when they introduced the personal computer in 1981. They allowed anyone to make PCs. They shouldn't have (1) _____ this. What they (2) _____ have done was to let other manufacturers make them, but under licence. In this way, they (3) _____ have forced other makers to pay them a royalty on each PC they sold. IBM (4) _____ have controlled and sold the software under licence too, but another mistake was to allow Microsoft to write the software that became dominant: MS-DOS. However, IBM (5) _____ have foreseen how big the mistake would be. If it had avoided this error, it (6) _____ have (7) _____ to be the most important company in computing, but instead Microsoft was.

1 a do   b doing   c done
2 a could   b shouldn't   c should
3 a should   b could   c shouldn't
4 a could   b couldn't   c shouldn't
5 a shouldn't   b couldn't   c didn't
6 a couldn't   b could   c should
7 a continued   b continue   c continuing

▶ Grammar overview page 168

B Simon has just left his job because he was unhappy there. Give him advice about what he *could have done* or *should have done* in order to improve the situation.

1 I didn't earn enough money. *You should have asked for a salary increase.*

2 I wasn't promoted fast enough.

3 I didn't have my own office.

4 I only took one week's holiday a year.

5 I didn't have a company car.

6 I agreed to do all the worst jobs.

7 I worked until midnight every night.

Grammar

Second conditional

A Look again at the rules and examples on page 83. Work in pairs. Take turns to ask each other what you would do in each of these imaginary work situations.

1 a fire breaks out
   A: *What would you do if a fire broke out?*
   B: *If a fire broke out, I'd call the fire brigade.*

2 your computer system crashes

3 one of your sales people leaves to work for a competitor

4 the photocopier breaks down

5 the company is taken over

6 you invent a new product for your company

▶ Grammar overview page 169

7 your company goes bankrupt

mmunication Look again at the communication skills pages in Units 13–16. Then complete these exercises.

A Max Byton is presenting his company. Put the phrases (a–k) in the correct place in the text.

a that brings me to the end
b Let me introduce myself.
c If you look here
d let's move quickly on to
e I'll hand out these catalogues
f give you a quick overview of
g I've prepared this chart
h feel free to interrupt
i are there any final questions
j first let's look at
k as I said earlier,

Good morning, everyone. It's a pleasure to see you all here. (1) _____.

My name's Max Byton and I am the MD of Byton Electronics. I know you have a busy day, so I'd just

like to (2) _____ Byton and its main products. If you have any questions,

please (3) _____. OK, (4) _____ what we offer in

the mobile field.

... So, (5) _____, I know you have a busy day ahead of you, so

I'll (6) _____ our industrial electronics division.

(7) _____ to illustrate the main applications.

(8) _____, you can see that we've got two principal product areas.

So (9) _____. Before you leave, (10) _____.

You'll find more information in them So, (11) _____?

B Prepare and give a presentation on one of the topics below.

1 You want to convince your audience to buy a car like yours. Tell them why you bought it.

2 You want to tell your audience about the press in your country. Tell them about two or three of the biggest newspapers.

3 You want to give advice to the audience about setting up a business in your country. Tell them about the business and cultural factors.

4 You want to talk to your audience about films. Tell them about the film industry in your country – e.g. how often people go to the cinema, what kinds of films are popular, etc.

TIPS

Remember to include in your presentation:

- an effective opening – introduce yourself – mention your topic – timing – questions.
- a clear development – structure your points – tell the audience your objective(s).
- some visuals – remember most people prefer visual communication.
- a clear ending – close with a clear summary, conclusion, and invitation for questions.

▶ Writing resource 20
page 98

Job advertisement

A **Read this job advertisement.**

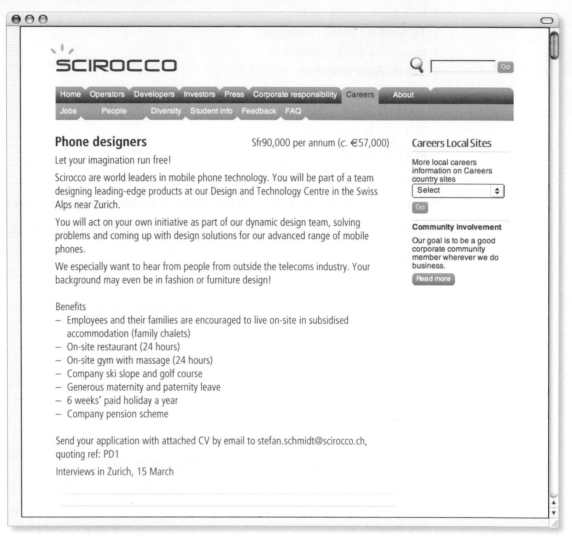

SCIROCCO

Home   Operators   Developers   Investors   Press   Corporate responsibility   Careers   About

Jobs   People   Diversity   Student info   Feedback   FAQ

Phone designers   Sfr90,000 per annum (c. €57,000)

Let your imagination run free!

Scirocco are world leaders in mobile phone technology. You will be part of a team designing leading-edge products at our Design and Technology Centre in the Swiss Alps near Zurich.

You will act on your own initiative as part of our dynamic design team, solving problems and coming up with design solutions for our advanced range of mobile phones.

We especially want to hear from people from outside the telecoms industry. Your background may even be in fashion or furniture design!

Benefits
– Employees and their families are encouraged to live on-site in subsidised accommodation (family chalets)
– On-site restaurant (24 hours)
– On-site gym with massage (24 hours)
– Company ski slope and golf course
– Generous maternity and paternity leave
– 6 weeks' paid holiday a year
– Company pension scheme

Send your application with attached CV by email to stefan.schmidt@scirocco.ch, quoting ref: PD1

Interviews in Zurich, 15 March

Careers Local Sites

More local careers information on Careers country sites

Select

Go

Community involvement

Our goal is to be a good corporate community member wherever we do business.

Read more

B **Are these statements about the job advertisement true or false? If there isn't enough information, choose 'Doesn't say'.**

a True   b False   c Doesn't say

The successful candidate will:

1 work with other team members.

2 be expected only to follow orders.

3 come from the mobile phone industry.

4 be forced to live on-site.

5 be able to use the company restaurant at 3 a.m.

6 be able to take time off if they have a child.

7 get money from the company after they retire.

8 pay 60 per cent of their salary in income tax.

CVs

A Look at this extract from Rosario Gomez's CV.

ROSARIO GOMEZ

Career goals
Looking for stimulating work in a design team in fashion, jewellery, or similar business.

Skills
- Enthusiastic self-starter
- Effective team player
- Good at problem solving
- Native Spanish speaker; fluent French and English
- Experience of working with clients from a wide range of cultures

Qualifications
1998–9 Master's degree specialising in jewellery design, *École des Arts Modernes*, Paris
1994–7 Degree in Art and Design from *Escuela de Bellas Artes*, Madrid

Experience
2001–now Buyer, women's jewellery, *Galeries Féminines* department stores, Brussels
1999–2001 Jewellery designer, *Bijoux Fulgurants*, Paris. (This small company of 20 employees produces high-quality mid-price jewellery for sale in shops and department stores.)

Interests
Skiing, flamenco dancing, cinema

B Now write your own CV using the same headings.

b application

A Complete this email applying for the job at Scirocco by choosing the correct word to fill each gap.

Send to: johann.schmidt@scirocco.ch
Subject: Phone designers, ref: PD1

Dear Mr Schmidt

I (1) _____ with reference to your advertisement for phone designers. As you can see from the (2) _____ CV, my background is in jewellery design, and I believe I can bring a fresh and innovative approach to your design team.

As my CV indicates, I (3) _____ _____ for more than 10 years in jewellery, of which the last five have been in retail, and now I (4) _____ _____ to move to a hi-tech company. I am willing to (5) _____ to Switzerland when my current contract (6) _____ in May.

I am available for interview on the date (7) _____

I look forward to (8) _____ from you.

Best regards,
Rosario Gomez

1 a write   b wrote   c am writing
2 a attachment b attaching   c attached
3 a have worked b am working c worked
4 a will like   b like   c would like
5 a remove   b relocate   c relive
6 a ends   b ended   c is ending
7 a mention   b mentioning c mentioned
8 a hear   b hearing   c heard

B Write a similar email to apply for the same job, this time from someone whose background is in car design.

18 Getting the go-ahead

Email exchange

Diretto is a multinational electronics company. One of its researchers, Susan Wang has developed a new navigation device. She had asked the company for more funding to develop the product further.

A **Choose the correct word to fill each gap in the email.**

Send to: Susan Wang
Cc: Paola Frascati
Subject: Navigation device project

Dear Susan,

Thank you for your memo of 2 March asking for (1) _____ for your new project. We have discussed this at board level, and I am (2) _____ to tell you that we have decided to go ahead with the project.

We discussed the possibility of spinning it (3) _____ into a new company, but decided not to. We will keep the project (4) _____.

You will be the project manager, and we will (5) _____ six new development staff to work with you. Your department will be (6) _____ in the new research building on our (7) _____ in Milan.

Please come to my office tomorrow morning at 10:00 a.m. to (8) _____ the project further. I have asked our marketing manager, Paola Frescati, to be present so that we can discuss the (9) _____ as well as the technical (10) _____ of your project.

Regards

Richard

1	a change	b funding	c coins
2	a delighted	b amused	c enjoy
3	a on	b off	c out
4	a in stock	b in store	c in-house
5	a personnel	b payroll	c recruit
6	a basing	b basis	c based
7	a sight	b site	c sighed
8	a argue	b talk	c discuss
9	a commercial	b commerce	c commerces
10	a possibility	b potential	c powers

B **You are Susan Wang. Write a reply to Richard Long.**

- Thank him for getting the go-ahead for your project.
- Say that are very happy to be working on it.
- Say that you have prepared a detailed development plan with dates for different parts of the project, and that this is attached to the email.
- Confirm that you will be in his office for the meeting at 10.00 a.m., but you might be slightly late (give a reason).
- End suitably.

To: Richard Long   Date: 31 March 20__
Cc: Paola Frascati
Subject: RE: Navigation device project
⌀ Attachment: technicalpotential.doc

_____

_____

_____

_____

_____

_____

_____

_____

_____

_____

C **You are Paola Frascati. Write an email to Richard Long.**

- Say that you cannot come to the meeting with Susan Wang – give a reason and apologise.
- Suggest that they have the meeting without you.
- Ask Richard Long to let you know what happened at the meeting after it has taken place.
- End suitably.

To: Richard Long   Date: 31 March 20__
Subject: RE: Navigation device project

_____

_____

_____

_____

_____

_____

_____

_____

19 Unhappy customers

A A passenger on a cruise organised by Seniorservices writes to the company. Read the letter and answer the questions below.

8 September 20_____

43 Acacia Gardens
South Melbourne, Vic. 3005

Customer Care Department
Seniorservices
412 Flinders Street
Brisbane 4000

Dear Sir or Madam

My wife and I have just come back from your Splendours of the Indian Ocean Cruise (1 Aug–3 Sept). This was supposed to be the holiday of a lifetime, but the whole cruise was a disaster from beginning to end. I am writing to make the following specific complaints:

The flight from Darwin to Colombo, Sri Lanka, where the cruise was to begin, was delayed, so the ship left port 24 hours late.

The scheduled stopover in the Seychelles was cancelled for 'mechanical reasons' which were never explained to passengers.

My wife caught a stomach bug – she thinks this was from the fish served on the evening of the 20 August – and she had to stay in her cabin for three days. The ship's doctor was straight out of medical school and could not help her in any way.

The dance band playing on board were not of sufficiently high standard – they played out of tune the whole time.

In view of these complaints, I would expect a refund of 50 per cent of the A$11,000 that we paid. If I do not receive a satisfactory response, I will hand the matter over to my lawyers.

I look forward to hearing from you.

Yours sincerely,

George Kinnear

1 The Kinnears' expectations of the cruise were
  a non-existent   b high   c low

2 Mr Kinnear thinks that the cruise was
  a a complete success   b a partial failure   c a total failure

3 The departure of the cruise was held up by
  a the late arrival of the plane from Darwin
  b technical problems on the ship
  c a strike at Darwin docks

4 The Seychelles stopover did not take place because of
  a technical problems   b bad weather   c political unrest on the islands

5 According to Mr Kinnear, his wife's illness was
  a definitely caused by bad fish   b might have been caused by bad fish   c imaginary

6 Mr Kinnear's dissatisfaction with the band was due to
  a the style of music they played   b the volume that they played at   c their lack of skill

7 Mr Kinnear is
  a asking for a replacement cruise
  b asking for a refund
  c threatening immediate legal action

B Amanda Grayson works in the Customer Care department at Seniorservices. She writes a reply to George Kinnear.

- Use the notes below to write the letter, putting the verbs in brackets into their correct forms.
- Write a suitable opening and ending to the letter.

seniorservices

Seniorservices
Customer Care Dept
412 Flinders Street, Brisbane 4000
Tel 07 8259 1900   Fax 07 8259 4301 Email: customercare@seniorservices.au

Mr George Kinnear
43 Acacia Gardens
South Melbourne, Vic. 3005

1 October 20_____

_____ ,

Thank you / letter / 8 September. We / (look) into / complaints.

We / aware / late departure / cruise ship / Colombo / and / (apologise) for this.
stopover / Seychelles / cancelled / because / engines not (work) properly / ship / (get) behind schedule. sorry / disappointment / caused
(have) no other complaints / passengers / food / dance band
willing / (make) / refund / 10 per cent / cost / cruise / late departure / lack / stopover / Seychelles
Please let / know / (be) acceptable / you.

_____ ,

Amanda Grayson

Amanda Grayson
Customer Care Manager

C You are George Kinnear. Write a short reply to Amanda Grayson, *either* accepting her suggested refund *or* refusing it, giving your reasons. Begin and end your letter suitably.

Fax exchange

A A French supermarket chain wants to expand abroad. Choose the correct word to fill each gap in the fax below.

Supermarchés Bertrand SA
BP 456, 92140 Issy
Tel +33 1 41 33 99 00, Fax +33 1 41 33 99 10
FAX

From: Marc Bertrand
To: Turkish Retailing Association
Attn: Mehmet Emin
Fax no.: +90 212 324 7209
No. of pages inc. this one: 1

May 2, 20_____

Re: Joint venture partner in Turkey

Dear Mr Emin

I am the founder of a chain of 79 supermarkets in France with annual (1) _____ of €10 billion. We are now looking to expand (2) _____ . We think that Turkey offers substantial opportunities for (3) _____ but we are aware of the dangers of setting (4) _____ operations in a country that we are not familiar with. As you know, our competitors have made some serious strategic (5) _____ recently.

I am writing to ask if you can (6) _____ an existing retailer in Turkey with whom we can work.

I would, of course, be more than (7) _____ to come to Istanbul to meet with anyone you could suggest as a local (8) _____, and I would be very grateful for any (9) _____ you could give me in this area.

I look forward to hearing from you.

Best regards

Marc Bertrand

Marc Bertrand
Chief Executive, Supermarchés Bertrand

1 a sold	b sales	c selling
2 a abroad	b foreign	c stranger
3 a grow	b capacity	c growth
4 a up	b down	c over
5 a faults	b defects	c mistakes
6 a recommend	b agree	c advise
7 a wanting	b desiring	c willing
8 a cooperator	b partner	c colleague
9 a advice	b advices	c advises

B **Write a fax reply to Marc Bertrand, including these points:**

- Thank him for his fax.
- Say that you have been in touch with a member of your association, Ms Dilek Saray, who is based in Izmir.
- She will be in touch with Marc Bertrand soon to take things further.
- End suitably.

Turkish Retailing Association
Istlikal cadd. 42
34018 Istanbul, Turkey
Tel +90 212 324 7200, Fax +90 212 324 7209
FAX

From: Mehmet Emin
To: Supermarchés Bertrand
Attn: Marc Bertrand
Fax no.: +33 1 41 33 99 10
No. of pages inc. this one: 1

Dear Mr Bertrand

C **You are Dilek Saray. Write a fax reply to Marc Bertrand, including these points:**

- Say that Mehmet Emin has been in touch with you about Marc Bertrand's enquiry.
- Talk about your company's history: small, successful chain of supermarkets, founded by your father in 1945 – started with one shop in Izmir, now has seven supermarkets in cities in western Turkey.
- Say that you are looking for an international partner to develop further.
- Invite Marc Bertrand to Izmir next week to discuss things (suggest a date).
- Say that you look forward to meeting him.
- End suitably.

Millikutuphane cadd. 318
35100 Izmir, Turkey
Tel +90 232 484 5000, Fax +90 232 484 5010

FAX

From: Dilek Saray
To: Supermarchés Bertrand
Attn: Marc Bertrand
Fax no.: +33 1 41 33 99 10
No. of pages inc. this one: 1

Dear Mr Bertrand

A Read this transcript of an engineer talking about himself.

Hi, my name's Serguei Bronovski. I'm into opera, football, and ice hockey. I was born on 10 December 1975 in Ekaterinburg, Russia, but now I'm living in London. When I was at school, I wanted to be a professional ice hockey player; that didn't work out, but I'm still interested in it and I watch all the matches on satellite TV. In fact, ice hockey is the main thing I'm interested in outside work! After secondary school in Ekaterinburg, I went to Moscow University to do a degree in civil engineering, and after a four-year course I graduated in 1999. Immediately after that, I did a PhD at the University of London on special steels used for construction. I know it won't mean much to non-specialists, but the title was 'High-strength steel in wind-exposed high-rise buildings.' I finished it in 2003, and have been working for Astrup, a construction company in the UK since then, but now I'd like to go to the United States for a few years to work as a research engineer in the construction industry, in a company that specialises in the use of hi-tech materials. I'm a native speaker of Russian, of course, and my written and spoken English is fluent after my years in the UK. My German is pretty good, too. People tell me that I'm good at working in teams but I prefer to use my initiative and do research on my own. Once a project has started, I prefer to hand it over to others.

B Write a CV for Serguei based on the information above using these headings:

Career goals   Skills   Qualifications   Experience   Interests

C Roberto Campi, a manager at Diretto, submits a proposal to Richard Long asking for funding for a new type of headphone stereo. Complete the gaps using the correct form of the words in brackets.

Date: 1 April 20_____

From: Richard Long

To: Roberto Campi

Subject: New headphone stereo

Thank you for your memo of 20 February asking for (1) _____ (fund) for your new project. We have discussed this at board level, and (2) _____ (unfortunate) I have to (3) _____ (information) you that we have decided not to go ahead with the project. The board decided that there are already enough portable stereo-type (4) _____ (production) on the market, for example the Walkman and iPods.

I know that you have put a lot of (5) _____ (energetic) into developing your product so far, but I hope you will find other projects at Diretto that you can work on. For example, your colleague, Susan Wang, is (6) _____ (development) a new navigation device. I'm sure that she would really (7) _____ (beneficial) from someone with your experience (8) _____ (work) in her team.

If you're interested in working on her project, please don't (9) _____ (hesitation) to get back to me.

Best wishes,

Richard Long

Student B Material

3 Incentives

Communication

Student B

You are travelling with Student A to a trade fair. Some of Student A's information about the trip is incorrect. Clarify and confirm the correct information with Student A.

MEMO

MAJESTIC TRADE FAIR

Dates:	16 – 18 February?
Cost:	$220 per delegate per day (corporate member rate)
Accommodation:	booked into the Adelaide Hotel for four nights (15–18 February inclusive)
Travel:	return flights from Hamburg to Chicago
Depart:	15 February, 18:15. Flight number LH 25768 Transfer from airport to hotel – taxi, booked in advance. Cost $55.

4 Work and leisure

Communication

Student B

1 Tell Student A about your work–life balance. Talk about:
working hours holidays time with family leisure time

2 Listen to Student A tell you about his / her work–life balance. Respond and develop the conversation by making comments and asking questions.

Business scenario 1 Improving morale

Speaking

Student B

You are James Murdo. Give Roxanne Simon the information from your report that she asks for.

FAX

	Agree	Disagree
Management understands our problems.	15%	85%
The work is well organised by managers.	25%	75%
Working hours are reasonable.	36%	64%
The company is family-friendly.	41%	59%
The company building is in a good location.	49%	51%
Our offices are attractive.	7%	93%

The company also has these problems:

High staff turnover: About 10 people leave the company every year, and have to be replaced. Many of those leaving go to work in Sydney for a higher salary.

Days off for illness. About 5 per cent of working days are lost because of it. (The national average is 2 per cent.)

Role play

Student A

You are Roxanne Simon, CEO of Province Advertising. You chair the meeting.

- Start by summing up the findings of the questionnaire.
- Ask the General Manager and the Human Resources Manager for their comments.
- Discuss the options (see notes below).
- At the end of the meeting, sum up the arguments and say what your decision is.

You calculate the costs of possible changes as follows:

More flexible working hours: People need to be in the office at the same time in order to work together and flexible working hours will require more people, so flexibility will cost A$500,000 per year.

Open company restaurant: A$150,000.

Company crèche for parents with young children: Cost: A$100,000 per year.

Moving location to Melbourne city centre: Cost: A$200,000 per year in extra rent and running costs.

Redecorate the present offices: One-off cost of A$50,000.

You have a total budget available for this year of A$400,000.

6 Creativity

Communication

Student B

1 Respond to Student A.

2 Get the right response from Student A in these situations:
   a Give Student A a gift.
   b Tell Student A your opinion about a film / play.
   c Request extra time to complete a task.
   d Suggest going out to a restaurant.
   e Say goodbye after visiting the restaurant.

Group 2

One of you is leaving for a new job. Prepare a short farewell speech to your colleagues. Use these notes to help you:

Thank your colleagues and your manager.

Thank everyone for the gift they gave you.

Say goodbye.

You should also respond to some of the comments in your colleague's farewell speech to you. You won't be able to prepare this in advance so you must listen carefully and improvise!

Business scenario 2 Pitching for finance

Procedure

Team A

You are a team of entrepreneurs. You want financial backing for Helitaxis, which provides a helicopter service for business people.

Use the information below as the basis for your pitch, adding more detail where necessary.

> **Helitaxis**
>
> • You will use areas in open spaces and car parks in and around big cities for helicopter flights. (You already have permission from the authorities to use sites around five European capitals.)
>
> • You want to lease 25 helitaxis each costing €100,000 per year in leasing costs. (You don't intend to buy them.) These are small, low-cost helicopters for up to four passengers with advanced technical equipment for navigation, etc.
>
> • You need an additional €2.5 million for other costs, mainly pilots' salaries and fuel.
>
> • All flights to be booked on the internet. Bookings will be picked up directly by pilots – no call centres needed.
>
> • Total costs: €5 million a year.
>
> • You calculate that you need 50,000 passengers a year at an average fare of €100 in order to break even.

Use the notes in the box to help you prepare your pitch.

> **Making a pitch**
> Be ready to talk about:
> • the details of your product and / or service
> • the competition, and how your product / service is different / better etc
> • your management team
> • the company's operations
> • the financial aspects
> • the chances of success

9 Kids as consumers

Information exchange

Student A

1 Find out from Student B what percentage of parents say they talk to their children about:
 • important family decisions
 • how the children should spend their money
 • advertisements they see on TV

2 Find out what percentage of parents say it makes shopping easier when their child knows what brand he or she likes.

3 Use the following information to answer Student B's questions.

 Percentage of children who report helping their parents pick out the following:
 • clothes – 84 per cent
 • movies, DVDs and videos to rent – 77 per cent
 • sit-down restaurants – 63 per cent
 • stores to shop in – 58 per cent
 • family holiday spots – 50 per cent

4 Discuss the statistics you have exchanged. Are they typical of your experience?

Communication

Student B

Practise responding to Student A in these situations. Just practise the opening of the call.

1 Student A calls to speak to Susan Barker. She is out of the office. Find out why Student A is calling.

2 Student A calls to speak to Greg Sayer. You are Greg Sayer and you know Student A because he / she is one of your suppliers. Find out what he / she wants to speak about.

3 Student A calls your company, Filtons. You answer the phone. Student A wants to speak to someone in Accounts. You don't know anybody in Accounts but put Student A through to this department.

Now practise calling Student A in these situations. Just practise the opening of the call.

4 You want to speak to Max Clifton. You have been given his name as someone who can help you to organise an exhibition.

5 Call the company Milligans. You want to speak to someone in the order despatch department about an order which has not arrived.

6 You want to speak to Dan Peters. He is in charge of Purchasing and you are a supplier. You want to discuss his company's new purchasing contract.

10 Selling yourself

Communication

Student B

1 Practise taking Student A's messages.

 a Patrick Sullivan is not in the office this week.

 b Pretend to be voicebox of Garfield Tober. Say 'Please leave a message and I'll get back to you as soon as possible.'

2 Practise leaving the following messages with Student A.

 a You would like to speak to Kate O'Brien. You have invited her to dinner and you would like to arrange to pick her up after work. Leave a message.

 b You want to speak to Pascal Durand. He is supposed to confirm a meeting tomorrow morning at 08.30. You want him to call you back as soon as possible.

11 Think global, act local

Communication

Student B

1 Student A is responsible for organising an important meeting next week but you are taking care of the arrangements. Student A will call you to confirm the arrangements:
  • Timing: start 9.30 a.m. finish 16.00; lunch – buffet lunch in meeting room.
  • Dinner arrangements – provisionally booked a French restaurant, *Le Bistro*.

2 Call Student A to discuss a project he / she is responsible for. You need an update on:
  • the progress of the project
  • the budget

You need to receive this information by the end of the week. You don't want to talk about anything else during the call.

12 The grey market

Communication

Student B

1 You are starting a new job next month as a member of Student A's team. He / she has called you to discuss the arrangements for your first day. He / she has invited you to lunch one day next week.

2 You are Student A's boss. You need a report from him / her urgently. You have discussed this and want to close the call by getting a commitment from Student A to deliver it very quickly.

Business across cultures

R&D

Your department developed the Protector XP. You are very proud of the innovation and, following the licensing of pepper spray in your country, you are sure that this product has a great future. You feel that you can't stop criminals from attacking women. If the criminal hadn't used your product, he might have used a knife or gun.

Marketing

Your department has been responsible for launching and promoting the Protector XP. You have carried out a very successful advertising campaign. You feel that the PR Manager should be able to deal with this little crisis. Your company cannot be blamed for every criminal incident.

Finance

You have made a big investment in this product – total development costs of €250,000, investment in the production line and stock of nearly €400,000. You have financial targets for sales of 25,000 units in the first year, delivering a gross margin of €250,000. If sales are affected by this incident, it could seriously damage your figures. On the other hand, this incident could have a negative effect on the whole business, and it might be better to withdraw the product quickly.

[handwritten: gross: amount of sales 250.000 before taken production]

[handwritten: Future]

[handwritten: move back / go back]

Production

You have put in a new production line for the Protector XP and you are pleased with it. When you heard about this incident, you wondered whether the product has a fault – the pepper spray can be activated without the alarm and therefore a criminal can attack somebody silently. You want to ask R&D whether the product can be modified so that the alarm and spray only work together. You realise this would mean withdrawing all existing stock and also offering existing customers a replacement product.

Logistics

You are very worried about this incident. You have already produced 15,000 products – around 5,000 have been sold, 5,000 are with retailers, and the rest are in your warehouse. It will be very difficult to withdraw the product from the market. You think you should stress the product's qualities and continue selling it.

Business scenario 3 Bolton Bikes

Group interview

Student B

You are Susie Chang. Use the notes below to help you prepare for the group discussion.

> **Susie Chang, 37**
> - You joined Bolton Bikes 10 years ago as a designer.
> - You were born in Canada of Chinese parents. You speak Mandarin, but not Cantonese (the language spoken in Shanghai), but could learn it.
> - You have a degree in Engineering Design from Vancouver University.
> - You are an excellent designer – you were Bolton Bike's chief designer for their latest, most successful model.
> - You have management potential but so far you have managed only small teams of three or four designers.
> - You are single, with no children.
> - You would be willing to move to Shanghai for up to five years.
> - You know and like Jim Kolowski, another of the candidates, whom you work with. You don't know the other candidate, Lee Kong.

In addition, be ready to talk about yourself in relation to these qualities:

language skills	openness	drive	patience
communication skills	flexibility	emotional strength	sensitivity
cultural understanding	autonomy	physical stamina	

Useful Language

I think I'm quite open – for example, when colleagues have problems, they often come to me for advice.

People tell me that ...

I like to think that ...

I have the reputation of being ...

In the past I've always ...

Review and development 9–12

Communication

Student B

Practise making two telephone calls. Use the information below, and add your own ideas.

1 You are Ms / Mr Chu, manager of an air-conditioning service centre in Kuala Lumpur, Malaysia. You act as an agent for various suppliers of air-conditioning equipment. You receive a call from the Export Manager of Biltons, an air-conditioning supplier in the UK. They are looking for representation in your market and want to arrange a meeting.

2 You work for Maisey and Cooper, a recruitment agency in London. You receive a call from a client in Dubai, who wants to speak to Ms Cooper. Unfortunately, she is on holiday this week. Take a message and do your best to help this important client.

14 Something for nothing?

Reading and speaking

Student A

There are only two developed countries that Tornberg rules out. One is Singapore, where the media are restricted and foreign ownership is limited to 3 per cent. The other is Australia, where Rupert Murdoch is already publishing free commuter dailies in Sydney and Melbourne. "It's probably the most competitive market in the world, with very emotionally driven, strong, rich players," Tornberg says.

Business scenario 4 Seniorservices

Expanding the business

Team A

Present this information to the management team. Think of more pros and cons.

> **Business parks**
>
> - This idea is for a chain of business parks designed specially for seniors.
> - You have seen figures that show that 50 per cent of people who retire from their careers continue to work, often in their own businesses. They need somewhere to work, surrounded by people of their own age. Each business park will have a social centre, golf club, and a shopping centre with shops, restaurants, etc.
> - Cost of investment: A$5 million per business park. Estimated return on investment: 7.5 per cent (A$37,500) per year per park.
> - Pros: Attractive activity with big growth potential.
> - Cons: This is a totally new concept – you have no idea if it will work.

Business scenario 1 Improving morale

Role play

Student B

> You are the General Manager.
> - You want the company to stay where it is, in the suburbs. Many employees with children live nearby and they don't want to commute to the centre.
> - You think that investment in the crèche, a new company restaurant, and possibly redecoration of the offices would help to improve employee morale.
> - You think staff turnover and staff absence will decrease if the right investments are made. Find out how much they would cost.
>
> Try to persuade the CEO (Student A) and the Human Resources Manager (Student C) that these are the best investments to make.

9 Kids as consumers

Student B

1 Use the following information to answer Student A's questions.
   - 73 per cent of parents say they talk to their children about important family decisions.
   - 77 per cent of parents say they talk to their children about how the children should spend their money.
   - 52 per cent of parents say they talk to their children about advertisements they see on TV.

2 Use the following information to answer Student A's question.
   Parents have recognised the benefits of listening to what their children have to say, with 70 per cent saying it makes shopping easier when the children know what brand they like.

3 Find out what percentage of children report helping their parents pick out the following:
   - clothes
   - movies, DVDs and videos to rent
   - sit-down restaurants
   - stores to shop in
   - family holiday spots

4 Discuss the statistics you have exchanged. Are they typical of your experience?

Business scenario 3   Bolton Bikes

Student C

You are Jim Kolowski. Use the notes below to help you prepare for the group discussion.

> **Jim Kolowski, 44**
> - You are Deputy Manager of Manufacturing at Bolton Bikes in Vancouver.
> - You came to Canada with your parents from Poland when you were five.
> - You are bilingual in English and Polish. You also speak Spanish fluently after only six months of evening classes. You think you could learn Cantonese very quickly.
> - You have a degree in Manufacturing Engineering from Toronto University.
> - You are known as a tough but popular manager. You are not always tactful in dealing with workers and suppliers, but you get results.
> - You are married to Janice, an engineer at Bolton Bikes. You have two sons, 12 and 14.
> - You would be willing to move to Shanghai for one year only.
> - You know and like Susie Chang, another of the candidates, whom you work with. You don't know the other candidate, Lee Kong.

In addition, be ready to talk about yourself in relation to these qualities:

language skills	openness	drive	patience
communication skills	flexibility	emotional strength	sensitivity
cultural understanding	autonomy	physical stamina	

Useful Language

I think I'm quite open – for example, when colleagues have problems, they often come to me for advice.

People tell me that ...

I like to think that ...

I have the reputation of being ...

In the past I've always ...

14 Something for nothing?

Reading and speaking

Student B

Metro has conquered most of continental Europe, most recently arriving in Russia and Portugal, but so far Germany has been impossible. Competition is much tougher there, and the Germans have proved more disciplined than their neighbours at banding together to keep *Metro* out of the market.

Business scenario 4 Seniorservices

Expanding the business

Team B

Present this information to the management team. Think of more pros and cons.

Cruise ship

- Seniorservices could extend its activities by buying a small cruise ship (200 passengers).
- The cruise market has been growing by 20 per cent a year generally and 30 per cent among the over-60 age group.
- You want to offer 'active' cruises with lectures, study groups, and so on.
- Each cabin will have Internet access, enabling passengers with business activities to continue them while on board. It will also allow all passengers to keep in touch with their families and the outside world in general.
- Cost: A$10 million.
  Return on investment: 10 per cent a year (A$1 million a year).
- Pros: Natural extension of our existing resort activities.
- Cons: In an economic downturn, consumers will not spend money on luxury holidays.

Business scenario 1 Improving morale

Role play

Student C

You are the Human Resources Manager.

- To improve employee morale, you think the company should move to the city centre with its shopping, bars, restaurants, etc. More than half the agency's staff are under 35 and many of them would prefer this.
- You think staff turnover and staff absence will decrease if this investment is made. Find out how much it would cost.
- Try to persuade the CEO (Student A) and the General Manager (Student B) that this is the best investment to make.

Business scenario 2 Pitching for finance

Procedure

Team B

You are a team of entrepreneurs. You want financial backing for Autoflowers, which sells flowers from a vending machine.

Use the information below as the basis for your pitch, adding more detail where necessary.

Autoflowers

- You plan to put flower vending machines in 100 locations in five European cities.
- Machines to cost €5000 each. Permission for the machines has already been granted by the cities' authorities. You will pay average rent of €1000 per machine per year.
- There will be a choice of five types of bouquets at €30 each. Payment by credit card only – no cash handling.
- Special system keeps flowers fresh for up to three weeks.
- Each city's machines to be serviced and refilled by just one technician.
- The outside of machine will have a large screen for TV advertising from a consumer shopping channel, showing 24 hours per day. Income: €5000 per machine per year.
- You need €3 million to start your company (to pay for machines and first year's rents).

Use the notes in the box to help you prepare your pitch.

Making a pitch

Be ready to talk about:

- the details of your product and / or service
- the competition, and how your product / service is different / better etc
- your management team
- the company's operations
- the financial aspects
- the chances of success

Business scenario 2 Pitching for finance

Procedure

Team C

You are a team of entrepreneurs. You want financial backing for Firenze Jewellery, a range of modern designer silver jewellery.

Use the information below as the basis for your pitch, adding more detail where necessary.

> **Firenze Jewellery**
> - You were at art school together and now you want to set up your own business making silver jewellery at reasonable prices for everyday wear.
> - You have been successfully making and selling your jewellery at street markets for two years. Now you want to make it on a large scale, selling through department stores, fashion stores, etc.
> - You want to make your jewellery in Italy, not Asia, despite lower costs there.
> - The global jewellery market is worth €60 billion a year. You think that you can easily get 0.1 per cent of this market, giving you sales of €60 million a year. You estimate break-even at €40 million.
> - You need €10 million to develop your business: factory and machinery (€9 million); recruitment and training of specialist workers (€500,000); other costs (€500,000).

Use the notes in the box to help you prepare your pitch.

> **Making a pitch**
> Be ready to talk about:
> - the details of your product and / or service
> - the competition, and how your product / service is different / better etc
> - your management team
> - the company's operations
> - the financial aspects
> - the chances of success

Business scenario 3 Bolton Bikes

Group interview

Student D

You are Lee Kong. Use the notes below to help you prepare for the group discussion.

Lee Kong, 47

- You were born in the USA of Chinese parents.
- You are bilingual in English and Cantonese. You also speak Mandarin.
- You have a Master's degree in Automotive Engineering from Detroit University.
- You have spent your whole career so far at General Motors in the USA in production management. You now want a new challenge in a different but related industry.
- You have two grown-up children who are studying at college in the US. Your wife (also Chinese-American) is a restaurateur – she owns a chain of ten Chinese restaurants in the US and would like to open a restaurant in Shanghai.
- You would be willing to move to Shanghai for up to two years
- You don't know the other candidates, Susie Chang and Jim Kolowski, who already work at Bolton Bikes in Vancouver.

In addition, be ready to talk about yourself in relation to these qualities.

language skills	openness	drive	patience
communication skills	flexibility	emotional strength	sensitivity
cultural understanding	autonomy	physical stamina	

Useful Language

I think I'm quite open – for example, when colleagues have problems, they often come to me for advice.

People tell me that ...

I like to think that ...

I have the reputation of being ...

In the past I've always ...

Business scenario 4 Seniorservices

Expanding the business

Team C

Present this information to the management team. Think of more pros and cons.

Insurance

- You want to sell insurance – for example, car and home insurance – to seniors.
- The insurance market has been growing by 5 to 10 per cent a year recently.
- Seniors are well known for driving safely and having fewer accidents. They also make fewer claims on home insurance.
- Cost of investment: A$1 million. Estimated return on investment: 15 per cent (A$150,000) a year.
- Pros: Low initial investment – the operations and claims could easily be paid out of premiums.
- Cons: Seniorservices has no expertise in the insurance business.

AUDIO SCRIPT

1 Happiness at work

1.1 1 I'm a lawyer. I work in property law – I do all the legal work connected with buying and selling buildings and land. My job is always interesting. I especially like meeting different clients – every day is different, in fact. I work 60 hours a week and sometimes I get very stressed, but most of the time I feel very positive about my job.

2 I'm a fitness instructor. I run fitness classes at gyms and leisure clubs but I have some private clients too. I plan exercise programmes for them and go to their homes to help them get fit. I like this job a lot because I can organise my own time. And it's very rewarding to see people get fit and healthy. It's more satisfying than my old job – I used to work in an office. I hated that!

3 I'm an accountant. I specialise in bankruptcy – so I spend all my time dealing with companies that have gone out of business. My job is pretty varied. I like the flexibility – in my company, you can start work when you want and leave when you want, as long as you're there during the core hours, from ten to three every day. That's a real bonus for a working mother. It's much more flexible than some of the larger accountancy firms. And it's well-paid so I'm very lucky, really.

4 I'm a civil servant. I work in regional government. I'm in a department with ten other people. Our job is to attract investment into the area. In the past five years, we've persuaded more than 20 overseas companies to set up operations here. I love the teamwork – I'm at my best working in a team. This is the most stimulating job I've ever had, and I'm happier in my work than most people I know. And, of course, as a civil servant, my job is very secure.

1.2 1 My name's Françoise. I'm 38 and I live in Paris. I have three children under the age of ten. When I'm not at work, I spend all my time with them.

2 Let me say a few words about myself. My name's Harvey. I'm from Wisconsin. I was born in Milwaukee, on Lake Michigan. Now I work on the East Coast, but I love going back to my hometown whenever I can.

3 My name's Lyn. I work in sales and I love my job! I work for Digicom – it's a big IT distributor. It's a great company to work for.

4 Hi, my name's Michael but everybody calls me Mick. My passion is bridges. I always spend my holidays visiting them. Last year we went to the south of France to see the new bridge at Millau. It's absolutely fantastic.

5 Hello, my name's Lucy. I was brought up in the north of England. My family moved south when I was a teenager and I've lived near London ever since.

6 My name's Ludwig. I'm in retail. I work for a large chain of furniture stores. We're based in Frankfurt but I travel all over the world for my job.

1.3 1 I'm not so good at structuring my day. I take time to sort things out and sometimes I find it difficult to decide on my priorities.

2 People tell me that I'm a good listener. Some of my colleagues talk to me when they have problems. I'm happy to help if I can.

3 I get on well with my colleagues and I really enjoy working with my team. We go out together a lot – for a meal or a drink after work.

2 Motivation

2.1 1 I'm a call centre manager in the financial services industry. I believe it's important to let people work without constant supervision – you have to let them use their initiative. Otherwise they feel they're being treated like children. Of course, there are procedures to follow, but we like to give employees as much flexibility as possible within those procedures.

2 I'm a section manager in an insurance company. We do the paperwork relating to insurance claims. The employees must be here by 8 a.m. and they can't leave before 5 p.m. I want to see what they're doing the whole time. That way I can be sure they're doing the work we're paying them to do.

3 I'm a senior manager in an oil company. I encourage younger managers in my department to use their initiative. They respond to this well – it motivates them and you can see their work improving. It's also a good way to identify potential future managers among them – the ones who are going to reach the top of the organisation in the future.

4 I work in the retail industry for a large chain of department stores. I'm in charge of 20 sales assistants. All they're interested in is getting to the weekend, and doing as little as possible. I have to keep an eye on them the whole time. We don't allow any sort of initiative – it just leads to problems when people start ignoring the established procedures.

2.2 1 I've worked in the oil industry since I graduated. I like the way they do things in this company. We're encouraged to use our initiative – to think for ourselves and solve problems. We get our own projects to look after – I think they realise that people with MBAs need that kind of independence. And we're judged on results, not by the amount of time we spend on the job.

2 The manager's breathing down my neck all the time! He walks around the different departments, checking on the sales people – you never know when he's going to appear. The only thing he's interested in is reaching his sales targets. We can't do anything without asking him first!

3 In this organisation, like in all insurance companies, you just follow established procedures. Decisions are imposed from above – there's no consultation. And don't ever dream about working from home, not even one day a week! That would never be allowed – they want to see what you're doing the whole time.

4 I've worked in other places where they measure your work very precisely – they don't want you to spend more than three minutes on each call. But here there's more flexibility, and you can spend as much time as you want with each customer, within reason, of course. As a team leader, I get a lot of responsibility, which I like, and I get a lot of satisfaction from my work. I think that motivates people. And valued employees make for valued customers!

2.3
Michael: Would you like coffee or tea?

Susanne: Coffee, please.

Michael: It's over here. Just help yourself. Where do you come from, Susanne?

Susanne: I was born in Germany, in Freiburg, in the south of Germany.

Michael: Really? I thought you were American.

Susanne: Well, I was brought up in the States. My father worked there.

Michael: Oh, that explains the accent! Where did you live?

Susanne: We moved around, but mostly we lived on the East Coast.

Michael: Did you go to university there?

Susanne: No, I studied in London. And I've been in England since I graduated.

Michael: Do you miss your family?

Susanne: Well, my sister is in England, too, and my parents come over to visit sometimes.

Michael: Do you get back to the States much?

Susanne: Once or twice a year. In my first job after graduation, I used to travel a lot so I saw my parents more often.

Michael: What were you doing?

Susanne: I was a trainee buyer for a fashion house in London.

Michael: That sounds fun!

Susanne: It was, but after a couple of years, I decided the fashion business wasn't for me.

Michael: Why was that?

Susanne: Oh, I don't know. The fashion business is very ...

Michael: I guess it's very competitive? Lots of beautiful people?

Susanne: That's right. It's all about image, as you would expect.

Michael: So how exactly did you end up in this line of business?

Susanne: Well, that's a long story ...

2.4 For us, the family is the most important element in our lives. I used to work for a local investment banking company, Asian Finance. It was a Singaporean company, run by a local family - the father and two sons. At Asian Finance, family ties were very important. Many of the people who worked there were related to each other. Now I work for Finvest, an international finance company. The head office is in France and some of the managers are from there, but there are also some Americans, one or two other Europeans, and some from other parts of Asia as well. So family doesn't count for much here. The Americans tell me that the company is very French, but I can't really tell. I have some friends who work for American multinationals and they are very different, that's true. Finvest is quite a traditional company, maybe that's a European thing, I don't know. It certainly has its own culture – people dress very formally and there's a lot of handshaking!

2.5 As I was saying, everybody dresses very formally – that's true for the men and the women. And I notice that the French managers tend to shake hands or even kiss when they meet each other. It's a well-established business – it's been going for generations. There are pictures on the walls of some of the founders and key people over the years. I notice the formality in letters and reports – the expressions they use are much more formal than I'm used to and generally when you write, even emails, you need to be careful what you say.

3 Incentives

3.1 A: ... So what exactly are the incentives if I exceed my performance target?

B: If you reach 110 per cent of your target for the year, you'll get a performance bonus of €1000. But you won't get a bonus unless you reach the target.

A: What will the benefits package contain if I join the company?

B: Well let's see ... health insurance, gym membership ... We have an excellent new gym on-site with all the latest equipment ...

A: I see. Could you tell me more about the health insurance?

B: The company will pay all hospital bills, unless you do something that's not covered by the policy, such as participating in dangerous sports.

A: What happens if I'm ill?

B: If you're ill, you'll be able to take sick leave. But unless you phone your manager, you won't be able to take more than three days off.

A: How much does the company contribute to the company pension scheme?

B: The company pays 80 per cent of the contributions, and the employee is responsible for 20 per cent. Our financial advisor will advise you if you need help with financial planning.

A: How much paternity leave will I get if we have children?

B: Fathers can take three months' paid leave, unless they decide to work instead, of course!

3.2 **Nikos:** Could we go through the details again, please?

Phil: Of course. We will supply the circuit boards on an annual contract, delivering once a month, unless you request extra deliveries or you want to postpone.

Nikos: Could you clarify that? We need to be sure that we can change the order, if necessary.

Phil: Yes, that's OK. We will deliver on the fifteenth of each month, according to the agreed schedule. If you contact us by the 28th of the previous month, we will accept a change of order.

Nikos: So, this means that we can increase or decrease the quantity?

Phil: Yes, that's correct. But, of course, there will be a knock-on effect on price.

Nikos: What do you mean by 'knock-on'?

Phil: I mean that we have agreed a unit price based on the schedule of monthly orders. If you decrease the quantity, we can't offer you the same price.

Nikos: Yes, I understand. So will you charge us at list price if we decrease our monthly order by more than 20 per cent?

Phil: That's right. On the other hand, at the end of the year, you may qualify for a further discount if you have exceeded the planned quantity significantly.

Nikos: Sorry, I'm not with you. What do you mean by 'significantly'?

Phil: You will qualify for a further 10 per cent discount if orders exceed the planned quantity by more than 20 per cent.

Nikos: Right. And we would expect to receive this as a credit note at the end of the year.

Phil: That's fine.

Nikos: So, let me just confirm that. We will contract you to deliver 250 circuit boards per month, on the 15th of each month. This will be invoiced at the end of each month at a rate of $15 per unit.

3.3 **Project leader A:** Thanks for coming to the meeting today. We're at a critical stage of the project, as you know, and I'd like to give you all some feedback. I think we're on track but there are some difficulties. How do you think it's going? Peter?

Peter: Pretty well. As you say, there are a few problems but my side of things is going OK.

Project Leader A: I am pleased to hear that, Peter. What about you, Marta?

Marta: Well, I've got some problems with my contractor in Spain.

Project Leader A: That's what I've heard. I'm worried about this, Marta. The markets are not sure if you can deliver on time. I think you need to put pressure on your contractor. Otherwise we're going to miss the deadline. Miguel, what about you?

Miguel: I've been getting good feedback.

Project Leader A: That's good. You've been doing a great job, Miguel. OK, let's move on and look at the ...

3.4 **Project leader B:** Thanks for coming to the meeting today and thanks for all your hard work on this project. We're at a critical stage of the project, as you know, and we're starting to run into some problems. We have some tight deadlines to meet and I'm sure we all want to stay on track. So I want to use this meeting to look at the problems and try to work out some solutions. OK, let's start with ...

4 Work and leisure

4.1 **Interviewer:** What do people mean by 'work–life balance'?

Jack Stevens: Well, many people these days feel that work takes up too much of their time and energy, so it's the idea that people want a balance between work and life outside the office – family, friends, leisure activities, and so on.

Interviewer: Aha ...

Jack Stevens: Of course, there are laws in many countries to limit the number of hours that people can work. In the EU, for example, there is a law that prevents people working more than 48 hours per week. It's widely known that working long hours can have serious negative effects on people's health and well-being – working long hours can cause illness and reduce life expectancy.

Interviewer: Right ...

Jack Stevens: And in some countries, the weekly limit is much lower. For example, France has a 35-hour week.

Interviewer: But aren't people spending more on leisure activities? Businesses like gyms and travel companies have benefited enormously ...

Jack Stevens: That's true. Of course things have improved since the 19th century ...

Interviewer: Aha ...

Jack Stevens: In those days people often worked 18 or 20 hours a day, and sometimes slept in the factory next to their machines – no gyms or weekends away for them! So we've come a long way since then.

4.2 *Interviewer:* So, have working hours gone down all over Europe?

Jack Stevens: Yes. If you look at the figures from 1996 onwards, they remained steady at about 38.7 hours per week and then they fell quite quickly, to 38.3 in 1999 and 37.9 in 2000.

Interviewer: Aha ...

Jack Stevens: The number of hours worked rose slightly in 2001 – that year people worked 38 hours a week on average ...

Interviewer: OK.

Jack Stevens: But then the figures started falling again: they fell to 37.9 in 2002, then they decreased to 37.4 in 2003 and went down again slightly to 37.3 in 2004.

Interviewer: So, since 1996, the number of working hours has decreased from 38.7 to 37.3 per week?

Jack Stevens: That's right. Now some people may find this ...

4.3 *Frank:* We started nearly 20 years ago. It was very tough at the beginning to establish the business and build our client base. We worked night and day.

Dieter: That must have been hard.

Frank: It was. It took us nearly three years to get established. Our first big breakthrough was when we won a contract to supply the Ministry of Health.

Dieter: Really?

Frank: Yeah. To begin with, we supplied a couple of hospitals with alarm systems but now this has grown, and we now cover the whole country. And we also supply hospitals abroad.

Dieter: I didn't know that. So, is the Ministry of Health your biggest customer?

Frank: Yes, it is. But we've worked hard to find other customers, especially in the private sector. In fact, almost 60 per cent of our work is in the private sector now.

Dieter: Is that where you see your business developing?

Frank: Yes, I think so. At the moment, we're trying to break into new markets in south-east Asia.

Dieter: Oh that can't be easy.

Frank: No, it isn't. You need to have good local partners. Luckily, we've found an excellent partner in Malaysia.

Dieter: That's interesting. I wonder if it's the same people we work with.

Frank: I've got their card here somewhere ... here it is ... Sunset Trading Company.

Dieter: I don't believe it! I was just talking to them yesterday ...

5 Entrepreneurs

5.1 *Interviewer:* Gabbie, you founded one of the most successful airlines on the continent. What, in your opinion, makes a good entrepreneur?

Gabbie Kung: Well, entrepreneurs have to be excellent communicators. You need to persuade investors to invest in your idea. Then, when you start your business you have to communicate your vision to the people who work for you. And then, of course, you have to communicate your product or service to potential customers.

Interviewer: What other characteristics do successful entrepreneurs need?

Gabbie Kung: Entrepreneurs have to be self-confident individuals. They have to have confidence in themselves and their idea. They also have to be persistent as they'll need to overcome all sorts of obstacles to achieve success.

Interviewer: And what about vision, which you mentioned earlier?

Gabbie Kung: Yes, it's vital to be innovative and creative. You need to offer something new, something that isn't already on the market. You need to be able to grasp ideas and opportunities that other people may miss.

Interviewer: Why do you think so many entrepreneurs fail?

Gabbie Kung: There are all sorts of reasons. If we look at personal characteristics, some entrepreneurs are over-cautious – they just aren't prepared to take risks. Or they're unrealistic – their goals and plans for the business and themselves just won't work in practice. Or they might be inflexible – sometimes you have to be prepared to change your plans and strategies to make sure the business succeeds.

Interviewer: And what about the businesses themselves– why do so many new businesses fail?

Gabbie Kung: There are all sorts of reasons: perhaps the product or service doesn't really offer anything new, or people don't need or want it, or the general economic situation may not be right.

Interviewer: And why do you think a lot of successful business ideas start with individual entrepreneurs, and not in large companies?

Gabbie Kung: Well, many large companies are very bureaucratic, and new ideas have to go through lots of committees before a decision is taken. There may even be active resistance to doing something new and unfamiliar. Individual entrepreneurs have a lot more freedom to act.

5.2　1　*A:* We moved recently. We used to live in a small flat in London. Now we have a big house in the country.

　　　B: That's quite a change. Do you like the country?

　　　A: Yes, I do. We have so much space and it's really quiet. I love it.

　　2　*A:* Have you seen the latest Spielberg film?

　　　B: No, I haven't. Is it any good?

　　　A: It's had good reviews. We were thinking of going to see it this evening.

　　　B: I'm not keen on action films. I prefer a good horror film.

　　3　*A:* How's the business going?

　　　B: Very tough, at the moment. Sales are pretty flat.

　　　A: Same for us. There's not much growth and it looks like higher taxes again next year.

　　　B: I can't believe it. I thought this government was meant to be pro-business.

　　4　*A:* How's the family?

　　　B: Fine, thanks. Our daughter has just started at university. She's having a great time. How are things with you?

　　　A: Well, did you know that Jane and I separated a few months ago? I'm living in a flat on my own.

　　5　*A:* We went on a cruise for the first time this year.

　　　B: Wasn't it boring? Being on a ship all the time?

　　　A: No, there was plenty to do. And we stopped at a number of different places ...

　　6　*A:* Did you see the match yesterday?

　　　B: No, I didn't. What was the score?

　　　A: Four three. It was a great match. City scored first and ...

　　7　*A:* I really must give up. For one thing, it's costing me a fortune.

　　　B: You should. You'd feel much better.

　　　A: I know, but I'm worried that I'd just put on weight.

　　　B: I don't think you will. I didn't.

　　8　*A:* Have you always worked in the public sector?

　　　B: No, I used to work for an IT company. They made me redundant two years ago. It took me nearly a year to find this job.

　　　A: Yeah, it's not easy these days. How is the new job?

　　　B: It's OK, but sometimes I get a bit bored.

5.3　1　I thought the meeting was a waste of time. What did you think?

　　2　You look really tired.

　　3　You've got some time. Join me for a drink.

4　You didn't mention it, but are you married?

5　I thought you were very good in that meeting – very well prepared and clear.

6　I'd like to invite you home. You could meet my wife and family.

6 Creativity

6.1　*Interviewer:* ... As we were saying earlier, creativity is very highly valued in business. Could you give us some examples?

Jackie Lang: When you think of creativity in business, you tend to think of brilliant new innovations like the Apple personal computer, the Internet or the cell phone.

Interviewer: Aha.

Jackie Lang: But creativity can come in much simpler forms, such as a metal box.

Interviewer: A metal box? How do you mean?

Jackie Lang: I'm thinking of the shipping container.

Interviewer: Oh ...

Jackie Lang: In 1956, Malcolm McLean, the boss of an American road transport company had the idea of putting goods into metal containers that could be transported by ship and offloaded onto trucks or railway wagons.

Interviewer: It's odd that no one had thought of containers before.

Jackie Lang: Well, they had, but the boxes were mixed with other cargo, and they weren't of a standard size so they couldn't be handled easily.

Interviewer: Right ...

Jackie Lang: No one realised how containers would change patterns of trade around the world. In 1968, there were consultants who confidently said: 'Five container ships will be enough for all the trade between Britain and the United States.'

Interviewer: That's incredible!

Jackie Lang: No one foresaw the expansion of trade that took place because containers made it cheap enough to trade goods that weren't traded before.

Interviewer: Right. So no one in the 1950s said 'Containers are going to change the world'?

Jackie Lang: Exactly. Creativity produces new products and services, but you can't always be sure of the impact.

6.2　1　I'd like you to have this small gift.

　　2　Could you send me the file when you get back?

　　3　I'm sorry, but I've lost the report.

　　4　Bye for now. Have a great weekend.

　　5　I hope we can work together again in the future.

　　6　Would you like to join us later for dinner?

7 My flight leaves at four o'clock. May I leave early?

8 Thanks for your support.

9 Why don't we take a taxi?

10 I saw *King Kong* on TV last night. I thought it was fantastic!

6.3 1 I work for the National Health Service. It's a huge, bureaucratic organisation with a lot of management layers. The problem is that the top management are a long way from the reality of nurses and doctors working in hospitals.

2 I work for a small family company called Thorntons. There are only three layers in the company. We all know the boss, that's Mrs Thornton. She took over from her father a couple of years ago. Then there are the supervisors, who report to Mrs Thornton, and then the workers. It works pretty well. We don't need middle managers, really.

3 I work for a medium-sized company. It's called TLC Ltd. We don't have so many layers but we are still fairly structured. The managers have their own offices and they keep their distance. I guess there are around four layers but there are fairly big differences between the layers.

4 We set up our company nearly ten years ago – it's called 'The Metal Cooperative'. It's totally flat. Everybody is an owner. It's a registered limited company but all the members of the cooperative have the same number of shares, so we share the profits equally.

7 Start-ups

7.1 *Maya Newman:* Come in, Mr Graham. Please sit down.

Jay Graham: Thank you.

Maya Newman: I've had a look at your business plan and it seems as if your idea has a lot of potential.

Jay Graham: I think so, too. I've been working on it for two years now. What I need now is some advice on where to go from here.

Maya Newman: Well, that's what I'm here for. This advisory service is intended for people just like you.

Jay Graham: That's great. Well, of course, I know I need a backer. Where should I go for financial backing?

Maya Newman: Well, you could try a venture capital company. These are organisations that invest in new entrepreneurial ideas. They know that some of the ideas they back will fail, some will do OK, and some, hopefully, will be very profitable. The profitable ones should make up for any losses on other investments.

Jay Graham: Are venture capitalists the only potential investors?

Maya Newman: No, there are also business angels. These are individual investors, typically business people who've already made money from previous ventures and are looking for new businesses to invest in.

Jay Graham: Right.

Maya Newman: Some business angels may just want to be a sleeping partner – they won't want to get involved in the day-to-day running of the company. Others will want to get actively involved in your business. They will help you develop the business ...

Jay Graham: I see ...

Maya Newman: But whether you go to a venture capital firm or a business angel, a good pitch is essential.

Jay Graham: A pitch?

Maya Newman: Yes. You have to present your ideas to investors, and it's important to do it briefly and clearly. You should be able to awaken their interest in just a couple of minutes. If they're interested, they'll ask you to make a longer presentation.

Jay Graham: So let's say I get some investment, everything goes well, and the company starts to grow. What about future expansion?

Maya Newman: Hmm, if you succeed, and that's a very big 'if', you may reach a point where you need much more investment to expand. In that case, the company is floated on the stock exchange in an IPO – that's an initial public offering. Then the company is listed on the stock market. Shares in the company are bought and sold by investors on the stock market.

Jay Graham: Right ...

Maya Newman: But that's a long way off yet! Concentrate for the moment on finding investors for your start-up!

7.2 1 A: That brings us to the last item on the agenda – the budget for the maintenance programme. George, I think you've prepared some figures.

B: That's right. I've got them here.

2 A: I'd like to fix a meeting for next week.

B: Of course. When would you like to hold it?

A: How about Thursday afternoon or Friday morning?

B: Do you want all the team to attend?

A: If possible. Could you email them and check their availability?

B: OK. What about the agenda?

A: I'll do that today and you can send it out tomorrow morning.

3 A: Did you get the minutes of the last meeting?

B: No, I didn't.

A: It's important that everyone reads the minutes. Peter <u>agreed to circulate</u> them after the meeting.

B: He's been on sick leave.

A: Well, there are some important actions to follow up ...

4 Good morning, everyone. Nice to see you all. Let's <u>get down to business</u>, shall we? We have a lot to cover today. Have you all seen the agenda? Good. By the end of the meeting, I'd like to finalise our plans for the new product launch. Melanie, could you start, please.

8 Inventions

8.1 *Interviewer:* How did you get the idea for the Anywayup cup?

Mandy Haberman: I first had the idea for a totally non-spill cup when I saw a little girl drinking from a conventional trainer cup. She dropped the cup and her mother dived to catch it before it hit the floor. This made me think that it must be possible to make a cup that would close and wouldn't spill or drip when the child wasn't drinking from it.

Interviewer: How did you go about producing the cup?

Mandy Haberman: Well, I had some experience of working with plastics, and, starting in my kitchen, I made a series of prototypes. After about a year I was ready to look for a financial <u>backer</u> to develop and sell the product.

Interviewer: How did you go about finding one?

Mandy Haberman: I had applied for a patent before I went to see possible backers, and over a period of a couple of years I showed my prototypes to about 20 companies.

Interviewer: Aha. How did companies respond when you went to see them?

Mandy Haberman: Responses varied. Typically, companies wanted to hold on to the prototypes while they <u>assessed</u> the product. Months would go by and I'd become very nervous about it until finally I would demand that they returned the product.

Interviewer: Mmm ...

Mandy Haberman: Those that were interested were either not prepared to invest enough money or were not prepared to commit to the sort of minimum sales figures that I considered possible.

Interviewer: So where did you go from there?

Mandy Haberman: I <u>exhibited at</u> trade shows. We showed prototypes which were convincing as real product samples. We demonstrated our samples by one moment drinking from them, and the next moment shaking them over people's clothes! Not a drop came out.

The shows were a huge success. We took about £10,000 of advance orders.

Interviewer: What happened next?

Mandy Haberman: With the £10,000 from the advance orders, I set up my own company – The Haberman Company Ltd. – to make the cups, and we rocketed into business. Later on, I licensed my product to V & A Marketing Ltd. in the UK, and a company called The First Years in the U.S.

Interviewer: How did you establish your routes to market?

Mandy Haberman: We realised that we needed to get the product into the supermarkets but this wasn't going to be easy – we had already been in contact with all the big chains, but they weren't interested.

Interviewer: Aha ...

Mandy Haberman: So we filled a cup with fruit juice and put it loose inside a white box and posted it to the buyer at Tesco, with a note to say that if it arrived without spilling, she should give us a call. A few days later, the telephone rang – we were into Tesco!

8.2 1 Thank you for coming to this meeting at such short notice. We have a small crisis and I want to make sure it doesn't become a big one. One of our packaging suppliers is in financial trouble and can no longer guarantee deliveries. We need to consider the options. Peter will present two alternative suppliers and Susan has costs for bringing the work back in-house. Peter, will you start ...

2 I'm delighted to welcome you all to our third meeting. Let me start by introducing a new member of the team. This is Pedro Rodríguez – he's the Marketing Manager in Venezuela – and he'll be representing our South and Central American markets. I've asked Pedro to start today's session with an overview of the market. Then we'll go around the table with the usual reports. Let's aim to stop for lunch around twelve thirty ...

3 A: Great to see you all today. Stephen is going to facilitate today's meeting. Stephen, let me hand over to you straight away.

B: Thanks, Sarah. We've got a fantastic new product and what we need now is a new name. We've had a few ideas but nothing really exciting. So let's see what we can come up with today. We have plenty of coffee and doughnuts, and I hope they'll help! I'll write your ideas up here first and then later we can see which ones we prefer ...

8.3 *Chairperson:* As you know, we're going to the Electronica trade fair again this year. We want our stand to have a big impact. I want to hear your ideas on this. I'll list the ideas as we go. So, the topic is Electronica stand ... Susie, what do you think?

Susie: I think we need to change the colour. Last year, we used very boring dark colours. We need something light and bright.

Chairperson: OK. Cathy, what's your opinion?

Cathy: As I see it, the main problem is there's nothing for visitors to do on the stand, just read and talk. In my opinion, we should have something interactive ...

Doug: I don't agree. People come to the stand to learn about us and what we have to offer, and I think reading and talking are ...

Chairperson: Excuse me, Doug, you may be right, but at the moment we're brainstorming new ideas. Is there anything you think we should change?

Doug: Well, we could change the design and layout of the stand – to make it more attractive.

Danny: Yes, we could have one area where people sit and maybe have access to our website ...

Chairperson: Do you mean we could break the stand into two parts, Danny?

Danny: Yes, that might be good. One area for talk and questions, maybe with something interactive, and another area to sit, read, access the internet ...

Chairperson: Susie, do you have anything to add? No?

Susie: No, I don't think so.

Chairperson: This all sounds great. So let me summarise what we have so far ...

9 Kids as consumers

9.1 1 **A:** Marketing Department.

B: Hi, Max. This is Patrick.

A: Patrick, how are you?

B: Not bad, and you?

A: OK. What can I do for you?

B: I want to ask you a favour.

A: Fire away.

B: Well, I was wondering if you could sit in on the project review meeting for me on Wednesday ...

A: I suppose so. What time does it start?

2 **A:** International Properties. How can I help you?

B: Could I speak to your General Manager, please?

A: Who's calling, please?

B: This is Gerard Manley from the Inland Revenue.

A: Could you tell me what it's about?

B: It's confidential but it's to do with your annual tax return.

A: I'll see if I can connect you ... I'm afraid he's not answering his phone. I think he's in a meeting. Could you call back later?

3 **A:** Mo Jacob speaking.

B: Hello, Mo. This is Helen.

A: Hi, Helen. How are you?

B: Fine, thanks. Listen, this is just a quick call. I thought you should know – Steve Johnson has got the job.

A: Really? I don't believe it ...

4 **A:** Good morning. Key Supplies.

B: This is Morgan Benton, calling from Bachelors. Could you put me through to Accounts, please.

A: Just a moment ...

C: Accounts.

B: This is Morgan Benton. I'm calling about a payment.

C: Hello, Morgan. I thought I recognised your voice. This is Jason. Can you give me the reference number?

B: The date on the invoice is the 11th of January and the number is 2901.

C: Have you got a purchase order number?

B: I don't think so.

C: Well, that could be the problem. All invoices have to have a purchase order number ...

5 **A:** Customer Service. How can I help you?

B: I'm calling about a delivery.

A: Can I take your name, please?

B: It's Susan Freeman.

A: One moment, please ... I'm afraid the line's engaged. Can I get them to call you back?

B: Look, this is the third time I've phoned and ...

10 Selling yourself

10.1 **Interviewer:** What do human resources specialists mean when they say that you should be able to sell yourself? Surely it's not like selling cars or washing machines?

Rebecca Sands: Well, in a way it is. In the same way that sales people have to communicate the benefits of their product and persuade people to buy it, someone in the job market has to communicate with potential employers and persuade them about what they have to offer.

Interviewer: I see ...

Rebecca Sands: Of course, in order to sell yourself, you have to know yourself. So self-awareness is where it all starts. For example, there are free psychometric tests on the Internet that you can take to check your skills – by answering the questions, you get feedback on how good you are at working with others, how well you manage stress, and so on.

Interviewer: Right ...

Rebecca Sands: This will help you write a personal mission statement – this states what you have to offer, and how you would like your career to evolve in the medium and long term. You can put this mission statement at the top of your CV.

Interviewer: So potential employers can see what your career goals are?

Rebecca Sands: Exactly. Another thing you can do is keep a work diary. Note down important things that happen to you at work and try to draw lessons from them.

Interviewer: We hear a lot these days about keeping your skills up-to-date ...

Rebecca Sands: Yes, that's very important. A lot of professions are changing constantly, so it's important to stay up-to-date, for example, through training. Some employers send their employees on courses, but training will increasingly be the responsibility of individuals, if they want to remain marketable.

Interviewer: Right. Any other tips?

Rebecca Sands: Yes. I know this will sound like a luxury to a lot of people, but getting a personal coach can be a good idea – someone who can give you advice on developing your career, help you build your confidence, and so on.

Interviewer: Aren't these coaches quite expensive?

Rebecca Sands: Well, a good personal coach will give you good advice on how to sell yourself, so you could see it as an investment for your future.

10.2 1 It's very useful. I like the specialist journals and the articles in them. It's good to keep up with what's going on in the industry. Last month, I saw an advertisement for a job that I'd really like to get.

2 It's helped me focus on what I want to do in my career. Putting something on paper has helped me clarify my ideas. I think my CV will really stand out from the crowd now.

3 It's helped me build my confidence. I went for an interview last week and I felt much more confident than last time. We spent two whole sessions preparing for the interview. She went through the kinds of questions that they were likely to ask, we talked about how to sit, what to wear, and so on. It was so helpful.

4 It's made me see some patterns in the way I interact with other people. I wrote something down today that's almost exactly the same as something I wrote last year. It's helped me understand how I can avoid making the same mistakes next time.

10.3 1 Hi, this is Susan. I tried calling you on your landline but I guess you must be out. I'd like to talk about the meeting this afternoon. Could you call me back? My number is 021-3567-2804. Speak to you later. Bye.

2 A: ... Can I take a message?

B: Yes, please. This is John Hacker.

A: Could you spell that, please?

B: H-A-C-K-E-R. I'd like to leave a message for Rosemary Finnigan. Could you tell her that I called and that I need to speak to her urgently about the software budget?

A: Of course. Has she got your number?

B: Let me give you my mobile number – it's 07882-393-978.

A: Let me just repeat that – 07882-393-978.

B: That's right. Could she call me back this afternoon? It's really urgent.

A: I'll make sure she gets the message.

B: Thanks.

3 A: Would you like to leave a message?

B: Yes, could you tell Gordon that Peter McEnery called. Shall I spell that for you?

A: Please.

B: It's M-C-E-N-E-R-Y. I'd like Gordon to know that we've won the contract. And could you ask him to give me a call?

A: Could I have your number?

B: That's OK. He's got it.

A: Fine. I'll tell him you called.

B: Thanks.

11 Think global, act local

11.1 *Interviewer:* Can you give us an example of a global advertising campaign?

Jane Williams: Yes, HSBC Bank ran a very interesting campaign recently. The slogan was 'Never underestimate the importance of local knowledge'. The advertisements demonstrated the brand idea of 'local knowledge' by looking at different customs and practices around the world.

Interviewer: Right ...

Jane Williams: For example, they looked at the meaning of gestures in different countries. One of these was the upturned hand with fingers closed. In Egypt, this means 'be patient'; in Greece, it means 'that's perfect'; in Italy, it means 'what exactly do you mean?'. They called this the cultural collisions campaign.

Interviewer: I see ...

Jane Williams: The idea was to show that the bank has a global presence, but also has local knowledge. The strapline was 'HSBC: the world's local bank'. The message was that customers are treated as individuals, and that HSBC cares about them as individuals, and recognises their particular needs.

Interviewer: Was the campaign successful?

Jane Williams: Yes, it increased global awareness of the HSBC brand. HSBC had been built up largely by the acquisition of banks in different countries, and this was a great way of showing it as a global brand with local interests.

Interviewer: I see ...

11.2 *Jane Williams:* They followed it up with a multimedia campaign that focused on the brand idea: 'the bank that values different points of view.' The first batch of 'different points of view' TV commercials was shown on global TV channels such as BBC World, CNN International, CNBC, Discovery, and National Geographic Channel. These ads present views from around the world on different topics, such as art, technology, food, sport, and so on. They aim to engage with viewers and send them to a website – yourpointofview.com – where they're asked to give their own views.

Interviewer: How do you mean?

Jane Williams: Well, on the website, you choose from a list of words that describe your point of view on a particular topic. So, for example on modern art, you have to say if you think it's 'fascinating', 'beautiful', 'confusing', 'rubbish', and so on. It's a very good way of engaging with people and encouraging the idea that HSBC is comfortable with different ideas and different ways of thinking about things.

Interviewer: And the Internet is, by definition, a global medium ...

Jane Williams: That's right. This website is not an advertisement in the ordinary sense, but it engages with, and involves people all over the world and makes them think about HSBC ...

Interviewer: Do HSBC intend to continue with ads like this?

Jane Williams: Yes. They'll have the same campaigns all over the world, but translated into the local languages of the countries where the campaign appears.

11.3 *Lucy:* Lucy Chen speaking

Mike: Hi, Lucy. This is Mike Brent here. How are you?

Lucy: I'm fine, Mike, and you?

Mike: Good, thanks. Listen, the reason I'm calling is to discuss the product launch next month.

Lucy: For the new headsets?

Mike: That's right. I'd like to cover two main points – logistics and promotion. Is this a good time to talk about this?

Lucy: Yes, that's fine.

Mike: Thanks. So firstly, logistics. We've decided to hold the main stock in our regional supply centres and ship to you locally on a weekly basis.

Lucy: Won't that lead to delays? I mean if it sells well, we could run out.

Mike: I don't think that will happen. The regional supply centre will have the headsets by the end of next week. You should receive the first shipment on the 4th of March. Is that OK with you?

Lucy: That sounds fine.

Mike: Good. Now on the promotion side, I'll email you the point-of-sale material later today. This will give you time to translate it, do any other local adaptations and get it to your printers by the beginning of next week.

Lucy: Fine.

Mike: OK, that's it for now. Is there anything else?

Lucy: I'd like to have a word with you about my transfer.

Mike: Don't worry, I haven't forgotten. I'll get back to you about that.

Lucy: OK, Mike.

Mike: Bye for now.

Lucy: Oh, Mike, before you go – could you send me an email to confirm the details we've discussed?

Mike: OK. I'll do that now.

Lucy: Then I'll let the team know about the schedule.

Mike: Great. I'll leave that to you. Lucy, I really must go now ...

11.4 1 *A:* It's your shot.

 B: OK, here goes ... Oh dear!

 A: Never mind. At least we can still see the ball.

2 *A:* Have you heard the one about the Englishman, the Welshman and the Scotsman?

 B: Probably, but go ahead.

 A: Well an Englishman, a Welshman, and a Scotsman form a lottery syndicate, and would you believe it, they win. It's a big pay-out – over ten million ...

3 *A:* You must let me get this.

 B: No way. It's my turn.

 A: No, I'd like to treat you.

 B: Well, if you insist. But next time, it's on me.

4 *A:* You really shouldn't have. Can I open it?

 B: Of course. Go ahead.

 A: Oh ... It's lovely. Is it from your part of the world?

 B: Yes, it is. In fact, it's made in ...

5 *A:* Cheers. Here's to a successful project.

 B: Yes, cheers. Umm ... That's good. I needed that.

 A: Me, too. It's been a long day. But I'm really pleased that ...

12 The grey market

12.1 1 *A:* It's been good to talk to you.

B: Yes, it's been very helpful. We should do this more often. Talking things through is so much better than emailing.

A: That's true. Anyway, can I just confirm that we've agreed to double deliveries for the next two months?

B: Yes, we've agreed that there will be one delivery mid-month and another at the end of the month. We can adjust these with two weeks' notice.

A: That's right. Would you like me to put that in writing?

B: An email would be good, and then I can forward it to the relevant people.

A: Fine, I'll do that.

B: OK, Pete. Nice to speak to you.

A: You, too. And thanks again.

B: You're welcome. Goodbye.

2 *A:* Let me just go over that. You'll let me have a preliminary report by the end of the week and then the full report at the end of the month.

B: That's right. I'll get on with it straight away. Is there anything else?

A: No, that's it. Thanks for your support on this.

B: No problem. See you at the meeting on Monday.

A: See you then. Bye.

B: Bye.

12.2 1 Of course, people are our most important asset. We need to encourage and develop them. This is the only way to ensure the success of our company. We have to retain talent, not lose it to our competitors.

2 In the end, it comes down to the bottom line. We need to have tight control over the business. This means monitoring transactions, especially cash flow. If we become too exposed, we could easily become the target of a take-over bid.

3 If you haven't got any customers, you haven't got a business. Our job is to match the company's products to the needs and aspirations of consumers. The customer is king and the sooner we realise that the better.

4 In my view, the key competitive advantage comes from innovation. We can't compete on price but we can use our know-how to develop solutions for the future.

13 The industry of industries

13.1 *Interviewer:* The management guru, Peter Drucker, said that car manufacturing is the 'industry of industries.' What did he mean exactly?

James Evans: It's to do with the fact that cars are among the most desirable consumer products, and making them is one of the most complex industrial activities – a typical car contains 20,000 parts. To do this successfully requires a high degree of planning and organisation.

Interviewer: Right …

James Evans: Of course, the car industry is an important employer in advanced countries and in developing countries, too, such as Turkey, Brazil, and China. And, of course, this means not just the people who are directly employed in the industry, but also the jobs created among parts suppliers as well.

Interviewer: Yes…

James Evans: But the problem is overcapacity – there's too much capacity – there are too many plants turning out too many cars – output is too high in relation to demand. Already some of the big players like Ford and General Motors are cutting back investment and closing plants.

13.2 *Interviewer:* What about the future? We hear a lot about air pollution and traffic congestion, and the increasing price of oil …

James Evans: That's right. Cars aren't the status symbols they once were but car owners still find it difficult to accept limitations on their freedom to drive. However, some cities, such as Singapore and London, have introduced congestion charges which have helped to cut traffic and reduce pollution levels.

Interviewer: And the increasing price of oil is a concern …

James Evans: That's right. A few years ago, oil was $20 a barrel. Now industry analysts are predicting as much as $100 a barrel. And of course, people are beginning to think about a time when oil runs out completely.

Interviewer: How are car manufacturers responding to that?

James Evans: Well, for a long time electric cars seemed to be the future. But after many years of investment and development the technology is still not advanced enough to produce electric motors for cars. You have to charge the battery too often and the maximum speed is not very high …

Interviewer: Right …

James Evans: But we *are* beginning to see what are called hybrid cars – cars that run on petrol some of the time and electricity the rest of the time. These hybrid cars are really taking off, especially in the U.S., despite the higher prices – up to $8000 more for the hybrid version of some models.

Interviewer: Who are the big investors in the development of hybrid cars?

James Evans: Well, as so often, the Japanese are taking the lead. For example, Toyota said they're investing $10 million to start manufacturing the hybrid Camry model in Kentucky, with the engines supplied from Japan. They're making a massive investment there …

13.3 1 Good morning. I'm very pleased to see you all here this morning. I'm going to speak for about thirty minutes, and I'd be happy to answer any questions. My name is Grigory Spanek. I'm responsible for regional development in this part of the country. I was born here and I grew up here and perhaps I am biased, but I think this is a beautiful part of the world. This morning I aim to give you an overview of the region – its main landmarks, something about the economy, and also future infrastructure plans. By the end of this presentation, I hope that you will be convinced that this is a great area for investment.

2 Ladies and gentlemen, welcome to STS Solutions. It's a pleasure to see you all here and to have this chance to show you around. First, let me introduce myself. My name is Victoria Sanchez and I'm in charge of PR. This is an exciting business to be in right now and this new joint venture is a great opportunity. Before we take a look around, I'd like to tell you a little about the company and how it's organised, just to give you an idea of how we work. Of course, if you've got any questions, please ask. Then I'll hand you over to my colleague, Miguel Pires, who will show you around the facility and explain everything in more detail.

13.4 Giving a presentation to an international audience isn't easy but my advice is just to be natural and be yourself. However, there are also some useful guidelines you can follow.

Gestures with the hands and arms are very important in some cultures. In Egypt, where I come from, we use our hands and arms a lot to get our message across. In some cultures, this isn't so acceptable so it's probably a good idea not to use your hands and arms too much. Maybe if you want to emphasise a point – for example, if you have three points to make, you could use your fingers to indicate which point you're talking about.

Wherever you are, don't fold your arms – this looks defensive or even aggressive. Also, even though the British do this quite a lot, I wouldn't advise you to put your hands in your pockets. Try to keep your palms open and hold up your hands sometimes so that the audience can see them.

Some people walk around during their presentation. I wouldn't advise too much movement but, on the other hand, it's good to move a little so you don't look like a statue. We used to say it was good to stand up for a presentation – that it's better for delivering your message. But nowadays, it's sometimes more appropriate to stay sitting down, like your audience.

14 Something for nothing?

14.1 1 I travel a lot. I don't have time to read newspapers, so I catch up on the news when I'm in my hotel room or at the airport waiting for my plane. I usually watch [beep] like CTV – I like the presenters and the programmes.

2 I look at the news on the [beep] – I never buy a newspaper. I like the BBC site – it's very well organised. The amount of information on there is absolutely incredible.

3 I listen to the news on the [beep] when I'm in my car. The hourly news bulletin on a pop music station is more than enough for me!

4 I like old-fashioned [beep], the ones you pay for! I really like the book reviews in the *New York Times*, for example. They're excellent.

5 I pick up a [beep] at the underground station – the journalism's pretty good, just as good as you get in newspapers that you pay for.

6 I pick up the news on my [beep], you know, personal digital assistant. The Internet sites have special versions for people with mobile phones and you get the top stories very quickly. The *Financial Times* is my favourite.

14.2 In this presentation, I aim to give you an overview of the organisation. To do this, I'm going to cover three areas. Firstly, we'll look at the organisation and how it works; secondly, the people who work here; and thirdly, the local community. So, let's start with the organisation. As you can see from this slide, there are four departments …

… As I mentioned earlier, we are in the middle of a major restructuring and that brings me to the second part of my presentation – the people …

… So it's important to remember that most of our employees live in this area. Let's move on now to the third and final part of my presentation – the local community. It's a critical part of our success in …

… On the one hand, we have a good relationship with the town and its people but on the other hand, we are sometimes seen as being too dominant. I'll come back to that later …

… OK, so let me just summarise. We've changed the organisation to meet the needs of our customers, and we have developed our people from a group of mainly unskilled workers into a highly skilled workforce. And finally, we can thank the local community for continuing to support our business …

15 In search of new markets

15.1 *Interviewer:* Carrefour is one of the world's leading retail chains, with operations in many parts of the world, but it didn't do too well in Japan. Can you explain some of the reasons for this?

Robert Dussollier: Yes, of course. As you know, Carrefour withdrew from the Japanese market after three years by selling its eight stores to the Japanese chain Aeon for one billion yen – that's about 70 million euros, and much less than they paid for them. I think they failed in Japan because they misunderstood the business culture and they misunderstood their clientele. They should have studied the market more carefully.

Interviewer: Right.

Robert Dussollier: Carrefour was encouraged by what had happened with Renault. Renault bought a large stake in Nissan – the car maker which had been making heavy losses but Renault turned it round. However, Carrefour didn't realise that these two markets are very different. They shouldn't have assumed that the car industry and the retail industry were the same.

Interviewer: Of course ...

Robert Dussollier: When Carrefour opened their first store in the suburbs of Tokyo in 2002, they thought they would benefit from the crisis in Japanese retailing – at that time some chains had gone out of business completely. But what Carrefour offered didn't appeal to Japanese consumers. They could have done more research into the Japanese retail market.

Interviewer: What do you mean?

Robert Dussollier: Japanese consumers are very demanding, but they are also price-conscious. Carrefour didn't offer anything new, except perhaps a slight 'French' flavour. They didn't offer lower prices and the quality of their products was nothing special. They could have paid more attention to product quality.

Interviewer: What about Japanese shopping habits? Do they drive to the supermarket once a week for the big family shopping expedition, like in Europe or the U.S.?

Robert Dussollier: No, Japanese consumers tend to go shopping more frequently, and buy smaller quantities. There are a lot of small local shops, many of them open 24 hours a day. In Japan, there are 90 shops per 100,000 inhabitants, compared to only 55 in the United States.

Interviewer: Aha ...

Robert Dussollier: And another problem was that Carrefour wanted a quick return on its investment in Japan. They didn't realise that to make a profit in Japan you need to be in for the long haul. They weren't prepared to wait. They should have expected to wait longer for a return on investment.

Interviewer: So has this affected Carrefour's plans for the rest of Asia?

Robert Dussollier: No, they're now trying to get into Korea.

Interviewer: Have they learnt any lessons from their Japanese experience?

Robert Dussollier: Yes, but of course the lessons learnt in Japan may not be applicable elsewhere ...

15.2 1 So, we've brainstormed what your customers have in common and here, on this chart, you can see the connections. They are very much around quality and brand image. Can I draw your attention to these two customers, which, as you know, represent around 25 per cent of your business.

Now here on this chart you can see the typical route to market they use – following their customer trials, they move on to a local launch and then, if this is successful, they start to roll out nationwide.

2 I've prepared some charts to illustrate my points. Here, on this chart, you can see the main segments in the market. By far the largest slice is the personal security sector. Not only is it the largest but it's also growing the fastest, which you can see on this chart. Here are the three main segments, showing total sales over the last three years. If you look here, you can see the corporate sector remains stagnant and the industrial sector is actually declining, but the personal security sector has grown by nearly 20 per cent over the last three years.

15.3 1 I think the most important quality for a leader is to be able to understand people. You need to be in touch with them, understand their concerns, needs and ambitions. If you understand them, you can then motivate them, direct them, and get great performance from them. It's important for a leader to stay close to people.

2 Being a leader is a lonely job. You have to make difficult, sometimes unpopular, decisions. You also have to have a vision – to know where you're going and to take your people with you. It's hard but you need to keep your distance. This is what allows you to make the right, but difficult decisions.

3 Nowadays, the key factor is how you manage change. Do you recognise what needs to change, when it needs to change and how it needs to change? Are you able to implement these changes? It's no good having a great vision, if you can't push through change.

16 Bollywood goes global

16.1 *Ruby Bennett:* There's increasing interest in Indian films around the world. Why do you think that is?

Bharat Mistry: Well, I think there is a market among international audiences for the singing and dancing, the colourful costumes, and the storylines that you find in Indian films. International audiences and Indian audiences are very similar in that respect.

Ruby Bennett: But there are some differences, too?

Bharat Mistry: That's right. For a film aimed at overseas markets, we would produce versions in two languages – Hindi and English – for release in India and in Europe. In the international version, there would be fewer songs and the story would be more complex. And the international version might have one big climax, whereas for Indian audiences we would have a series of climaxes throughout the film. That's what they expect.

Ruby Bennett: What about finance for Bollywood film productions?

Bharat Mistry: Finance has traditionally been informal, through family contacts and cash flow from earlier films. But some Indian film-makers are raising money now on the Mumbai stock exchange. A big international Bollywood production would need to gross between $25 and $30 million overseas in order to make a profit. But that's possible, if global audiences can relate to the content. That's what we have to get right.

Ruby Bennett: What else are you doing to make Bollywood a global industry?

Bharat Mistry: Well, we need to promote higher standards of production to meet the demands of an international audience.

Ruby Bennett: How is that being achieved?

Bharat Mistry: Traditionally, we've relied on natural talent, but now we're introducing training in all areas of film-making. One important development is a new $3 million training centre at Film City, just north of Mumbai, called Whistling Woods International.

Ruby Bennett: Whistling Woods?

Bharat Mistry: Yes, it's a training school for the entertainment industry, where film-makers can learn their trade. The school will place great emphasis on scriptwriting. Scriptwriters have never had much status in Bollywood, but the screenplay should be the foundation of a professional film production. And the whole industry needs to become more cost-effective – in terms of budgeting, scheduling, planning locations and working out the entire logistics. The training school will address all of that, and more.

Ruby Bennett: Before we finish, can you tell me about your latest film project?

Bharat Mistry: Well, I have very provisional plans for a film about an Indian woman who ...

16.2 1 That brings me to the end of my presentation. I said at the start that I wanted to convince you to invest in this area and I hope I've done that. This is a great region with a big future. Thank you for your attention. I've prepared a folder with more information about the region. Please pick one up as you leave.

2 That's all I have to say as an introduction to STS Solutions. I hope that gives you a good overview of the business. There are some handouts here, which I'll pass around. Please help yourself. There will be a chance to ask questions during and after the tour. So shall we get started ...?

3 So to sum up, for us our workforce is the key to the future. That's why we invest so much in training and recruitment. Are there any questions? No? Well, if you would like to know more, please contact me – you all have my email address. You've been a very attentive audience. Thank you.

16.3 1 In this presentation, I aim to show you how we set up a new project. I'll cover three main areas: the selection of personnel, the use of software, and the project reporting system. By the end of this presentation, you should be able to start setting up your own projects. Right, let's start with the selection process.

2 My objective today is to convince you to upgrade your system. I've had a look at your current system and there is no doubt that it needs upgrading. I'll look at this from two points of view – firstly, user needs and secondly, system design. Please ask any questions as I go along. When I started this survey, I ...

3 Welcome to Castle Electronics. It's a pleasure to have you here. Before we have a look round, I'd like to take ten or 15 minutes to explain a little about the company. I thought it would be helpful to give you a short history and tell you something about our product range. After I've finished, we'll start the factory visit, which will take about an hour.

ANSWER KEY
1 HAPPINESS AT WORK

Listening and speaking

 1.1

A

	Job	Speciality	What they like about the job
1	Lawyer	property law	meeting different clients
2	Fitness instructor	fitness classes / exercise programmes	organising own time seeing people get fit and healthy
3	Accountant	bankruptcy	flexibility well-paid
4	Civil servant	regional investment	teamwork security

B varied _3_   interesting _1_   secure _4_   well-paid _3_

stressed _1_   stimulating _4_   rewarding _2_   satisfying _2_

Speaking

B
3 Chefs / cooks
6 Mechanics
10 Fitness instructors
18 DJs
23 Accountants
27 Estate agents

Grammar

A

Type of adjective	Base form	Rule	Comparative	Superlative
One syllable	*long*	Add *er* / *est*	longer	the longest
Two syllables ending -y	*happy*	Change *-y* to *-ier* / *iest*	happier	the happiest
Two or more syllables	*rewarding*	Put *more* / *the most* before the adjective	more rewarding	the most rewarding
Ending in -ed*	*stressed*	Add *more* / *the most*	more stressed	the most stressed
Irregular	*good* *bad*	~ ~	better worse	the best the worst

B 2 Lawyers are more stressed than fitness instructors.
3 I worked in IT for three years but I hated it. It was the worst job I've ever had!
4 Builders have noisier working conditions than bankers.
5 I'm in R&D. I love developing new products. It's the most fascinating work in the company.

C 1 e   2 a   3 c   4 b   5 d

D 2 Scientists are as happy as pharmacists.
3 Teachers are not as happy as mechanics.
4 IT specialists are slightly happier than estate agents.
5 Hairdressers are much happier than civil servants.

Communication

 1.2/1.3

A 1 c   2 b   3 a   4 d   5 b   6 a

C 1 organisational skills
2 communication skills
3 people skills

Business across cultures

B geography   climate   politics   work   festivals

2 MOTIVATION

Reading and vocabulary

A 1 g 2 d 3 f 4 a 5 c 6 h 7 b 8 e

B 1 supervision 2 satisfaction 3 responsibility 4 initiative 5 commitment

C commitment – to be committed to, to commit to
satisfaction – to be satisfied, to satisfy
responsibility – to be responsible for, to take responsibility for
initiative – to take the initiative, to initiate
supervision – to supervise , to be supervised by
motivation – to be motivated, to motivate
imagination – to be imaginative, to imagine
encouragement – to encourage, to give encouragement, to be encouraged by

Listening and speaking

🎧 2.1/2.2

A

	Organisation	Industry	Theory X or Theory Y?
1	Call centre	Financial services	Y
2	Insurance company	Insurance	X
3	Oil company	Oil	Y
4	Department store	Retail	X

B 1 oil company
2 department store
3 insurance company
4 call centre

C Speaker 1: Expressions 2 9
Speaker 2: Expression: 4
Speaker 3: Expressions 3 6 7
Speaker 4: Expressions 1 5 8

D Theory X organisations: 3 4 6 7
Theory Y organisations: 1 2 5 8 9

Communication

🎧 2.3

A place of birth – Freiburg, south Germany
education – studied in London
family – father worked in the States, parents still in the States, sister in England
first job – trainee buyer for fashion house in London, travelled a lot with this job, very competitive

B Use the audio script to check your answers.

C 1 do 2 mean 3 Could ... tell 4 do 5 sounds 6 exactly

Business across cultures

🎧 2.4

A

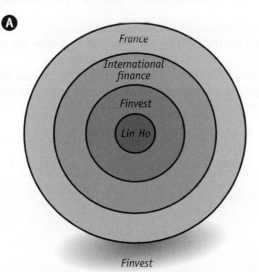

🎧 2.5 **C** dress body language organisation communication history

3 INCENTIVES

Reading and speaking

B The article mentions: a c d e f g
The company already provides: c d f g

C 1 True
2 False, employees can stay at home to care for sick family members.
3 False, the company has adopted a seven-hour workday.
4 True
5 False, they are analysed according to three criteria.

Vocabulary and listening

🎧 3.1

A 1 b 2 a 3 g 4 c 5 d 6 e 7 f

C health insurance
gym membership
sick leave
company pension scheme
financial planning advice
paternity leave

Grammar

A 1 What will the benefits package contain if I join the company?
2 We'll pay all the bills, if you need hospital treatment.
3 If you become seriously ill, the company will give you up to four months' sick leave on full pay.
4 If you need to have your clothes cleaned, our on-site laundry service will take care of it.
5 You'll get fired if you call in sick six Mondays in a row!

B 2 You can't go to dance classes unless you finish your work first.
3 Employees will not get the end-of-year bonus unless they arrive on time in the mornings.
4 You can't take more than three days off sick unless you phone your manager.
5 Unless you tell your boss about your summer holiday dates by 31 January, you will not get the dates you want.

Communication

🎧 3.2

A 1 15th of each month
2 250 units
3 $15 per unit
4 28th
5 20
6 10
7 20

B Use the audio script to check your answers.

Business across cultures

🎧 3.3/3.4

A They are on track but there are some difficulties.
The project leader doesn't give Peter any feedback. Marta is given negative feedback and Miguel is given very positive feedback.

B The project leader thanks all the team for their hard work, but says that they are starting to run into some problems.
It is different from the feedback given by project leader A because it focuses on the team and how the team can solve the problems together. Project leader A focussed on the individuals not the team.

4 WORK AND LEISURE

Listening and speaking

 4.1/4.2

A 1 A balance between work and life outside work
2 48 hours per week
3 Serious negative effects on health and well-being
4 France, 35 hours a week
5 The 19th century, 18 or 20 hours a day

B

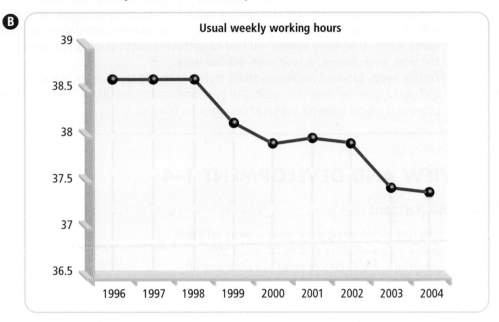

Usual weekly working hours

Grammar

A In 2001 people <u>worked</u> 38 hours a week on average. Past simple
Since 1996 the number of working hours <u>has decreased</u> from 38.7 per cent to 37.3 per cent. Present perfect

B You use the past simple tense to talk about actions and events that happened at a specific time in the past.

C rise – rose – risen
go up – went up – gone up
increase – increased – increased
remain steady – remained steady – remained steady

fall – fell – fallen
go down – went done – gone down
decrease – decreased – decreased

D 1 has fallen
2 went up
3 has increased
4 has risen
5 has gone down
6 remained

Communication

 4.3

A

```
SOUTHERN SECURITY SYSTEMS

Founded: ..20.. years ago

First big client: ...Ministry of Health.........

Ratio of private to public sector business: ..6:10...

New target markets: ...south-east Asia..........

Key to breaking into these markets: ..good local partners....
```

B Use the audio script to check your answers.

Business across cultures

(A) Norway: a c   The Netherlands: d f   Japan: j b g   India: g i

(C) Most of Patrick's experience is in more masculine cultures (see page 153). In these cultures, he will have been encouraged to be assertive and directive in his management style. He also comes from a sales and marketing background where the working culture tends to be fast-paced and results-oriented. He is now working with mainly women from an HR background. They will favour a more mutually supportive way of working and will not appreciate his directive approach. They will also see the value of giving time to people and making sure that everybody is involved in decisions. There is also a strong feminist dimension to life in the UK which means that many women will find compliments about their appearance inappropriate in the work environment, maybe even outside work.

Patrick needs to adapt his management style. He should try to involve everybody in decisions and make sure he does not push his own personality too much. He should avoid making comments about women's appearances when he is at work.

REVIEW AND DEVELOPMENT 1–4

Grammar

Comparisons

(A) b efficient – two syllables or more – more efficient
c pretty – two syllables ending in -y – prettier
d powerful – 2 syllables or more – more powerful
e relaxed – ends in -ed – more relaxed

(B) 1 thicker   2 prettier   3 more powerful   4 more efficient   5 more relaxed

(C) 1 b   2 a   3 c   4 c   5 b   6 a

Vocabulary

Motivation

(A) 1 motivation   5 encouragement
2 consulted   6 Discussion, decision
3 supervision   7 initiated
4 committed

Grammar

First conditional

(A) 3 We'll promote you quickly if you have management potential.
4 If you improve your communication skills, we'll put you in charge of a team of engineers.
5 We'll increase your budget if you win the contract.
6 If you exceed your sales targets, we'll give you a top-of-the-range BMW.
7 You'll go far if you produce results.

(B) 2 Unless you complete the first year successfully, we won't send you to our Paris office.
3 We won't promote you quickly unless you have management potential.
4 Unless you improve your communication skills, we won't put you in charge of a team of engineers.
5 We won't increase your budget unless you win the contract.
6 Unless you exceed your sales targets, we won't give you a top-of-the-range BMW.
7 You won't go far unless you produce results.

Vocabulary

Company incentives

2 c The benefits package
3 f The company pension
4 e The perks
5 a a performance bonus
6 b maternity leave

Grammar

Past simple and present perfect

B
1 first became	4 left	7 lent	10 has made
2 was	5 has raised	8 has needed	11 has she ever had
3 did not finish	6 invested	9 have now reached	12 has always shown

mmunication

A 1 i 2 c 3 e 4 k 5 h 6 l 7 f 8 a 9 g 10 j 11 b 12 d

B
1 born	5 sounds
2 brought up	6 tell
3 worked	7 move
4 based	8 mean

5 ENTREPRENEURS

Reading and speaking

B 1 He worked as a record producer with rock bands, in theatre stage design and in TV programme distribution.
2 He set up Yo! Sushi in 1997.
3 Selling sushi on conveyor belts like restaurants in Japan and staffing the café with girls in short PVC skirts. He introduced the conveyor belts.
4 There were 13 restaurants and three bars in Britain and a branch in Dubai.
5 He sold his stake for £10 million.
6 It means idea.
7 From flying first class on British Airways – he saw the way comfort can be created in a very small space.
8 They are small but the space is well used. They have mood lighting and wi-fi facilities.
9 Professionals who want to work, play and then sleep in luxury that is affordable.

ocabulary and listening

A 1 d 2 f 3 i 4 h 5 c 6 g 7 a 8 e 9 b

B **Possible answer:** Innovative, bold, self-confident

 5.1

C 1 self-confident   persistent   innovative
2 over-cautious   unrealistic   inflexible
3 She gives three reasons: the product or service may not offer anything new; people may not want it or need it, the general economic situation may not be right.
4 Because individuals have much more freedom to act. They do not have to wait for people on committees to make a decision.

D
Adjective	Noun
independent	independence
innovative	innovation
self-confident	self-confidence
inquisitive	inquisitiveness
persistent	persistence
bold	boldness
reliable	reliability
strong	strength
competitive	competitiveness

E 1 inquisitive
2 independent
3 Innovation
4 persistent
5 reliability

Communication

 5.2

A 1 c 2 e 3 f 4 b 5 h 6 d 7 g 8 a

C
1 applied
2 joined
3 redundant
4 look
5 promoted
6 married
7 had
8 work
9 divorced
10 partner
11 see
12 share
13 buy
14 build
15 move
16 commute
17 fit
18 shape
19 lose
20 diet
21 exercise

Business across cultures

5.3

A 1 c 2 e 3 f 4 b 5 d 6 a

6 CREATIVITY

Listening and speaking

6.1

1 The Apple personal computer, the Internet, the cell phone.
2 Malcolm McLean.
3 In 1956.
4 They weren't mixed with other cargo, and they were of a standard size so they could be handled easily.
5 Five container ships would be enough for all the trade between Britain and the United States.
6 No.
7 Containers made it cheap enough to trade goods that weren't traded before.
8 Containers are going to change the world.
9 It's difficult to foresee how things are going to develop.

Grammar

A
2 We are going to have the most successful product on the market. / We aren't going to have the most successful product on the market.
We will have the most successful product on the market. / We won't have the most successful product on the market.
3 Scientists are going to find new sources of energy. / Scientists aren't going to find new sources of energy.
Scientists will find new sources of energy. / Scientists won't find new sources of energy.
4 People are going to live to be 100. / People aren't going to live to be 100.
People will live to be 100. / People won't live to be 100.
5 Company employees are going to have more leisure time. / Company employees aren't going to have more leisure time.
Company employees will have more leisure time. / Company employees won't have more leisure time.

B
2 He's going to do a lot of research.
3 CS employees are going to sign a confidentiality agreement.
4 They are going to work directly for CS.
5 CS are going to pay a big penalty if they don't reach the targets.

Communication

6.2

B Use the audio script to check your answers.

business across cultures

 6.3

A The Metal Cooperative   Thorntons   TLC Ltd   National Health Service

B flat   lean   transparent
network   bottom-up

hierarchical   many-layered   bureaucratic
top-heavy   slow   climb the ladder
complex   top-down

7 START-UPS

Listening and vocabulary

 7.1

A 1 Business advisor and entrepreneur. They are talking about a business start-up.
2 A venture capitalist invests in new entrepreneurial ideas.
3 Because they hope that some will be very profitable and this will make up for the losses made on those ideas that fail.
4 A business angel invests in new businesses.
5 No, some just want to be a sleeping partner.
6 It should be brief and clear and awaken investors' interest in a couple of minutes.
7 It can be floated on the stock market.

B 1 The company is floated on the stock exchange in an IPO.
2 IPO stands for initial public offering.
3 Then the company is listed on the stock market.
4 Shares in the company are bought and sold by investors on the stock market.

Grammar

A 2 e   3 a   4 b   5 c

B 1 The company was founded by an entrepreneur.
2 The new product was developed by a mechanical engineer.
3 $75,000 was invested in the business by a business angel.
4 Sometime in the future, more investment will be needed by the company.
5 The company will be floated on the stock market by the founders.
6 More money could be raised on the stock market.

C 2 Large amounts of money could be made in this market in the next ten years.
3 Forecasts of future sales can be found in our business plan.
4 Our profits could be affected by changes in the tax laws.
5 The company might be taken over by a stronger competitor.

Communication

 7.2

A 1 c   2 a   3 d   4 b

B a items
b fix
c attend
d circulate
e get
f minutes
g hold

8 INVENTIONS

Vocabulary and listening

A 1 f 2 c 3 a 4 e 5 g 6 d 7 h 8 b

B a d e g h

🔊 8.1

C 1 When she saw a little girl drop a cup and her mother dived to catch it.
2 In plastics.
3 No. She looked for companies to make her product.
4 When she exhibited at trade shows, she shook the cups over people's clothes.
5 She sent a non-spill cup full of fruit juice to a buyer at Tesco.

D 1 b 2 d 3 e 4 c 5 g 6 a 7 f

Grammar

A 1 b 2 a

B 1 a 2 b

C *had* past participle

D 2 did not apply had made
3 made had seen
4 started had already set up
5 sent had contacted
6 started had already met

Communication

A 1 c 2 a 3 b

🔊 8.2/8.3

C/D Use the audio script to check your answers.

Business across cultures

B Reduce the number of layers in a company
Recruit creative people
Don't punish mistakes

Additional ideas:
Google recruits a mix of risk-takers and people who know if something is too risky.
Project management rotates around team members.
It observes and listens with ten employees reading e-mails from users full-time.

REVIEW AND DEVELOPMENT 5–8

Vocabulary

Personal characteristics

A 1 e 2 f 3 c 4 d 5 a 6 g 7 b

C 1 strength
2 Innovation
3 competitive
4 ✓
5 Persistence
6 ✓
7 Self-confidence

Grammar

Will and going to

A 1 c 2 b 3 a

B 1 won't be / isn't going to be
2 are going to cut
3 will lose
4 won't recover / isn't going to recover
5 will go up / are going to go up
6 will promote
7 are going to recruit
8 will finish
9 are going to increase

C 1 a 2 c 3 b 4 a 5 a 6 b 7 c 8 b 9 c

Grammar

Passives

A 2 An advertisement is placed on appropriate websites.
3 Candidates' applications are sorted and analysed.
4 A shortlist is drawn up.
5 Shortlisted candidates are interviewed.
6 References are checked.
7 The successful candidate is notified.

C 1 have been logged   3 might be planted   5 should be poured
2 have been cut down   4 be developed   6 will be made

Grammar

Past perfect

A 1 had, invented   4 had built
2 had worked   5 had developed
3 had, been

Communication

A to share a flat   to live with your partner   to move house
to apply for a job   to be on a diet   to keep in shape
to commute to work   to join a company

C 1 c   2 e   3 h   4 a   5 f   6 g   7 d   8 b

D 1 hold   5 fixed   9 actions
2 agenda   6 copy   10 circulate
3 items   7 get down   11 follow up
4 attend   8 taking

9 KIDS AS CONSUMERS

Reading

A 1 Phrases that describe the way children persuade their parents to buy things.
2 Parents and children often like the same things.
3 Cookies, cars, video games, snack foods, the latest electronic gadgets, blockbuster film hits, evergreen food and drink brands.
4 International example: Coca-Cola, Heinz (canned foods) / Nestlé (various food products).
5 Students' own answers.
6 It means they can take advantage of the fact parents and children are making decisions together about what to buy.

Grammar

A influence – both   decision – count   advertising – uncount
enjoyment – uncount   purchase – count   information – uncount
power – both   factor – count
popularity – uncount   gadget – count

B 1 lots of
2 many
3 a lot of
4 a lot of
5 plenty of
6 many
7 much

Communication

A 1 d   2 e   3 b   4 c   5 a

 9.1

B Use the audio script to check your answers.

Business across cultures

B 1 It means that employees won't take advantage when deciding their own salaries.
2 They are motivated to make the company successful, and therefore keep budgets in line.
3–5 Students' own answers.

10 SELLING YOURSELF

Listening

🎧 10.1/10.2

A g f a e b c
d is not mentioned

B Use the audio script to check your answers.

C 1 d 2 a 3 c 4 e

Vocabulary and speaking

A

Noun	Adjective
2 numeracy	numerate
3 motivation	motivated
4 flexibility	flexible
5 creativity	creative
6 energy	energetic
7 commitment	committed
8 cooperation	cooperative

1 h 2 d 3 f 4 b 5 c 6 a 7 e 8 g

B 1 energy
2 creative
3 committed
4 numeracy
5 motivated
6 Flexibility
7 cooperative

C 1 He's inflexible. He's not very flexible.
2 He's not very creative.
3 He's not very energetic.
4 He's not very committed.
5 He's uncooperative. He's not very cooperative.
6 He's innumerate. He's not very numerate.

Communication

🎧 10.3

A 1 Name of caller: Susan
Message: would like to talk about the meeting this afternoon
Action: Please call back
Contact number: 021 3567 2804

2 Name of caller: John Hacker
Message: for Rosemary Finnigan. Needs to speak about software budget. Urgent.
Action: Rosemary Finnigan to call him this afternoon
Contact number: 07882 393 978

3 Name of caller: Peter McEnery
Message: For Gordon. Have won the contract
Action: Gordon to call
Contact number: Gordon already has it

Business across cultures

B c

C to neglect a customer
to lose a customer
to under-promise
to treat a customer badly
to be uncompetitive
to be unhelpful
to not smile / to frown
to be rude

11 THINK GLOBAL, ACT LOCAL

Listening and vocabulary

 11.1

A Company: HSBC bank
Countries: Egypt, Greece, Italy

B **Slogan:** Never underestimate the importance of local knowledge
Brand idea: the bank has global presence and local knowledge
Outcome: Successful. Increased global awareness of HSBC brand
What the ad consisted of: different customs and practices around the world
Strapline: HSBC: the world's local bank

11.2

C **Brand idea:** the bank that values different points of view
Media: TV, then website
What the ad consisted of: different views from around the world on different topics e.g. art, technology, food, sport
Example from website: Choose from a list of words to describe your point of view on a topic such as modern art

D global advertising b   global brand c
global presence e   global TV channels f
global awareness a   global medium d

Grammar

A 1 f   2 d   3 b   4 c   5 e   6 a

B 1 to run   4 to do   7 to conduct
2 producing   5 producing   8 to design / designing
3 having worked   6 to make   9 to wait

Communication

11.3

A 1 reason for call: new product launch
2 logistics
3 delivery date of headsets
4 promotion
5 point-of-sale material

B a The reason I'm calling is ...
b I'd like to cover two main points ...
c Is this a good time to talk about this?
d So, firstly ...
e Now on the promotion side ...
f Is there anything else?
g I'll get back to you about that.

Business across cultures

11.4

A 1 d   2 c   3 b   4 a   5 e

B a Australia   c China   e Brazil
b Egypt   d Japan   f Poland

12 THE GREY MARKET

Reading and speaking

1 20 million
2 80 per cent
3 A quarter
4 They want it to be informative
5 Older people have formed their tastes by the age of 40 and don't respond to advertising vs older people are just as changeable as the young. The second view.

Grammar

A 1 've been studying,   've decided
2 have been running,   have increased
3 has been selling,   have invested
4 have portrayed,   have been considering

B 1 ✓   2 ✗   3 ✓   4 ✗   5 ✓   6 ✗   7 ✓

Communication

🔊 12.1

A 1 Double deliveries for the next two months – one mid-month and one at the end of the month.
2 Delivery of preliminary report by the end of the week, full report by the end of the month.

B Use the audio script to check your answers.

Business across cultures

🔊 12.2

A 1 e 2 d 3 f 4 a 5 c 6 b

B 1 Human Resources 2 Finance 3 Marketing 4 R&D

REVIEW AND DEVELOPMENT 9–12

Grammar

Count and uncount nouns

A influence – both experience – both employment – uncount
progress – uncount information – uncount behaviour – both

B 1 employment
2 behaviour
3 influences
4 information
5 experience
6 progress

Vocabulary

Personal qualities

A 1 commitment 4 honesty
2 responsibility 5 maturity
3 literacy 6 capability

B 1 committed 4 honest
2 responsible 5 mature
3 literate 6 capable

C 1 inflexible 4 illogical
2 impatient 5 disloyal
3 uncreative 6 irreplaceable

D

dis-	il-	im-	in-	ir-	un-
disloyal	illogical	impatient	inflexible	irreplaceable	uncreative
dishonest	illiterate	immature	incapable	irresponsible	uncommitted

Grammar

Infinitives and *-ing* forms

B 1 c 2 c 3 b 4 a 5 b 6 a 7 c 8 c

Grammar

Present perfect simple and continuous

A 1 have finished
2 have worked
3 has had
4 have been learning
5 have been talking, haven't decided
6 have known

A

Receptionist:	Good morning, Crystal Lighting. How can I help you?
Peter:	Could I speak to someone in Sales?
Receptionist:	Of course. Who's calling, please?
Peter:	It's Peter Menzies from Galtons.
Receptionist:	Just a moment, Mr Menzies. I'll put you through.
Jim:	Sales, how can I help you?
Peter:	This is Peter Menzies from Galtons Appliances. I'm calling about an order I placed last week.
Jim:	Do you have the reference number?
Peter:	Yes, it's 456/IND/MC.
Jim:	Oh yes, that's one of Maggie's. I'm afraid she's out of the office at the moment. Can I get her to call you back?
Peter:	Yes, please. Could you tell her that we were expecting a delivery this morning and nothing has arrived.
Jim:	I'm sorry to hear that. I'll get her to call you as soon as she gets back. Has she got your number?
Peter:	I'm sure she has, but just in case – it's 0355 634 4577.
Jim:	OK. I'll make sure she gets the message. Goodbye.
Peter:	Goodbye.

13 THE INDUSTRY OF INDUSTRIES

Reading

A/**B**
1 a It goes very fast.
2 d It has to have space for as many children as possible.
3 c It's the manoeuvrability that I really like.
4 e I need a vehicle I can use off-road.
5 b I like to drive in comfort.

Listening and speaking

13.1/13.2

A 1 b 2 e 3 d 4 c 5 a

B 1 F. It's also because car manufacturing is one of the most complex industrial activities.
2 T
3 F. There is overcapacity.
4 T

C 1 $20 a barrel a few years ago. $100 a barrel predicted for the future.
2 When there is no more oil.
3 The technology is still not advanced enough to produce electric motors for cars. You have to charge the battery too often and the maximum speed is not very high.
4 Cars that run on petrol some of the time and electricity the rest of the time.
5 Up to $8,000 more expensive.
6 Toyota.
7 No. The engines are made in Japan.

Vocabulary

A 1 a 2 e 3 b 4 c 5 d

ommunication

13.3

A Presentation 1 includes all five elements.
Presentation 2 does not include a clear objective or timing.

B They both start with a welcome.

C Use the audio script to check your answers.

Business across cultures

Body Language	Country	Meaning
Smile	All countries	I'm pleased.
Tip head back, suck air in	China	That's difficult.
Bow very low	Japan	Shows great respect.
Males stand close and make contact	Saudi Arabia	Shows trust.
Males go though door first, ahead of women	Korea	Shows males are dominant.
Palm facing in, index finger moving	USA	Come to me.
Constant eye contact in one-to-one communication	UK	I'm interested.

 13.4 **D** Use the audio script to check your answers.

14 SOMETHING FOR NOTHING?

Reading and speaking

A 1 59   83
  2 5.1m
  3 From $9.6m in 1995 to $302m
  4 Young urban professionals
  5 Its strict editorial formula and its scientific approach to success.
  6 It is distributed to "high commuter traffic zones." It is delivered by trucks to hand distributors and racks.
  7 No. There were problems in the Czech Republic because old women were taking 100 copies at a time from railway stations to sell on.

Listening and speaking

A 1 f   2 d   3 a   4 c   5 e   6 b

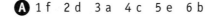 14.1

Vocabulary

B

Type 1	Type 2
– local newspaper – public transport – huge operation – international expansion	– distribution system

Type 3	Type 4
– combined circulation	– shopping malls – teething problems

C high commuter traffic zone

D Model answers
  2 Do you expect continued international expansion? *Yes, we're opening five new plants in three different countries this year alone.*
  3 What's the distribution system? *Our trucks deliver products overnight to supermarkets all over Europe.*
  4 Were there teething problems? *Only small ones. Our first plants didn't operate with 100 per cent of potential output at the beginning, but this was soon solved.*
  5 Are young urban professionals among your customers? *No, our products are targeted mainly at older people living in the country.*

mmunication

 14.2

A Objective: to give an overview of the organisation
Part 1: the organisation and how it works
Part 2: the people in the organisation
Part 3: the local community
Summary: have changed organisation to meet needs of customers; developed unskilled workers into highly skilled workforce; local community has supported the business

B Use the audio script to check your answers.

siness across cultures

A **Model answers**
The first email is very short and direct. It is very task–oriented.
The second email is more indirect. It asks about the addressee and uses very polite language.

C saying 'no'   low-context
being very polite   high-context
pleasing everybody   high-context
saying 'yes'   high-context
criticising   low-context
disagreement   low-context
getting to the point quickly   low-context
reading between the lines   high-context
packaging the message with a nice beginning and end   high-context

D

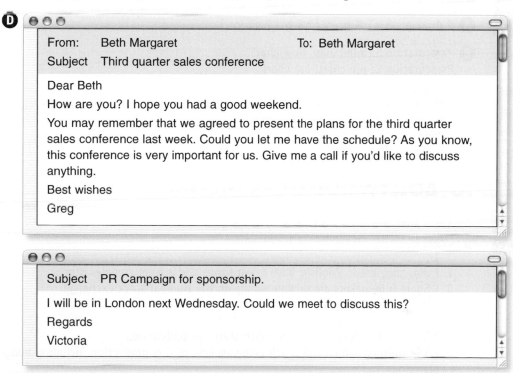

From: Beth Margaret   To: Beth Margaret
Subject   Third quarter sales conference

Dear Beth

How are you? I hope you had a good weekend.

You may remember that we agreed to present the plans for the third quarter sales conference last week. Could you let me have the schedule? As you know, this conference is very important for us. Give me a call if you'd like to discuss anything.

Best wishes

Greg

Subject   PR Campaign for sponsorship.

I will be in London next Wednesday. Could we meet to discuss this?
Regards
Victoria

15 IN SEARCH OF NEW MARKETS

Listening and speaking

🔊 15.1

A Year Carrefour entered Japanese market: 2002
Year Carrefour withdrew from Japan: 2005
Price paid by Aeon for Carrefour's stores: ¥ 1 bn/ €70 m
Company whose success Carrefour wanted to copy: Renault
Reasons for Carrefour's failure in relation to customers: didn't offer anything new, quality of goods was nothing special
Number of shops per 100,000 people in Japan: 90
Number of shops per 100,000 people in U.S.: 55
Reasons for Carrefour's failure in relation to Japanese business culture: they wanted a quick return
Market that Carrefour is now trying to get into: Korea

C 1 should have studied
2 shouldn't have assumed
3 could have done
4 could have paid
5 should have expected

Grammar

A 2 Coca-Cola should have kept its traditional formula.
Coca-Cola shouldn't have dropped its traditional formula in 1985.
3 British Leyland should have used just one brand name.
British Leyland shouldn't have used two brand names for the same car.
4 Elf should have expanded abroad more slowly.
Elf shouldn't have expanded abroad so rapidly.
5 Siemens should have entered the mobile phone market with a partner who knew the market.
Siemens shouldn't have entered the mobile phone market on their own.
6 Gerald Ratner shouldn't have said that the jewellery he sold in his shops was rubbish.
Gerald Ratner should have kept quiet!

C 2 They could / should have used a market research company.
3 They could / should have talked to people who knew the market.
4 They could / should have worked with a local partner.
5 They could / should have advertised in the local press.
6 They could / should have listened to what people were telling them.

Communication

15.2

A 1 d 2 a 3 e 4 g 5 f 6 b 7 c

B Presentation 1: mind map, flow chart
Presentation 2: pie chart, bar chart

Business across cultures

15.3

B Speaker 1: a good listener (6)
Speaker 2: lonely, decisive and vision (4, 5, 9)
Speaker 3: none (+ managing change)

16 BOLLYWOOD GOES GLOBAL

Vocabulary

1 c 2 d 3 b 4 a 5 f 6 e 7 h 8 g

Listening

16.1

1 T
2 F No, they are in English, have fewer songs and a more complex story.
3 F Some film-makers are raising money on the Mumbai stock exchange.
4 T
5 T
6 F Scriptwriters have never had much status in Bollywood.
7 F The training school will teach many aspects of film production including budgeting, scheduling, planning.

Grammar

A 1 would you cast   would use   was / were
2 would you shoot   would go   didn't cost
3 would you choose would ask   accepted
4 would you pay   would give
5 would we   would start

Communication

16.2

A Presentation 1 does not include objective 4.
Presentation 2 does not include objective 5.
Presentation 3 meets all objectives.

B Use the audio script to check your answers.

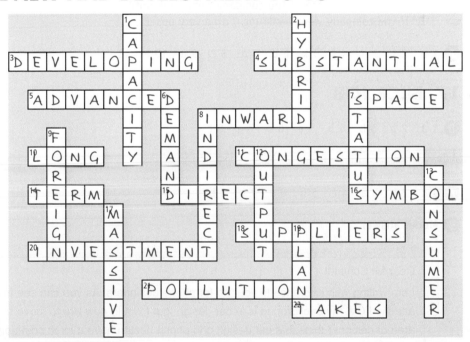 16.3 **D** **Model answers**

1 That brings me to the end of my presentation.
I hope that gives you a good overview of how to set up a project. I have some handouts here, if you'd like to take one. Thank you very much for your attention. I'd be happy to answer any questions.

2 I said at the start that I wanted to convince you to upgrade your system. I hope I have done that. I've prepared a folder which goes into more detail. Are there any more questions? ... You've been a very attentive audience. Thank you and goodnight.

3 That covers everything I wanted to say. I hope that gives you a good overview of the company and our product range. I'm happy to take any questions now and as we look around the factory. Any questions?
Let's take a look around now.

siness across cultures

C The Swedes took a task-oriented approach to winning the contract. They assumed they would get it and did not pay enough attention to building a personal relationship with the Venezuelans whose culture is person-oriented.
They should not have expected a decision during the meeting as in more person-oriented cultures decision-making is less structured. The Swedes need to take time to build the relationship, and not focus immediately on the task. They should not try to force a decision but accept that this will be made by those in a more person-oriented culture in their own time.

REVIEW AND DEVELOPMENT 13–16

Vocabulary

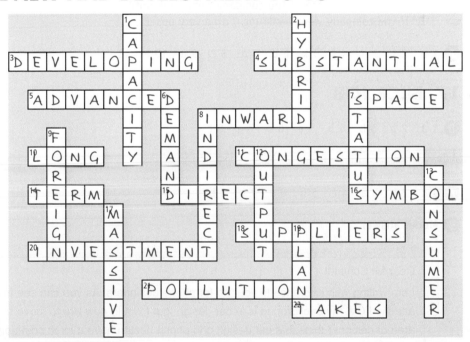

B 1 domestic expansion
2 reduced growth
3 private transport
4 combined sales
5 advertising rates
6 shopping catalogues
7 ongoing problems
8 complex operation
9 distribution network
10 national newspaper
11 restaurant chain

Grammar

Should / shouldn't have, could have

A 1 c 2 c 3 b 4 a 5 b 6 b 7 a

B Model answers
2 You could have / should have asked for promotion.
3 You could have asked for an office.
4 You should have taken your full four weeks' holiday.
5 You should have asked for a car.
6 You shouldn't have agreed to do all the worst jobs.
7 You shouldn't have worked so late / should have left at six every evening.

Grammar

Second conditional

A Model answers
2 A: What would you do if the computer system crashed? B: I'd call the computer manager.
3 A: What would you do if one of the salespeople left to go to work for a competitor?
  B: A: If one of the salespeople left to go to work for a competitor, I'd be very angry.
4 A: What would you do if the photocopier broke down?
  B: If the photocopier broke down, I'd contact the photocopier company.
5 A: What would you do if the company was taken over?
  B: If the company was taken over, I'd leave.
6 A: What would you do if you invented a product for the company?
  B: If I invented a new product for the company, I'd ask to be the product manager for it.
7 A: How would you feel if the company went bankrupt?
  B: If the company went bankrupt, I'd be very upset

Communication

A 1 b 2 f 3 h 4 j 5 k 6 d 7 g 8 c 9 a 10 e 11 i

17 NICE JOB

Job advertisement

B 1 a 2 b 3 b 4 b 5 a 6 a 7 a 8 c

Job application

A 1 c 2 c 3 a 4 c 5 b 6 a 7 c 8 b

B Model answer

Dear Mr Schmidt

I am writing with reference to your ad for phone designers. As you can see from the attached CV, my background is in car design, but I would now like to move to another area of design. I think that car design and phone design have a lot in common.

As my CV indicates, I have worked for more than seven years at Renault, of which the last five have been in its design office outside Paris and now I would like to move to a hi-tech company. I am willing to move to Switzerland: I can do this at any time from September onwards.

I am available for interview at any time except the last week of March, when I will be on holiday.

I look forward to hearing from you,

Best regards,

Jens Jensen

18 GETTING THE GO-AHEAD

mail exchange

A 1 b 2 a 3 c 4 c 5 c 6 c 7 b 8 c 9 a 10 b

B Model answer

> Dear Richard
>
> Many thanks for getting the go-ahead for my project. I am very happy to be working on it. I have prepared a detailed development plan with a schedule, which I am attaching here.
>
> I will be in your office for the meeting at 10:00 am, but I might be slightly late, if that's OK, as I'm seeing a supplier at 9:00 am for an hour, and it may run over slightly.
>
> Best wishes
>
> Susan

C Model answer

> Hi, Richard.
>
> Thanks for asking me to come to your meeting with Susan tomorrow. Unfortunately, I can't make it – I have an important meeting with an advertising agency. My apologies for this. Please have the meeting without me and let me know what you discuss.
>
> Best regards
>
> Paola

19 UNHAPPY CUSTOMERS

Letter of complaint

A 1 b 2 c 3 a 4 a 5 b 6 c 7 b

B Model answer

> Dear Mr Kinnear
> Thank you for your letter of 8 September. We have looked into your complaints.
> We are aware of the late departure of the cruise ship from Colombo and we apologise for this.
> The stopover in the Seychelles was cancelled because the engines were not working properly and the ship was getting behind schedule. We are sorry for any disappointment that this caused.
> We have had no other complaints from other passengers regarding the food and the dance band.
> We are willing to make a refund of 10 per cent of the cost of the cruise because of its late departure and the lack of a stopover in the Seychelles. Please let me know if this acceptable to you.
> Yours sincerely
>
> *Amanda Grayson*
> Amanda Grayson
> Customer Care Manager

C Model answer

Dear Ms Grayson

Thank-you for your letter of 1 October, offering 10 per cent of the cost of our cruise in compensation for the problems that occurred. Although this is less than the 50 per cent I was hoping for, I have decided to accept this offer. I look forward to receiving your cheque.

Yours sincerely

George Kinnear

Dear Ms Grayson

Thank-you for your letter of 1 October, offering 10 per cent of the cost of our cruise in compensation for the problems that occurred. This offer is totally inadequate. You will be hearing soon from my lawyers.

Yours sincerely

George Kinnear

20 LOCAL PARTNERS

Fax exchange

A 1 b 2 a 3 c 4 a 5 c 6 a 7 c 8 b 9 a

B Model answer

Dear Mr Bertrand,

Thank you for your fax of 2 May. I have been in touch with a member of our association, Ms Dilek Saray, who is based in Izmir. I have asked her to contact you with reference to your enquiry and she will be in touch with you soon.

I hope she will be able to help you with your enquiry.

Best wishes

Mehmet Emin

C Model answer

Dear Mr Bertrand

Mr Mehmet Emin of the Turkish Retailing Association has given me your name. He has told me that you wish to find a local partner in Turkey.

My company, Saray Markets, is a small but successful chain of supermarkets. The company was founded by my father in 1945. He started with one shop in Izmir, and the chain now has seven supermarkets in various cities in western Turkey.

We are currently looking for an international partner to develop further. Would it be possible for you to come to Izmir next week to discuss things? How about Wednesday 22 May? Please let me know if this is suitable.

I look forward to meeting you.

Yours sincerely

Dilek Saray

REVIEW AND DEVELOPMENT UNITS 17–20

B Model answer

SERGUEI BRONOVSKI

Career goals

Looking for stimulating research and development work in a US construction company

Skills

- Enthusiastic self-starter
- Good at independent research
- Native Russian speaker; fluent English, good German

Qualifications

1995–1999	Degree in civil engineering, Moscow University
1999–2003	PhD: 'High-strength steel in wind-exposed high-rise buildings', University of London

Experience

2003-now   Research engineer, Astrup Engineering, London

Interests

Ice hockey

C

1 funding	4 products	7 benefit
2 unfortunately	5 energy	8 working
3 inform	6 developing	9 hesitate

COMMUNICATION

All learners of English need to develop good communication skills. Some people have a good knowledge of English grammar but don't communicate effectively; other people have a poor knowledge of English grammar but communicate well. Communication depends on clear messages, feedback and confirmation. It depends on developing a two-way channel: both speaker and listener need to communicate in order to achieve understanding.

The Communication section of each unit and these notes will help you improve your communication skills in the key areas of two-way communication, socialising, telephoning, meetings and presentations.

Units 1–4 focus on developing two-way communication.

UNIT 1 TALKING ABOUT YOURSELF

It is vital in the business world that you are able to introduce yourself well – first impressions are important. You also need to be sensitive to the culture you are doing business in. In some cultures, it is acceptable to discuss personal details early in the relationship; in others, it is usual to maintain distance and choose more impersonal topics of conversation, such as your job.

You also need to be sensitive about how much you should 'sell yourself.' In some cultures, a business card will include job title (e.g. Vice President International. Marketing) and also qualifications (e.g. MBA London Business School); in other cultures this information is not advertised. In some cultures people may be more open about discussing their strengths and weaknesses than in other cultures, believing that this shows knowledge about yourself. (See Unit 5 Communication, page 28 for other aspects of this topic.)

UNIT 2 FINDING OUT ABOUT PEOPLE

Showing an interest in someone is a sure way to build a business relationship. Nobody likes someone who just talks about themselves. The skill you need to develop is in asking questions and responding to the answers that people give. There is a wide range of types of questions you can ask and comments you can make. Some of the most useful ones are covered in this section:

Open questions / comments

This type of question or comment encourages people to talk freely, for example, *I'd be interested to hear about your experience of doing business in Latin America* or *Could you tell me something about your storage facilities?*

Closed questions

This type of question leads to a short answer and may not develop the conversation. Some *wh-* question words produce closed questions, for example, *When did you leave Germany? Did you go to university?*

Probing questions

This type of question tries to find out more detail, for example, *What exactly are the plans for the new product launch?*

Reflecting questions

This type of question is very important because it shows you are listening and actively trying to understand what is being said, for example, *So, you mean that we can't meet this deadline without extra resources?*

Encouraging comments

This type of feedback is also important in building a relationship. It shows that you are listening and interested. For example, the comment *That sounds interesting* encourages the speaker to say more.

UNIT 3 BUILDING TRANSPARENCY

Sometimes you may not always understand what is being said, and you may feel that you can't interrupt and say 'I'm sorry, I don't understand.' However, sometimes, it is very important to check, clarify and confirm details. Your business partners would almost certainly prefer to take a little more time to explain than risk delays and mistakes later on because of a misunderstanding. When you interrupt or want to ask for clarification or confirmation, the right tone of voice will help you to do this successfully and without appearing rude. You can help yourself to achieve the right tone by phrasing your sentences in this way:

Front	Qualifier	Polite question
I'm sorry,	I didn't *quite* understand.	*Could* I go over that again?
I'm afraid,	I'm *not sure* I got that.	*Would you mind* repeating that?

UNIT 4 RESPONDING AND DEVELOPING COMMUNICATION

Showing that you are listening and interested is critical in building rapport. This type of communication will vary from culture to culture. Making positive responses (e.g. *That sounds great! / Well done! / Good work!*) is more appreciated in U.S. culture than European cultures. Silence, as a response, is more appreciated in some Asian cultures, showing that you are thinking and reflecting. In most Western cultures, silence is not appreciated because it makes people feel uncomfortable. In these cultures, the silence is filled with responses, such as *Uh Uh / Um / Really / Right.*

Units 5–6 focus on socialising. Building business relationships often depends on the ability to talk socially with your business partners.

UNIT 5 SOCIALISING 1: SMALL TALK

In some cultures, it is important to spend a lot of time socialising and getting to know business partners and colleagues. This is sometimes more important than talking about work and business. In other cultures, people get down to business much more quickly and don't spend time socialising. It is also important to be sensitive about the topics you talk about, for example, sharing intimate details about your family is appreciated in some but not all cultures. (See Unit 5, Business across Cultures, page 29 and Unit 11 Business across cultures, page 59 for other aspects of this topic.)

UNIT 6 SOCIALISING 2: POSITIVE RESPONSES

The language we use to express positive responses is supported by intonation and body language such as smiles, gestures and eye contact.

Positive questions and responses tend to have more noticeable rising or falling tones. Practise asking the questions on page 32 with a marked rising tone and then practise the responses with a high tone at the start and then falling at the end, for example:

Would you like to come for dinner?

I'd love to, but I'm afraid I can't.

Smiling and other facial expressions can show interest, surprise and gratitude. You can also reinforce your verbal response with head movements, for example, by nodding when you make a positive response. Making frequent eye contact can help to support a verbal response. However, it may be advisable not to hold eye contact with one person for too long as in some cultures this can make people feel uncomfortable.

Units 7–8 deal with communication skills at meetings.

UNIT 7 MEETINGS 1: RUNNING A MEETING

A simple but effective way to run meetings is to manage the 3 'Ps':

Purpose: Make sure you communicate the objectives before the meeting and again at the start of the meeting. Keep your objectives in mind throughout the meeting and this will help to keep things on track.

Process: All meetings should have a transparent process, for example, a problem-solving meeting might consist of four steps:
Step 1: Collect all available information
Step 2: Analyse the data
Step 3: Draw conclusions
Step 4: Plan action

People: Besides the role of chairperson, other roles which might need to be allocated for a meeting are minute-taker (who takes notes about what was said and decided) and

specialist (who contributes to a particular item). It is also important to manage people who talk too much and those who don't say enough.

UNIT 8 MEETINGS 2: PARTICIPATING IN MEETINGS

There is a strong cultural dimension to brainstorming. Individualist cultures tend to encourage people to express their opinions directly and defend their positions. Collectivist cultures tend to encourage people to be more modest and not express their opinions. In collectivist cultures, people tend not to interrupt, but focus more on listening and reflecting. (See Unit 3, Business across Cultures, page 15 for more on this topic.)

If you come from an individualist culture, you need to adapt your communication style when working with more collectivist-oriented cultures, for example, don't push people to express an opinion if they appear reluctant to do so. Pay attention to any rules about behaviour in meetings, for example, in some cultures it would be unacceptable to disagree with your boss at a meeting.

If you come from a collectivist culture, you will also need to adapt your communication style when working with more individualist-oriented cultures. For example, expect individualists to enjoy dominating the discussion and expect to see confrontation and disagreement at meetings.

Units 9–12 focus on communication skills for telephoning.

UNIT 9 TELEPHONING 1: OPENING AND RESPONDING

To make sure that your telephone calls get off to a good start, greet the person who has answered and identify yourself clearly. Ask for the person you want to speak to and be ready to spell the name, if necessary. Give a clear reason for the call.

In some cultures, people like to start a telephone call with some small talk. In other cultures, people will get down to business immediately. In any situation, it's a good idea to check that the person has time to talk, before you launch into the details of your call.

UNIT 10 TELEPHONING 2: LEAVING AND TAKING MESSAGES

If you have to leave a message on an answer phone or voice mail, planning what you want to say in advance will make sure that your message is clear and easy to follow. If you have planned what you want to say, you are more likely to speak clearly and without hesitation or unnecessary repetition. This creates a good impression and may even help to build relationships.

When you leave a message on an answer phone or voice mail, make sure you leave your name, the date and time of the call and any action that needs to be taken. Remember to repeat important information like telephone numbers or addresses. It may also be helpful to give some information about your movements, for example, *I'm at my desk tomorrow morning until 11:30, if you'd like to call back then. After that I'm in a meeting for the rest of the day.*

UNIT 11 TELEPHONING 3: STRUCTURING A CALL

Before you make a telephone call, especially an important one, it is a good idea to prepare for it. Think or make notes about what you want to say and what you hope to achieve by the end of the call. Make a checklist of important points that you want to cover. Make sure you have all the information that you might need during the call – reports, prices, catalogues, etc. You could also warn someone of an important call by sending them an email first.

During the call, listen actively – check, repeat, clarify and confirm. Take notes during the call to help you remember what has been discussed. Some people like to stand up during a telephone call – it keeps you alert and may make you feel more in control.

UNIT 12 TELEPHONING 4: CLOSING A CALL

Closing a call well is as important as opening a call well. Closing a call well helps to leave a positive impression with the person you have called.

At the end of the call, summarise any actions that need to be taken or decisions that have been made. Aim to close on a positive note. If appropriate, this might include thanks or a personal touch, for example, *Thanks for taking time to explain things to me – I really appreciate it* or *Have a good weekend*.

After the call, write up any notes you have made before you forget what has been discussed. If appropriate, send a follow-up email to confirm in writing anything that has been discussed or agreed during the call.

Units 13–16 focus on communication skills for making presentations.
The key factor when making a presentation is to make contact with and satisfy your audience. You can achieve this by:
- delivering a clear message
- getting feedback from your audience

UNIT 13 PRESENTATIONS 1: OPENING

An important way of establishing contact with your audience when making a presentation is to make eye contact with them from the start. If you have notes, do not spend all your time reading them – look at them occasionally but maintain regular eye contact with the audience so that they continue to feel engaged and interested in you and what you are saying. If you are using slides or a board, make sure you do not stand with your back to the audience. If you have a big audience, make sure you make eye contact with a few people in different sections of the audience. Keep eye contact with one person for a significant time (e.g. 10 seconds). Do not allow your eyes to flit around the audience.

UNIT 14 PRESENTATIONS 2: DEVELOPING THE MESSAGE

Like all communication, presentations are best when they are well prepared. Using a transparent structure will help you as a presenter, and the audience, to follow the thread.

When you are confident about the structure and content, you can relax and be more natural when presenting. Rehearsing what you are going to say and checking the timing of each section of your presentation will also help you to give a more confident performance.

UNIT 15 PRESENTATIONS 3: USING VISUALS

All communication is improved with visual messages. However, it is important to make sure the visuals don't dominate. There is nothing worse than hundreds of dense PowerPoint slides. These guidelines will help you to use visuals effectively in your presentations:

- Don't use more than one slide per minute.
- Don't fill the slide with small text.
- Don't just repeat what you are saying on the slide– the slide should support or illustrate.
- Don't read from the slides.
- Don't block your audience's view of the visual.
- Don't talk with your back to the audience.

One way to reinforce the structure of the verbal part of your presentation is to follow the same structure in your visuals, marking them by section, for example, slide 1.3 = Part 1, slide 3.

UNIT 16 PRESENTATIONS 4: CLOSING

When you have finished your presentation, use the checklist below to evaluate your success.

CHECKLIST

Preparation
1 Was I well prepared?
2 Was I at ease with the subject?

Audience
1 Did I meet their needs / expectations?
2 Did I get their involvement / feedback?

Structure
1 Did I deliver a clear presentation?
2 Did the introduction and ending have a good impact?
3 Did I follow my structure?
4 Did I keep to the timing?

Visuals
1 Did my visuals help to get the message across?
2 Did I provide handouts as a follow-up?

Body Language
1 Did I use eye contact to engage the audience?
2 Was my body language relaxed and confident?

You could also ask a colleague to evaluate your performance. Use the feedback you collect to help you improve your next presentation.

BUSINESS ACROSS CULTURES

In order to work internationally, we need good English, good communication skills and also good intercultural skills. The *Business across Cultures* section of each unit and these notes aim to help you:

- understand the scope and importance of culture in business
- build a framework of key intercultural concepts
- understand the impact of your culture on your international business partners.

It can be difficult to talk about culture as we often do not have much experience of doing this. We have a lot of experience of our own culture, of course, but that does not mean we can share or explain it easily. Sometimes we may even be unaware that cultural factors play a part in our business dealings or relationships.

> **Units 1–4** aim to give you a clear picture of what culture is.

UNIT 1 UNDERSTANDING YOUR OWN CULTURE

When you brainstorm what culture means to you, you will probably think of a number of things ranging from food to values. The iceberg diagram helps you to put them into a simple framework.

Above the surface of the iceberg are the things we can see or observe in a culture, such as food, buildings, or landscape. Under the surface are the things that take much longer to understand, such as the history and the traditions of a culture. At the deepest level, some distance below the surface, are values, beliefs, and assumptions. The deepest level is the most difficult to understand because these things are mostly unspoken.

It is always important to remember that we are looking at the behaviour of groups, not individuals when we talk about cultures. When we observe a culture, we need to look at groups of people – on holiday, at work, or socialising.

Talking about your own culture makes you think about what is different or special about it. Doing this should help you to identify what people from other cultures might find difficult to adapt to. This will be easier if you have visited other countries – experiencing other cultures will help you to look at your own culture from a different perspective.

UNIT 2 UNDERSTANDING DIFFERENT TYPES OF CULTURE

When we talk about culture we usually think of countries. However, this is only one layer of culture. In one country, there could be regional, ethnic, or linguistic sub-cultures. The onion diagram gives us a way of thinking about different layers of culture. At work, we are influenced by country culture, but also by company culture. At home we may be very influenced by family or community culture. Understanding these different layers of culture stops us from thinking in simple national stereotypes.

UNIT 3 INDIVIDUALS AND GROUPS

Some cultures put a high value on the individual. These cultures tend to encourage individuals to prove themselves against other individuals – who is the cleverest, richest, most famous? Other, more group-oriented cultures do not expect individuals to solve problems and have successes – they look to the group to do this. In these cultures, motivation is more about what you can do for the group and less about what you can do for yourself. (This concept was developed by Geert Hosftede. Go to http://www.geert-hofstede.com for more information.)

UNIT 4 WOMEN AT WORK

Gender is an important area of cultural difference, and we see it very clearly in the business world. In the West, people talk about a 'glass ceiling' which stops women from reaching the top positions in companies. In the East, women often have a much more clearly defined role in society. In all cultures, this is an area of cultural change.

Masculinity / femininity: Some cultures are more masculine than others. A masculine culture values assertiveness, achievement, and acquisition of wealth, as opposed to caring for others, social support, and the quality of life. These cultures tend to have very clear expectations of male and female roles in society. Low-masculinity cultures focus more on quality of life issues such as helping others and sympathy for the unfortunate. Feminine cultures also prefer equality between men and women and less defined roles for each other. (This concept was developed by Geert Hosftede. Go to http://www.geert-hofstede.com for more information.)

> **Units 5–8** continue to build a framework to help you understand cultural differences.

UNIT 5 PUBLIC AND PRIVATE SPACE

Everybody has a public self and a private self, but in some cultures they are more separate than in others. The peach / coconut concept has been used to explain a key difference between American and German culture. The peach-like culture of the USA allows people to share their private space very easily. This means that Americans are more likely to tell you about their private lives, and also to enquire about yours. They will also allow you into the private territory (their home) quite quickly. In contrast, the culture is more coconut-like in Germany, where people prefer to protect their private selves for longer. They will maintain distance for longer; the language can also be more formal, allowing Germans to distinguish between close and less close contacts. (This concept was developed by Susanne M. Zaninelli. Go to http://www.ic-perspectives.net for more information.)

UNIT 6 THE CULTURE OF ORGANISATIONS

For some people, a key motivation in life is getting and holding onto power. Inside companies, there are always power differences between people. In a vertically structured company, the higher you are in the hierarchy, the more power you have. In a flatter organisation, power is less connected to position in a hierarchy and more to do with what you do and what you know. Many companies are moving towards flatter, less hierarchical organisations. In these types of organisation, people communicate in all directions – up, down, and sideways. The culture of flatter organisations is based more on cooperation and less on competition. (This concept was developed by Geert Hosftede. Go to http://www.geert-hofstede.com for more information.)

UNIT 7 ATTITUDES TOWARDS TIME

Some cultures consider time and its control very important. In these so-called monochronic cultures, punctuality is very important. You are judged by your punctuality, and arriving late is seen as a sign of inefficiency or lack of respect. Organisation of life into schedules is common in this type of culture. Working life is dominated by start times and finish times, structured agendas, and almost an obsession with time-keeping.

On the other hand, in polychronic cultures, time is not such an important resource. Finishing the topic and allowing everybody an opportunity to talk is much more important than finishing on time. In these cultures, people will be happy to do many things at the same time – for example, a business meeting won't be very structured, allowing for many more interruptions and diversions than would be possible in a monochronic culture. (This concept was developed by the anthropologist E.T. Hall. For more information, see his book, with Mildred Reed Hall, *Understanding Cultural Difference*, published by Intercultural Press. 2000.)

UNIT 8 DEVELOPING A CULTURE OF INNOVATION

Innovation has become very important for companies, especially in the developed world, where it is seen as one of the few ways that companies can continue to compete with emerging nations. It is easier to recognise an innovative company culture like Google's than to decide how to create a culture of innovation. It is also difficult to sustain innovative cultures.

Many large companies and organisations have a strong dislike of uncertainty – they try to plan and anticipate everything, so that nothing unexpected will happen, but avoiding the unexpected can discourage innovation. Cultures which can live with some uncertainty are more able to respond quickly when things change.

Units 9–12 focus on company culture.

UNIT 9 UNDERSTANDING CORPORATE CULTURE

The iceberg gives us a way of talking about corporate culture. When you first join a company, you notice things above the surface, such as the layout of the offices, the way employees dress and behaviour during lunch breaks. After some time, you may be able to grasp some of the company values which are just below the surface, especially if they are written down. However, many companies share the same values, such as integrity, honesty, performance and quality. The layer which tells you most about the company is at the deepest level of the iceberg. Here we find the hidden assumptions, for example, it may be important to be very modest in your behaviour or, on the other hand, it may be part of the culture to tell people about your successes. You may find that one particular function in the company is valued more than others, such as finance or marketing.

UNIT 10 CUSTOMER SERVICE CULTURE

From a national point of view, some countries seem to have a better customer service culture than others. For example, an Asian culture like Malaysia has a very well-developed attitude towards service; in many European countries, however, this positive attitude towards customers is not present. But all companies need to develop a customer service culture. This has always been understood in the retail sector, and gradually other sectors, such as the industrial sector, have tried to develop more customer orientation. The public sector (e.g. public transport, civil service, etc.) does not usually have a strong customer service culture. However, in some countries, this is beginning to change. The main focus in changing the culture is to improve communication with customers. The introduction of telephone helpdesks is a common first step.

UNIT 11 WORK AND PLAY

In some cultures, work is totally separate from personal life. You leave work and you enter another 'culture' outside work. In cultures which place a lot of importance on interpersonal relations at work, there is usually some overlap between work and personal life. In other words, socialising with your colleagues and business partners after work may be just as important as discussing business at the office.

Drinking alcohol can be an important part of this social interaction as it allows people to be more relaxed and uninhibited, thus showing their true personality. In this way, people understand and trust each other more. The events which form part of socialising, such as giving gifts, celebrating successes, or dining out are important as they mark the development of the relationship, just as much as moving to the next milestone in a business project.

UNIT 12 WORKING IN CROSS-FUNCTIONAL TEAMS

One key part of the silo mentality is failing to understand the concerns or priorities of colleagues in other departments: Finance has always been a difficult area for non-specialists to understand; R&D seems like science and not business; Human Resources is not really close to the hard side of business; people in Marketing are seen as being out of touch with the realities of day-to-day business. This may be reinforced by the use of terms and concepts that colleagues from other departments cannot understand.

One way to "talk the same language" is to brainstorm the key issues in each area and make sure they are understood by colleagues in other departments. For example:

Finance:	Profitability, return on investment, cash flow, liquidity
R&D:	Pure and applied science, innovation, renovation
HR	Turnover, manpower planning, talent spotting
Marketing	Segmentation, positioning

You could use these as a starting point to build up your own business dictionary of key concepts.

Units 13–16 focus on interactions across business cultures.

UNIT 13 BODY LANGUAGE

A key aspect of differences in body language is the display of emotion. In cultures where people are encouraged to show their feelings, it is important to use the body to reinforce the verbal message. This means more physical contact, such as touching and standing closer to your colleagues. It also means showing your feelings in your facial expressions – smiling when you are happy and even crying when you are not. In so-called 'neutral' cultures, people are not encouraged to show their emotions. People maintain a physical distance, rarely touch each other and their faces do not show what they are feeling. In these cultures, people are taught to hide their feelings and not to impose them on other people.

UNIT 14 COMMUNICATION STYLE

In high-context cultures, the environment (the way people sit, the shared cup of tea, the dress of the boss) is important in understanding the message. You need to be able to read these signals to understand the communication. Often, it is more important to understand what is not said, rather than what is said. In low-context cultures, people do not pay much attention to the context. They focus on what is said and expect the message to be transparent. (This concept was developed by the anthropologist E.T. Hall. For more information, see his book, with Mildred Reed Hall, *Understanding Cultural Differences* published by Intercultural Press. 2000.)

Email is a low-context communication tool, and it can be an excellent means of communication – it is available 24 hours a day; it is flexible, quick, and direct. However, it can be impersonal and can easily upset people. Because it is so easy to use, we sometimes reply too quickly, without thinking about the effect our message will have on the reader. When we speak face-to-face or on even on the telephone, we reinforce feelings and emotions by our expressions and tone of voice. In an email this can easily be lost. We may not be able to convey the same depth and range of meaning as we can in spoken interaction, especially if we are in a hurry, or if our writing skills are weak. If you rely on email a lot, you can make sure that you maintain good business relationships through occasional telephone calls or by sometimes including personal messages in your emails.

UNIT 15 LEADERSHIP

Leading people from different cultures is a real challenge because expectations of leaders and leadership can vary so much. Many companies have identified what they think are the key leadership competencies and they use these to assess and develop their leaders, for example, communication skills, customer focus, strategic focus, team building, decision-making.

Whatever their culture, all companies will want their leaders to be focused on results. However, many companies will also stress the ability to manage and develop people. Companies which have become flatter can no longer motivate their staff by offering one promotion after another. In this kind of company culture, the leader needs to motivate his or her staff by offering them opportunities for development, for example, through training and on-the-job experience.

Some cultures will expect leaders to stay close to their employees. Americans talk about 'practising what you preach' and 'managing by walking about,' both of which suggest that the leader should spend time with employees. However, in other cultures, leaders gain respect by keeping some distance between themselves and their staff. Cultural sensitivity is becoming more and more important. Leaders need to be able to adapt their style to the dominant culture.

UNIT 16 DECISION-MAKING

Cultures which are very task-oriented (i.e. focused on the transaction and process of a task) will want to clearly mark the moment of making a decision and put it in writing. In more person-oriented cultures (i.e. focused on the relationships between people), decision-making is a less structured process. It may not be so clear when a decision has been made or who has made it. It will be clearer from the actions and events which follow. Forcing a decision at a certain time in this type of culture will not work, as no action will follow from it.

GRAMMAR OVERVIEW

UNIT 1 Comparisons

Form

Comparatives

- One-syllable adjectives: add *-er*, or just *-r* if the adjective ends in *-e*: *cheaper, weaker, larger, safer*.
- One-syllable adjectives ending in *-y*: delete the *y* and add *-ier*: *busier, steadier*.
- Most two-syllable adjectives and all adjectives with more than two syllables: use *more* + the adjective: *more careful, more serious*.

Superlatives

- Instead of *-er* or *–r*, use *-est* or *-st*, and instead of *more*, use *most*.
- You put *the* before the adjective: *the brightest, the latest, the most famous, the most interesting*.

Use

- You use the **comparative** to compare two people or things, with or without *than*. Without *than*, the comparison is understood but not stated directly.

  *Work involving routine tasks is **more stressful than** varied and interesting work.*
  *Some workplaces are **noisier than** they should be, which also causes stress.*
  *Flexitime is getting **more popular** as people's family commitments increase.*

- You can use *as ... as* to say that two people or things are similar in some way.

  *For most people, job satisfaction is **as important as** a high salary.*
  *Working at home can be **as rewarding as** going to an office every day.*

- You use the **superlative** to say that someone or something has more of a certain quality than anyone or anything else.

  *We have created **the most attractive** working environment in the city.*
  ***The happiest** employees are usually **the most productive**.*

- You can use words like *much, a lot, nearly, slightly, far* and *by far* to make your comparison more exact.

  *I need to earn a **much better** salary than in my previous job.*
  *That was **by far the most enjoyable** job I have ever had.*

Practice

Rearrange the words below to make sentences. Use the comparative or superlative form of the adjective.

1 owning / and running / Nothing / satisfying / business / your own / than / is
2 often / than / Self-employed people / work / long / people / in / hours / offices / far
3 school-age / from home / good / for people / children / Working / may be / option / with
4 in business / successful / with / nothing / Some of / started / people
5 flexible / there / demand / a / for / is / Nowadays / hours

UNIT 3 First conditional

Form

- To form the **first conditional**, you typically use the present simple in the *if* clause and *will* + infinitive in the main clause. The clauses can come in either order.

  *If you **have** children in the future, you **will receive** vouchers to help with childcare.*
  *You **will get** paid leave if you **are** ill.*
  *What **will happen** to my pension if I **die** while I'm still working for you?*
  ***Will** I **be given** a company car if I **travel** on business?* (passive)

- You can also use **modals** such as *can, could, have to, might* and *may* in the main clause, or the imperative.

  *If you **achieve** your targets, you **could receive** quite a large bonus.*
  *If you **wish** to know more about all the perks, **phone** Jay Scott during office hours.*

- You can also use the **present continuous** or the **present perfect** in the *if* clause.

  *If the company **is making** good profits, the staff **will be** the first to benefit.*
  *Even if someone **has paid** regularly into the company pension fund, they **may** still **receive** an inadequate pension.*

Use

You use the first conditional to talk about possible situations in the present or future, and their results.

Negatives

- Either the *if* clause or the main clause can be negative, or both.

  *You **won't need** to pay for childcare if you **use** the company crèche.*
  *If you **don't want** to come into the office every day, we**'ll arrange** for you to work from home.*
  *You **won't get** a full pension if you **don't contribute** to the company scheme for the minimum period.*

- *Unless* means the same as *if not*. You don't normally use *unless* in questions.

  *We **can't expect** the company to be successful **unless** we **treat** our employees well.*
  ***Unless** you **want** time to consider, we**'ll go ahead** and prepare your contract.*

Practice

Match the clauses to make conditional sentences.

1 Patients will be the first to benefit	a staff may return to the private sector.
2 If nursing staff are well-motivated,	b Britain will be brought into line with much of Europe.
3 Unless we improve public service pay and conditions,	c if we improve conditions for medical staff.
4 We could lose many of our female staff	d fewer women will return to the company after having children.
5 If we don't provide on-site childcare,	e if we don't develop family-friendly employment options.
6 If fathers are granted paternity leave,	f they will provide a better service for patients.

UNIT 4 Past simple and present perfect

Past simple

- You use the **past simple** to talk about events in the past. You often ask or state the exact time that something happened.

  > I **decided** to change my job because the hours **were** too long. I simply **couldn't juggle** the demands of work and children!
  > When **did** you **leave**?
  > As soon as my resignation **was accepted**. (passive)

- When you are talking about the period of time since something happened, you use *ago*.

  > I **realised** a year **ago** that I had to do something to improve my lifestyle.

Present perfect

- The **present perfect** is different because it is basically a present tense. You use it when you want to state the connection between past events or situations, and the present or future.

  > I**'ve worked** hard and **put** all my energy into my career. But I feel it **hasn't** really **been appreciated**. (passive)

- You can use the present perfect with *since* or *for*, or *how long* in questions. *Since* is followed by a point in time, and *for* by a period of time.

  > Unbelievably, I**'ve worked** every weekend **since** joining the company.
  > **How long have** you **felt** resentful about this?
  > I suppose it**'s been** a serious problem **for** the last year or so.

- You can use the present perfect with *ever* and *never*, which indicate time up to now.

  > **Have** you **ever thought** of leaving London and living life at a slower pace?
  > No, never. I'm a city girl and I**'ve never liked** the country.

- You can also use *already* (typically in affirmatives) and *yet* (typically in questions and negatives).

  > I**'ve already used up** all my paid holiday, but I **haven't begun** to feel rested **yet**!

- Sometimes you begin a conversation about the past by using the present perfect to establish that an event is recent and relevant, often adding *just* in order to emphasise this. Then you fix the details in time using the past simple.

  > I**'ve just come** back from a well-earned break.
  > Where **did** you **go**?
  > Egypt. It **was** wonderful...

- Note that you cannot use the present perfect with adverbs that place the action at a definite time in the past. So you cannot say *I have worked hard yesterday.*

Practice

Underline the most natural tense.

In recent years the company (1) *took / has taken* important steps towards delivering a balanced package. We (2) *have extended / extended* maternity leave from six to nine months, and last year new fathers (3) *were given / have been given* the right to three months' paid leave. Measures (4) *have been drafted / were drafted* to improve conditions for carers of elderly or disabled relatives, although these (5) *have not come / did not come* into force yet. We (6) *installed / have installed* a gym on the premises six months ago, because we know that employees need to work out as well as work.

UNIT 5 Adjectives and nouns

Form

Many adjectives and nouns are closely related, and very often the only difference in spelling is the **suffix.** A suffix is a letter or group of letters added to the end of a word to form another word. Here are a few of the ways in which adjectives and nouns are related.

adjective → *noun*

-able, -ible → -ability, -ibility
*She founded the most **profitable** stationery company in Britain.*
*The company has achieved a high level of **profitability**.*

-ent → -ence, -cy
*There are many business opportunities for **competent** and **efficient** people.*
*Success depends partly on the **competence** and **efficiency** of the mangement.*

-ant → -ance
*Selling the company when she did was a **brilliant** tactical move.*
*He was known for his **brilliance** as a negotiator and headhunter.*

-ist, -istic → -ism
*Businesses are **optimistic** that economic conditions will slowly improve.*
*There was a mood of cautious **optimism** in the City.*

-ive → -ness
*A successful entrepreneur must be brave, **decisive**, and a very hard worker.*
*Staff respect his **decisiveness** and air of calm authority.*

But these are not fixed rules, and relationships can be unpredictable:

important → *importance*	but		*financial* → *finance*	
inflationary → *inflation*	but		*productive* → *production*	
amateurish → *amateur*	but		*entrepreneurial* → *entrepreneur*	

Participles

Many present and past participles are used as **adjectives.** The present participle is formed with *-ing* and the past participle with *-ed.*

our **recurring** *financial difficulties*	**accepted** *professional standards*
some of our **leading** *businesswomen*	*worse than* **expected** *profits*

Less frequently, present participles (but not past participles) are used as nouns.

*He was over-cautious and hated **risk-taking**.*
***Headhunting** and 'poaching' are often ruthless and unprincipled.*

Practice

Complete the sentences using the nouns and adjectives in the box.

entrepreneur	willing	culture	opportunity	existing
profit	essential	personal	optimistic	

A business (1) _____ is someone who starts up and runs a commercial enterprise. His or her company offers a new or (2) _____ product or service into a new or established market, usually with the aim of making a (3) _____ . Entrepreneurs are often (4) _____ to accept a certain level of (5) _____ , professional or financial risk to pursue what they see as a promising market (6) _____ . They are usually (7) _____ and hard-working, and are often highly regarded in U.S. (8) _____ as being an (9) _____ part of its capitalistic society.

UNIT 6 The future

Form

Will

- You form the **future** with *will* (*'ll*), + infinitive. The negative is *will not* (*won't*).

  The LifeStraw® is an invention that **will change** the lives of the world's poor.
  It **will filter** dirty water and **make** it clean enough to drink.
  It **won't cost** much to buy.
  Sanitation in the world's poorest regions **will be improved**. (passive)

Going to

- The form is *be* (*am, is, are*) *going to* + infinitive. The negative is formed with *not* (*n't*).

  It's **going to spread** throughout the developing world.
  Is it **going to reduce** the level of bacteria in water?

Use

- You use both *will* and *going to* to make **predictions** about the future.

- You use *will* for on-the-spot **decisions**, and *going to* for decisions that you have already made and for stating **intentions**.

  I know what to do – we'**ll hold** a brainstorming meeting.
  They'**re going to export** the LifeStraw® to large parts of Africa.
  How **are** they **going to persuade** people to buy it?
  They **aren't going to waste** any time.

- You use *will* for **promises**, **requests** and **offers**.

  I'**ll find out** more about it and **email** you as soon as possible.
  Will you **contact** Research and Development and **tell** me what they think?
  I'**ll think about** what we as a company can do to help.

- If an **offer** is in the form of a question, you often use *shall*.

  Shall I **go** and **ask** if anyone else has any ideas?

Other modals

You can also use *might*, *may* or *could* to talk about future possibilities.

  This invention **could play** an important role in the future.

Practice

Rearrange the words to make sentences.

---

1 changes / the / going to / health / make / countries / What / LifeStraw® / is / in / developing / to

2 water / prevent / The / diseases / are / by / carried / LifeStraw® / could / the / of / spread / that

3 supply / drinking / provide / Each / of / water / year's / a / straw / will / pure

4 electricity / spare / won't / never / It / use / and / will / parts / need / it / any

5 bacteria / As well as / improve / of / water / killing / will / taste / the / the / it

6 poorer / afford / Critics / not / said / may / people / be able to / it / have / that

---

UNIT 7 Passives

Form

- You form the **passive** using the verb *be* + past participle.

- The person or thing that is affected by an action is the **subject** of the sentence. The **agent** (the doer of the action) is often not mentioned.

    *The fund **is invested** in Singapore.*
    *The goods **are going to be marketed** overseas.*
    ***Will** economic recovery **be achieved** by the end of the year?*

- You can put a modal such as *can, could, would* or *should* before *be*.

    *Details of the deal **can be supplied** on request.*

- You form the negative with *not* (*n't*).

    *Unfortunately, the money that the company needs **has not been raised** in time.*

- You can often put an adverb after the first auxiliary.

    *He **has often been quoted** as saying that prices would recover rapidly.*

Use

- You usually use the **passive** when you don't know who or what the agent is, when you do not want to say, or when it is obvious.

    *More investment in green fuels **is** urgently **needed**.*
    *I**'ve been told** that your company is in financial difficulties.*
    *The company **will be floated** on the stock exchange next week.*

- When you want to say who the agent is, you use *by*.

    *The project **was funded** by private investors.*
    *Shares are **bought and sold** by investors on the stock market.*

You can also use the passive:

- to describe processes and procedures

    *Woven textile cloths **are manufactured** mainly from natural fibres.*

- for newspaper reports

    *A 30 per cent rise in pre-tax profits **has been reported**.*

- to make announcements

    *The convention **will be opened** at 2 p.m.*

Practice

Reorder the words below to make complete sentences. Put the verb into the most appropriate tense of the passive.

1 can find / Stock exchanges / major / of the world / most / capitals / in
2 Their debt / write off / probably / next month
3 consider / At that time / price fixing / offence / a civil
4 by / notify / of the deal / the Italian authorities / They / not yet
5 a private equity firm / A takeover bid / announce / from / yesterday
6 insider dealing / believe / complaints / to be looking into / The Bank of England / of / now

UNIT 8 Past perfect and past simple

Form

- To form the **past perfect,** you use *had* + past participle. You form the negative with *not* (*n't*).

  *They **had researched** waterproof paper, but they **hadn't developed** it fully.*

- You form questions by reversing *had* and the subject.

  ***Had** she **applied** for a patent for her invention by that time?*

- To form the **past perfect continuous**, you use *had* (*'d*) + *been* and the *-ing* form.

  *He**'d been working** on ways of making underwater cameras much smaller.*

Use

- You use the **past simple** to refer to an event in the past, and the **past perfect** to refer to what happened before that event.

  *In 2005, Lee Loree **came up** with an invention called the SLEEPTRACKER®. Some years before, he **had begun** to think about ways of getting a better night's sleep.*

- You can use the past perfect to say that something was (or was not) hoped for or expected before a particular time in the past.

  *She didn't get as much financial backing as she **had hoped**.*
  *He **hadn't expected** to make much money from the robot, but it made him rich.*

- You can use conjunctions such as *after, until, by the time* (*that*), *once* and *because* with the past perfect.

  ***Once** the patent application **had been filed**, there was little to do but wait. (passive)*
  *She was pleased when it was granted, **because** she **had worked** very hard on the project.*

- You often use *already* with the past perfect, or *just* to emphasise that an event happened soon before another.

  *We bought an inflatable tent, which **had already proved** successful in America.*
  *They**'d just invented** a piano that you can roll up.*

- You often use the past perfect to report what someone said or thought about a past event or situation.

  *They announced that they**'d developed** a robotic dancing partner.*
  *I thought I**'d explained** the principles of the design.*

- You use the past perfect continuous to emphasise the duration of a continuous activity that took place before another event.

  *She**'d been thinking** about the device for years before the big breakthrough.*

Practice

Underline the most natural tense.

> On April 3, 1973, a man called Martin Cooper (1) *made / had made* a phone call that (2) *changed / had changed* the world for ever. Cooper (3) *worked / had worked* for a company called Motorola and he (4) *just developed / had just developed* the world's first 'hand-held cellular telephone'. And who did he call? He (5) *called / had called* the head of research at Bell Labs – Motorola's direct competitor – to let them know that he (6) *beat / had beaten* them in the race to make the first mobile phone. Bell (7) *introduced / had introduced* the idea of cellular communications in 1947, but it was Motorola who (8) *got / had got* there first.

UNIT 9 Count and uncount nouns

Count and uncount nouns

- Nouns that have a singular and a plural form are called **count nouns**.

- In the singular, you can use them with *a / an*, or another determiner such as *the*, *this* or *my*, but not alone. In the plural, you can use them either alone or with a determiner.

  > Over 95 per cent of **kids** have pestered **their parents** for **a product** promoted on TV, according to **a new survey**.

- Nouns that have only one form are called **uncount nouns**. You can use them alone or with a determiner, but not usually with *a / an*.

  > **Research** has shown that children need **some protection** from constant **advertising**.

- Some nouns can be both count and uncount with the same meaning.

  > Some parents give in to their children simply to avoid **a confrontation** / to avoid **confrontation**.

- Many nouns are uncount when they refer to a substance, and count when they refer to a brand or type of substance.

  > Parents are often nagged to buy more and more **junk food**. (uncount)
  > **Junk foods** such as crisps and fries are very popular. (count)

Determiners

- You use *many* or *(a) few* with plural count nouns, and *much* or *(a) little* with uncount nouns.

  > **Few people** doubt that our society has become more and more commercial.
  > **How much persuasion** do parents need these days?

- You use *each* and *every* only with singular count nouns, and *both* only with plural count nouns.

  > No parent should give a child **every toy** she asks for.

- You use plural determiners like *these*, *those* and *several* only with plural count nouns.

  > **Several factors** account for so-called 'pester-power'.

- Most other determiners, like *some* and *any*, can be used with both types of noun.

Practice

Complete the sentences using the nouns in the box. Make them plural where necessary.

money responsibility consumer market day childhood season campaign

Companies have realised how powerful children and young people are as (1) _____ . Every (2) _____ , especially at Christmas, new toys and gadgets come onto the (3) _____ , and many advertising (4) _____ target children aggressively. As a parent, you have a (5) _____ to help your child become a sensible consumer. Don't give them too much (6) _____ to spend, and discuss the idea of waiting a few (7) _____ instead of rushing out to the nearest store. The principles they learn in (8) _____ will be the ones they carry through life.

UNIT 10 Prefixes

To form the opposite of a word, you can often add a **prefix** to the beginning.

Adjectives

dis-

> If you want to sell yourself, you must come across as **respectful**, **courteous** to clients, and extremely **organised**.
> He seemed **disrespectful**, **discourteous** and very **disorganised**, and he didn't get the job.

- Other negative qualities are:

  > **un-** unfriendly, unemployable, unhelpful, unreasonable, unreliable, unsympathetic, untruthful, unqualified.
  > **in-** inaccurate, incompetent, inconsiderate, indecisive, inefficient, inexperienced, insensitive, insincere, intolerant.
  > **il-, im-, ir-** illogical, illiterate, impractical, immoral, impolite, irrational, irresponsible.

- If the original adjective has a negative meaning, then the addition of a prefix makes the meaning positive, for example, *unafraid, uncomplaining, unselfish*.

Nouns

- You form opposites in the same way to refer to facts, states and behaviour that are negative.

  > Her CV has one **disadvantage**: it's 12 pages long!
  > Her **inability** to make a coherent presentation ... her **unwillingness** to take on board new technological developments ... her **uncertainty** about her commitment to the company ... her **dishonesty** about her past experience, ... not to mention her **untidiness** ... no, I wasn't impressed at all.

- The prefix **mis-** (used with some nouns and verbs but not usually with adjectives) adds the meaning that something is done badly or wrongly, as in *mismanagement* and *misuse*.

Verbs

- Verbs formed with negative prefixes refer to an action or process that is opposite to that of the original verb.

  > She was **distrusted** and **misunderstood** by her colleagues.
  > The truth of the matter may never be **uncovered**.

  The prefixes **in-**, **il-**, **im-** and **ir-** are not usually used with verbs.

Practice

Add a negative prefix to the words in the box. Then complete the sentences.

rational	employable	organised	considerate	reliable	qualified	competent	truthful

1 You can't trust him to get to work on time. He's _____ .
2 He doesn't always argue fairly or sensibly. He can be _____ .
3 He'll go as far as to lie to a client if he needs to. He's _____ .
4 He's very bad at arranging and planning his work. He's _____ .
5 Clients find he doesn't care about their needs or feelings. He's _____ .
6 His experience and qualifications don't meet our needs. He's _____ .
7 He's unable to do the job properly. In fact, he's completely _____ .
8 In fact he'll never get another job when he leaves here. He's _____ !

UNIT 11 Infinitives and *-ing* forms

Some verbs are followed by the *to*-infinitive and some are followed by the *-ing* form. Some can be followed by either.

Verbs followed by the *to*-infinitive

agree	aim	begin	compete	continue	decide	guarantee	hope
intend	manage	plan	prefer	pretend	promise	prove	want

> Some authors **prefer to use** the term 'internationalisation' rather than globalisation.
> Multinational companies **are aiming to increase** international trade at a faster rate.
> Generally, unrestricted free trade **has proved to benefit** the rich rather than the poor.

Verbs followed by an object and the *to*-infinitive

Some verbs are often followed by an object and then the *to*-infinitive.

advise	ask	believe	cause	challenge	employ	encourage	expect
force	invite	like	order	pay	persuade	remind	teach

> Financial services companies **expect their staff to dress** in a way that reflects
> the company's values.
> A cancer patient **has challenged an international tobacco company to**
> **admit** that cancer is linked to smoking.
> Which particular groups **believe globalisation to be** a negative development?

Verbs followed by the *-ing* form

avoid	deny	end up	enjoy	finish	go on	involve	(not) mind
postpone	practise	propose	regret	remember	risk	start	stop

> The company **ended up gaining** nearly all the marketing rights to the drug in
> Asia and Africa.
> Globalisation **involves developing** international financial systems.
> You **will not regret selling** your shares in that company.

Practice

Complete the sentences using the *to*-infinitive or *-ing* form of the verbs in the box.

remain	think	cause	sell	defer	buy	submit	discuss

1 We have invited six major consultancies _____ proposals.

2 The executives went on _____ the product launch all evening.

3 The funding of the new research promises _____ a difficult issue.

4 Manufacturers are encouraging us _____ faster machines with more storage capacity.

5 We hope that the lenders will agree _____ capital repayments until next year.

6 The nuclear industry has always denied _____ any damage to the environment.

7 The ecology debate has forced economists _____ harder about climate change.

8 I wouldn't mind _____ my offshore shares and investing in a small local business.

UNIT 12 Present perfect simple and continuous

Form

- To form the **present perfect continuous**, you use *has* or *have* + *been* and the *-ing* form.

    We **have been exploring** how elderly people view prime-time television commercials.
    Which issue **have** you **been investigating**?
    We **haven't been asking** younger people for their views on the issue.

- You don't often use the passive (*has been being explored*) with this tense.

Use

- You can often choose to use either the present perfect simple or the continuous.

    The importance of the grey market **has grown / has been growing** rapidly recently.

- You usually have a choice with the verbs *live* and *work*, for ongoing situations.

    I've **worked / have been working** in market research for several years.

But there is often a difference of focus. When you want to focus on an action that is completed and has a **result**, you use the simple.

    He's playing the Pink Floyd CD that he's just **bought** – his musical tastes
    haven't changed since the 60s.

- When you want to focus on the **action** itself, whether or not it is completed, you use the continuous.

    Advertisers **have been using** a range of older celebrities in some adverts.
    People in their sixties **have been buying** the latest digital technology.

- The continuous is more common when you want to ask or emphasise *how long*.

    How long **has** she **been researching** this question?
    Advertisers have woken up to the power of the grey pound, and for the last few years,
    they **have been targeting** the market.

- You use the continuous to talk about actions repeated over a period of time.

    She's **been playing** computer games since she was 60, and she's in her 80s now.

- You don't usually use the continuous with stative verbs like *know, believe, prefer, belong* and *seem*.

Practice

Put the verb in brackets into the most natural form, present perfect simple or continuous.

> 1 The industry _____ (know) about these market trends for years.
>
> 2 The change _____ (happen) for at least a decade.
>
> 3 Ageing pop stars _____ (appear) in at least six adverts aimed at the elderly this year.
>
> 4 How long _____ your grandfather (read) computer journals?
>
> 5 We _____ (hope) the product will sell to the older consumer.
>
> 6 Lately it _____ (seem) more urgent that we appreciate the needs of the elderly.

UNIT 14 Compounds

- A compound noun is a fixed expression that is made up of more than one word.
- Often the meaning of a compound is obvious from the words it consists of, but sometimes it is not. For example, a *leading article* in a newspaper gives the paper's opinion on a subject, but this is not obvious from the meaning of *leading*.
- Sometimes the meaning is even less transparent, for example, a *print run* is the number of copies printed.

  *The newspaper's initial **print run** was 5,000 copies.*

Form

Compound nouns are formed in several ways. These are a few of them.

- **noun + noun**

  There are several different kinds of relationship between the two nouns. For example, a *press release* is the release of information to the press, a *media event* is an event that the media gives a lot of attention to, and a *news agency* is an agency that collects and distributes news.

  *A good **press release** excites the editor's interest with the first sentence.*

- **adjective + noun**

  The adjective classifies the noun in some way, for example, *financial district, grey pound, foreign correspondent*.

  *They employ 120 distributors to hand out the paper in London's **financial districts**.*

- ***-ing* form + noun**

  The participle often tells you what the noun does, for example, *publishing company, managing director, training manual*.

  *The paper was owned by a small New York **publishing company**.*

- ***-ed* form + noun**

  The participle often tells you what has happened or been done to the noun, for example, *developed world, classified ad, printed matter*.

  *Circulation and revenues of newspapers in the **developed world** are under pressure.*

- **nouns related to phrasal verbs**

  Some compound nouns are related to phrasal verbs, for example, *passer-by, cover-up, phone-in*.

  *We hand out the newspaper to 90,000 **passers-by** every day.*

- Some compounds are quite complicated. For example, *takeover bid* is formed from a phrasal verb and a noun.
- New compounds are being formed all the time. *Handout newspaper* (a newspaper that is handed out free) is not in the dictionary, but it may be one day.

  *City AM has proved that a new **handout newspaper** can succeed.*

Practice

Match the words below to form compound nouns. Use a dictionary if necessary.

1	news	a	tax
2	general	b	bulletin
3	current	c	campaign
4	mass	d	columnist
5	labour	e	media
6	advertising	f	force
7	gossip	g	public
8	value-added	h	affairs

UNIT 15 Speculating about the past

Should have

- You use *should have* + past participle to talk about what someone didn't do in the past, although it would have been the right thing to do.
- You can use it to criticise someone.

    *You **should have formed** a much clearer idea about your business aims and goals.*
    *Many aspects of the business **should have been handled** differently.* (passive)

Should (not) have

- You use *should not (shouldn't) have* + past participle to say that it was important not to do something in the past, but that it was done.

    *You **shouldn't have spent** so much money on getting the business up and running.*

Continuous form

- The continuous form is *should have + been + -ing* and the negative is *should not (shouldn't) have + been + -ing*.

    *You **should have been concentrating** on building up your reputation with your clients.*
    *You **shouldn't have been spending** all your time on designing promotional material.*

Ought (not) to have

- *Ought to have* + past participle and *ought not (oughtn't) to have* + past participle is used in exactly the same way, but is much less frequent.

    *You **ought to have found out** much more about your target customers.*
    *You **oughtn't to have started** the project without gaining some management skills.*

- The continuous form is *ought to have + been + -ing* and the negative is *ought not (oughtn't) to have + been + -ing*.

    *You **ought to have been analysing** market trends more carefully.*

Other uses

- These forms are also used more generally to talk about desirable things that didn't happen, or undesirable things that did.

    *You **should have been making** a profit by now.*
    *You **shouldn't have had** such bad luck.*

Could have / couldn't have

- You use *could have* + past participle to talk about an opportunity that someone missed.

    *The government **could have consulted** nurses about the National Health Service IT project.*
    *They **could have addressed** the concerns of family doctors, too.*

- You use *could not (couldn't) have* + past participle to say that it was not possible for someone to do something.

    *The government **couldn't have known** that the cost of the scheme would rise to £20 billion.*

Practice

Fill in the gaps with *should, should not, ought, ought not* or *could*.

1 The NHS project _____ have been a great success.
2 They _____ to have investigated the funding more carefully.
3 The money already spent _____ have been used to run ten hospitals for a year.
4 Computer systems in 80 hospitals _____ to have crashed.
5 Far more research _____ have been done before the project started.
6 They _____ have put patient safety and public health at risk.

UNIT 16 Second conditional

Form

- To form the **second conditional**, you typically use the past simple in the *if* clause and *would* + infinitive in the main clause. The clauses can come in either order.

  *If biographical films **were** more profitable here, there **would be** many more of them.*
  *The industry **would prosper** if more people **invested** in it.*
  *If we **didn't censor** films so strictly (negative), more foreign films **would be shown** here.*
  (passive)

- In the *if* clause, *were* is often used instead of *was*, especially after *I*, and especially in the clause *if I were you*, used for giving advice.

  ***If I were you**, I'**d go** to see the film 'The Weeping Camel'.*

- You can also use *might* and *could* in the main clause, to talk about possibility or ability.

  *If we **managed** to ban pirated DVDs, the film industry **might make** more money.*
  *If you **had** good scriptwriters, **could** you **produce** better films?*

- You can also use the **past continuous** in the main clause.

  *If I **was / were working** in the film industry, I **would like** to direct.*

- Often you use a main clause on its own. The *if* clause is understood – here it is something like, *if I could make decisions about the country's film industry*.

  *I'**d build** a lot more cinemas. I'**d modernise** them and **make** them smarter and more comfortable. I'**d relax** the censorship laws.*

- You use *even if* to emphasise that one situation would have no effect on another.

  ***Even if** they **cut** the budget, we'**d go on** making the film.*

- You can use *if* without a verb in some expressions such as *if possible* and *if necessary*.

  ***If possible**, we'**d use** our own actors rather than big international stars.*

Use

You use the second conditional to talk about an imaginary present or future situation, and its consequences.

Practice

Complete the sentences using the verbs in the box. Change the form or add *would* as necessary.

watch	advertise	be	start	fail	produce

1 If I _____ a film promoter, I would plan my campaign carefully.
2 I _____ by identifying my target audience.
3 I _____ the film several times and list its main selling points.
4 If I _____ a good trailer, it would create a 'want-to-see' reaction in an audience.
5 If possible, I _____ the film online as well.
6 If the film _____ at the box office, a lot of people would lose their money.

ANSWER KEY

UNIT 1 Comparisons

1 Nothing is more satisfying than owning and running your own business.
2 Self-employed people often work far longer hours than people in offices.
3 Working from home may be the best option / a better option for people with school-age children.
4 Some of the most successful people in business started with nothing.
5 Nowadays there is a demand for more flexible hours.

UNIT 3 First conditional

1c 2f 3a 4e 5d 6b

UNIT 4 Past simple and present perfect

1 has taken
2 have extended
3 were given
4 have been drafted
5 have not come
6 installed

UNIT 5 Adjectives and nouns

1 entrepreneur
2 existing
3 profit
4 willing
5 personal
6 opportunity
7 optimistic
8 culture
9 essential

UNIT 6 The future

1 What changes is the LifeStraw® going to make to health in developing countries?
2 The LifeStraw® could prevent the spread of diseases that are carried by water.
3 Each straw will provide a year's supply of pure drinking water.
4 It won't use electricity and it will never need any spare parts / It will never need any spare parts and it won't use electricity.
5 As well as killing bacteria, it will improve the taste of the water.
6 Critics have said that poorer people may not be able to afford it.

UNIT 7 Passives

1 Stock exchanges can be found in most major capitals of the world.
2 Their debt will probably be written off next month.
3 At that time price fixing was considered a civil offence.
4 They have not yet been notified of the deal by the Italian authorities.
5 A takeover bid from a private equity firm was announced yesterday.
6 The Bank of England is now believed to be looking into complaints of insider dealing.

UNIT 8 Past perfect and past simple

1 made
2 changed
3 worked
4 had just developed
5 called
6 had beaten
7 had introduced
8 got

UNIT 9 Count and uncount nouns

1 consumers
2 season
3 market
4 campaigns
5 responsibility
6 money
7 days
8 childhood

UNIT 10 Prefixes

1 unreliable
2 irrational
3 untruthful
4 disorganised
5 inconsiderate
6 unqualified
7 incompetent
8 unemployable

UNIT 11 Infinitives and -ing forms

1 to submit
2 discussing
3 to remain
4 to buy
5 to defer
6 causing
7 to think
8 selling

UNIT 12 Present perfect simple and continuous

1 has known
2 has been happening
3 have appeared
4 has / been reading
5 have been hoping
6 has seemed

UNIT 14 Compounds

1b 2g 3h 4e 5f 6c 7d 8a

UNIT 15 Speculating about the past

1 should / could
2 ought
3 could
4 ought not
5 should / could
6 should not

UNIT 16 Second conditional

1 were
2 would start
3 would watch
4 produced
5 would advertise
6 failed

GLOSSARY

accounts *n* **1** the company department which keeps records of the money that the company spends and receives **2** an official record of all the money that a company has spent and received

adapt *v* to change something to make it more suitable for a different use

advertising *n* the business of trying to persuade people to buy particular products or services

advise *v* to tell someone what you think would be the best thing to do in a situation

agenda *n* a list of things that people will discuss at a meeting

appraisal *n* a meeting between an employee and a manager to discuss how well the employee is doing their job, **appraise** *v*, **appraisee** *n* the person who is being appraised, **appraiser** *n* the manager who appraises someone

average *n* an amount which is considered to be standard or usual

bankrupt *adj* if a company goes bankrupt, it officially admits that it has no money and cannot pay what it owes

benefits *n* advantages or extra money that an employee receives in addition to their salary

board *n* the group of people who are responsible for controlling and organising a company

boardroom *n* a room where the group of people who control a company hold meetings

bonus *n* extra money paid to an employee in addition to their usual salary

boss *n* (informal) a manager or someone who is in charge of other employees

bottom-up *adj* progressing from the lower ranks of a company through to higher and more important levels

brainstorming *n* a way of developing new ideas for a future activity by quickly making lots of suggestions before considering the best ones more carefully, **brainstorm** *v*

branch *n* part of a business or organisation located in a different area

brand *n* a recognised name for a product made by one particular company

breadwinner *n* the person who earns the money needed to support their family

break into *phrasal v* to become involved in a type of business activity, especially one that is usually difficult to enter

budget *n* **1** a plan to show how much money a company will need or be able to spend and how much it will earn **2** the amount of money a company or organisation has to spend on something

bureaucratic *adj* involving a lot of official rules and processes and people who are employed to make sure they are followed

business *n* the activity of buying and selling products or services, or a particular company that does this

business angel *n* an individual who invests in a new company

business environment *n* the situations, places, or conditions relating to business

campaign *n* a planned group of business activities which are intended to achieve something, especially activities that try to persuade people to buy a product or service

capacity *n* the total amount of goods that a company can produce or the amount of work that it can do

CEO (also **managing director**) *n* chief executive officer: the person with the most senior position in a company who has overall responsibility for managing the company

chain *n* a group of businesses, especially restaurants, hotels or shops, which all belong to the same company

chairperson *n* the person who is in charge of a meeting

channel *n* a way of communicating information or getting something done

check *v* to examine something in order to make sure that it is correct

clarify *v* to make something clearer and easier to understand by giving more details or a simpler explanation

client *n* a person who pays a company for products or services; a customer

climb the ladder *idiom* to progress through a series of increasingly important jobs within a profession

colleague *n* a person who works for the same company as you

collectivist culture *n* an approach to work which focuses on a group of people working together and supporting each other

commercial sector *n* an area of business activity which involves buying and selling products or services

commitment *n* determination to work hard at something because you believe in it

communication *n* the act or process of giving information to someone

commute *v* to travel regularly between work and home

company culture *n* the set of ideas, beliefs and practices belonging to a particular company

compensation *n* **1** something a person gets which makes them feel better about a difficult situation **2** an amount of money that a person receives because they have been injured or something has been damaged

competitor *n* a company that sells the same products or services as another company

confirm *v* to tell someone that something will definitely happen in the way that has been arranged

cons *n* reasons for not doing something; disadvantages

consult *v* to discuss something with someone before making a decision

consultant *n* an expert or professional person who gives advice on a particular subject

contract *n* a formal agreement between two different people or businesses, or a legal document which explains this agreement

corporate culture *n* the set of ideas, beliefs and practices belonging to a large company

cost-effective *adj* giving a good profit or advantage in relation to the amount of money spent

creativity *n* the ability to develop new and original ideas

criterion *n* a standard used for judging or making a decision about something

cross-functional team *n* a team of people with different skills who work together towards the same aim

culture *n* the set of ideas, beliefs and ways of behaving of a particular group of people

customer *n* a person or organisation that buys products or services from a company

decentralisation *n* the process of moving control of an organisation from a single place to several smaller or more local places

decrease *v* to become less, or to make something become less

degree *n* a course of study at a college or university, or the qualification given to a student who completes this

delegate *n* a person who is chosen to represent an organisation at a meeting or conference

delivery *n* **1** the process of bringing goods or letters to a place **2** goods or letters brought to a place

demand *n* the amount of products or services that people want to buy from a company

department *n* a part of a company which deals with a particular type of work

develop *v* to create a new product or service

discuss *v* to talk about something with another person and tell them about your ideas and opinions

disposable income *n* the amount of money left to spend after all bills have been paid

distribution *n* the process of supplying products or services to different shops, companies or other organisations

distributor *n* a company or person that supplies products or services to different shops, companies or other organisations

employ *v* if a person or company employs someone, they pay that person to work for them

employee *n* someone who is paid to work for a person or company

encouragement *n* actions or words that make a person feel good and give them confidence

entrepreneur *n* a person who starts their own business, **entrepreneurship** *n*

EU *n* European Union: an organisation of European countries whose aim is to improve economic, political and social links between its members

evaluate *v* to think carefully about someone or something and decide how good they are

exceed *v* to be more than a particular amount

expand *v* if a company expands, it grows by moving into new areas and selling more products or services.

expansion *n* the process of making a company grow by moving into new areas and selling more products or services

fall *v* to become lower in level, amount or value

feedback *n* comments about how well or badly a person has done something

finance *n* the department that decides how money is spent or invested

financial advice *n* suggestions about how a person or company should spend or invest their money

flexitime *n* a system of working in which employees must work a fixed number of hours in a week or month, but can choose when they start or finish work each day

float *v* to sell a company's shares on the stock exchange

forecast *n* a statement about what is likely to happen in the future

foresee *v* to expect or know that something will happen in the future

gender politics *n* ideas, activities and relationships which relate to the fact of being male or female

general manager *n* a manager at the highest level in a company

go down *phrasal v* to become lower in level or amount

go up *phrasal v* to become higher in level or amount

graph *n* a picture which uses lines or curves to show the relationship between changing measurements or numbers

gross *adj* a gross amount of money is the total amount before costs or taxes have been taken away

headquarters *n* the main offices of a company

hierarchical *adj* a hierarchical organisation is one in which people or things are arranged in order of importance

high power distance culture *n* a set of ideas, beliefs and practices with a strong emphasis on status and importance

high-context culture *n* a culture where communication is less explicit and being direct is seen as rude

HR *n* human resources: a company department that is responsible for employing and training people

imagination *n* the ability to think of clever and original ideas

incentive *n* something that encourages a person to do something or work harder

in-company *adj* within the offices of a company

increase *v* to become larger, or to make something become larger

individualist culture *n* an approach to work which focuses on people working independently as individuals

industrial sector *n* an area of business activity which involves producing goods for sale

industry *n* **1** the people and activities involved in a particular type of business **2** the companies and activities involved in the production of goods for sale

influence *n* **1** the power to affect how someone behaves or how a situation develops **2** someone or something that has an effect on another person or thing

initiative *n* the ability to decide what to do without being told

interview *n* a meeting in which someone asks another person questions to see if they would be suitable for a job

invention *n* something that someone has created or designed for the first time, or the process of creating or designing something for the first time

invest *v* to put money into a business in order to make a profit

investment *n* the money that someone puts into a business in order to make a profit, or the act of doing this

investor *n* a person or organisation who puts money into a business in order to make a profit

invoice *n* a document which describes the products or services that someone has bought and must pay for

IPO *n* initial public offering: when a company's shares are sold to the public for the first time

IT *n* information technology: the use of computers and electronic systems for storing and sending information

joint venture *n* an agreement between two companies to work together on something

key *adj* very important; crucial

launch *v* to start a new activity or introduce a new product or service, **launch** *n*

leadership *n* **1** the position of being in charge of an organisation **2** the qualities and skills of a leader

legislation *n* a law or set of laws

level off (also **level out**) *phrasal v* If an amount or rate levels off, it stops becoming more or less and remains the same

licence *n* an official document that gives someone permission to do or use something, **license** *v* to give someone official permission to do or use something

licensing agreement *n* an official agreement giving someone permission to produce and sell a particular product

logistics *n* the practical arrangements needed to successfully organise something, especially if this involves moving products or equipment

logo *n* a symbol or design used by a company to advertise its products

low power distance culture *n* a set of ideas, beliefs and practices with a strong emphasis on equality and respect for people at all levels

low-context culture n a culture where communication is explicit and being direct is appreciated

low-point n the lowest level or amount

management n 1 the control and organisation of a company 2 the group of people who control and organise a company

manager n a person whose job is to control and organise a company, **manage** v

managing director (also **CEO**) n the person with the most senior position in a company who has overall responsibility for managing the company

manufacture v to make products in a factory, **manufacturer** n

manufacturing n the business of making products in a factory

marketing n the methods a company uses to encourage people to buy its products, or the company department that is responsible for this

master's degree n a higher university qualification that a student gets if they study for one or two years after their first degree

maternity leave n time off given to a woman before and after the birth of her baby

mid-size company n a company that is average in size

minutes n an official written record of what is said and decided during a meeting, **take the minutes** v phr to write an official record of what is said and decided during a meeting

mission n an important aim for a person or company

monochronic culture n a structured approach to time with a strong emphasis on punctuality and good organisation at work

morale n the amount of confidence and enthusiasm a person or group of people feel about their situation at a particular time

motivation n a feeling of enthusiasm and commitment that makes a person determined to do something

negotiate v 1 to reach an agreement by discussing something in a formal way 2 to successfully deal with something difficult

on-site adj within or among the buildings occupied by a company

organisational culture n the set of ideas, beliefs and practices belonging to a particular organisation

output n the amount of something produced by a person or company

overtime n extra time that someone works after their usual working hours

patent n an official document that gives a person or company the exclusive legal right to make or sell a product for a particular period of time, **patent** v

paternity leave n time off given to a man after the birth of his child

peak n the time when something is at its highest amount or level, **peak** v to reach the highest amount or level

pension n money that is paid regularly by the government or a company to a person who has stopped working because they are old or ill, **pensioner** n someone who receives a pension

performance n 1 how successful a person or company is 2 the speed and effectiveness of a machine or vehicle

perk n an extra payment or benefit that a person gets as part of their job

pitch n a presentation that a person gives in order to persuade someone to buy something

plant n a large factory

plateau n the period of time when an amount or level stays the same

policy n a set of plans or actions agreed by a company or organisation

polychronic culture n an unstructured approach to time where more than one work task is dealt with at a time, and where timing is less important

position v 1 to make people think of a product in a particular way 2 to put something in a particular place

potential n 1 the possibility of developing or achieving something in the future 2 abilities that may develop so that someone is successful in a particular job

PR n public relations: 1 the relationship between an organisation and the public 2 the activity of creating a positive opinion among people about a company or product

pre-tax adj before taxes are taken out

proceeds n the money earned from an activity or event

production n the process of making products for sale, or the company department that is responsible for this

profit n money that a company makes by selling products or services and that is left after it has paid all its business costs and taxes

profit-sharing n a system in which all the employees of a company get a share in the profits

promote v 1 to give someone a more important job in a company 2 to help or encourage something to develop

proposal n a suggestion or plan

pros n reasons for doing something; advantages

prototype n the first model or example of a new product that can be copied or developed in the future

public sector n the industries and services, such as hospitals and schools, that are supported by taxes and controlled by the government

purchasing n the process of buying something, or the company department that is responsible for this

quantity n the amount or number of something

R & D n research and development: the department in a company that is responsible for developing new ideas and products

rank v to put someone or something in a position according to their importance or level of success, **rank** n someone's job or position in an organisation

ratio n the relationship between two things expressed in numbers or amounts

reach v to get to a particular level or amount

redundant adj not working because you are no longer needed in your job, **make someone redundant** v phr to tell someone that they must leave their job because they are no longer needed, **redundancy** n

reinvest v to give money that you have made in business to another company or business because you hope to get further profit

remain steady v to stay at the same level or amount

researcher n a person whose job is to do research

responsibility n something that you have to do, and are in charge of, because it is part of your job

results n success achieved by the efforts or actions of a person or organisation

retirement n the period of someone's life after they have stopped working

return on investment n profit on money that has been invested

revenue n money received from business activities

reward v to give something good to someone because they have worked hard, **reward** n

v to increase in level or amount

risk *n* the possibility that something bad might happen

salary *n* a fixed amount of money that someone receives each month or year from their employer

sales *n* **1** the activity of trying to sell products or services, or the company department that is responsible for this **2** the total number of things that a company sells within a particular period of time **3** the money a company earns by selling things

satisfaction *n* a pleasant feeling someone gets when they have done something well or when they get what they wanted

schedule *v* to plan that something will happen or be done at a particular time, **schedule** *n* a plan that shows events and activities and the time they will happen or be done

segment *n* one of the parts that something can be divided into

self-starter *n* a person who works effectively without needing to be told what to do

shares *n* the equal parts that the value of a company is divided into, and which can be bought as a way of investing money

shortlist (also **short list**) *n* a list of people who could be suitable for a job, chosen from a larger group of people, **shortlist** (also **short list**) *v* to put someone on a shortlist, **shortlisted** *adj*

silo mentality *n* the breakdown of communication and understanding between different departments

skill *n* the ability to do a job or activity well

slogan *n* a short phrase used to advertise something

soar *v* to increase to a high level very quickly

social democracy *n* the belief that society should change from capitalism to socialism in a gradual, peaceful way

social security system *n* a system by which the government regularly pays money to people who are old, ill or not working

society *n* a large group of people living together in an organised community, with laws and traditions controlling how they behave

software *n* the programmes used by computers for doing particular activities

stable *adj* not likely to change

staff turnover *n* the rate at which employees leave a company and new employees replace them

stagnant *adj* not growing or developing

stake *n* the part of a business that someone owns because they have invested money in it

start-up *n* **1** the process of starting a business **2** a small business that has recently been started

stock exchange also **stock market** *n* **1** the place where people buy and sell shares in a company **2** the activities related to buying and selling shares in a company **3** the value of shares being bought and sold

strapline *n* **1** a sub-heading in a piece of printed text, especially in a newspaper or magazine article **2** a short phrase which is associated with a brand name and used for advertising

strategic *adj* carefully planned in order to achieve a particular business aim

stressed *adj* worried

supervision *n* the process or activity of being in charge of someone and making sure that they do their job correctly

supplier *n* a company or organisation that supplies a product or service

survey *n* an examination of opinions or behaviour made by asking people questions

take over *phrasal v* to take control of something, **takeover** *n* a situation in which one company takes control of another company by buying the majority of its shares

target *n* something that a person intends to achieve

target *v* to try to persuade or influence a particular group of people, especially through advertising

tax *n* an amount of money that people have to pay to the government from what they earn, which is used to provide public services

team-building session *n* an organised activity which helps a group of people to work more effectively as a team

time off *n* time during the working week when you are not required to work

top-down *adj* controlled by the people at the highest level in a company or organisation

top-heavy *adj* a top-heavy company or organisation has a lot of employees at higher levels and not enough at lower levels

top-of-the-range *adj* a top-of-the-range product is the best and most expensive product from a group of products of the same type

trade *n* **1** the buying and selling of goods and services **2** a particular area of business

trade fair (US also **trade show**) *n* a large event at which companies display and sell their products

training *n* the process of learning the skills needed to do a particular job

trend *n* a general change or development in the way that people behave

value *n* **1** how useful or important something is **2** the amount of money that something could be sold for

value *v* to consider someone or something to be important, **valued** *adj*

venture capitalist *n* someone who invests money in a new business that may or may not be successful, **venture capital** *n* the money invested in a new business that may or may not be successful

word of mouth *n* informal communication consisting of spoken comments that people make to each other

work environment *n* the situation and physical conditions that people work in, and how these affect the way they feel

work–life balance *n* the amount of time a person spends working compared to the amount of time they spend relaxing and doing other things

Credits

The publishers would like to thank the following sources for permission to reproduce their copyright protected texts:

Page 04: Happiness at Work. The author and publisher would like to thank City & Guilds for permission to reprint The Happiness League Index. The City and Guilds of London Institute accepts no liability for the contents of this book. Please note that minor simplifications in language have been made in the tips. Copyright © City & Guilds 2005. **Page 12: SAS Institutes** from "Sanity Inc." by Charles Fishman from Fast Company, issue 21, page 84, January 1999. Copyright © 2005 Mansueto Ventures LLC. All rights reserved. Fast Company, 375 Lexington Avenue, New York, NY 10017; **Page 16:** Graph taken from: http://www.statistics.gov.uk/. Copyright © Office for National Statistics, material published under click-use licence. **Page 19:** "Employers and Work-life Balance" from www.employersforwork-lifebalance.org.uk. Copyright © THE WORK FOUNDATION 2006; **Page 26: Successful Entrepreneur** from "Yo! Man who's done his time", by Sarah Ryle. Copyright © Guardian Newspapers Limited 2005; **Page 38: Inventions** taken from "Background" on http://www.mandyhaberman.com. Copyright © Mandy Haberman 2006; **Page 41: Google** from "How google grows...and grows...and grows", by Keith H. Hammonds from Fast Company, issue 69, page 74, April 2003. Copyright © 2005 Mansueto Ventures LLC. All rights reserved. Fast Company, 375 Lexington Avenue, New York, NY 10017; **Page 48: Marketing Report** from "Leveraging 'pester-power' is no way to build a brand, according to Yankelovich Youth Study", by Danielle Runmore / Keenan Hughes. Copyright © Danielle Runmore / Keenan Hughes 2005; **Page 51: Semco** from "Guts! Companies that blow doors off business-as-usual", by Drs Kevin and Jackie Freiberg. Copyright © Kevin and Jackie Freiberg 2004. Used by permission of Doubleday, a division of Random House, Inc; **Page 55:** "Five Fundamental Rules" from www.cpwplc.com. Copyright © THE CARPHONE WAREHOUSE 2006; **Page 59: Work and Play** adapted from "Chinese Business Etiquette and Culture", by Kevin Bucknall, Boson Books Raleigh, NC. Copyright © Kevin Bucknall 2002. ISBN 0917990439, www.bosonbooks.com; **Page 60: The Grey Market,** extracts from "Ad nausea hits the grey market", by James Arnold. Source: http://bbcnews.com/business 2004; **Page 74: Pelle the conqueror** from "The Success of Metro", by Cosima Marriner. Copyright © Guardian Newspapers Limited 2005; **Page 82: The Indian Film Industry** from "Bollywood takes lessons in going global", by Khozem Merchant. Copyright © The Financial Times Ltd. 2004; **Page 160: LifeStraw®.** Copyright © Vestergaard Frandsen S.A, Switzerland 2006.

Photos sourced by Pictureresearch.co.uk

Illustrations by Mark Duffin p 63

The publishers would like to thank the following sources for permission to reproduce their copyright protected photographs:

AKG p 46ct; **Alamy** pp 22bl (Motoring Picture Library), 29cl, 29cr (foodfolio), 35t (Sean David Baylis), 48b (plainpicture GmbH & Co. KG), 49 (Zak Waters), 55b (uk retail Alan King), 56br (Nigel Hicks), 70a (Mark Scheuern), 70b (Motoring Picture Library), 70c (David R. Frazier Photolibrary, Inc.), 100b (Gondwana Photo Art); **Anthony Blake Photo Library** p 17r (Dominic Dibbs); **Corbis** pp 8b (Jagadeesh/Reuters), 9 (Catherine Karnow), 15b (Walter Hodges), 16b (Larry Williams/zefa), 19c (Natalie Fobes), 35b (TWPhoto), 46t (Bettmann), 46c (Hulton-Deutsch Collection), 50, 54, 58, 62 (Jim Craigmyle), 51r (James Leynse), 56bc (Jean-Philippe Arles/Reuters), 87cr (Gene Blevins/LA Daily News), 87b (Bob Krist), 87t (Rolf Bruderer), 89 (Reuters), 97 (Martin Harvey); **Fairfaxphotos** pp 70t, 74t, 78t, 82t ,86t, 88 (Rob Homer); **Getty Images** pp 4tr, 8t, 12t, 16t, 20t, 22t (ColorBlind Images), 4bl (Daniel Bosler), 4br (Marc Romanelli), 6b (Britt Erlanson), 7c (J W Burkey), 18b (Eric Audras/PhotoAlto), 23 (John Turner), 24 (James Porter Photography), 28 (Ghislain & Marie David de Lossy), 30b (Peter Ginter), 33b (Shannon Fagan), 34b (Rob Van Pellen), 36, 40 (Seizo Terasaki), 37b (Justin Pumfrey), 43tr (Rob Brimson), 43b (Joanna McCarthy), 43tl (Gulfimages), 44b (Mike Powell), 46b (Steve Mercer), 48t , 52t, 56t, 60t, 64tr, 66t (Romilly Lockyer), 52b (Trinette Reed), 56bl (Harald Sund), 57r (David McLain), 59b (David Harrison), 60b (Zigy Kaluzny), 64b (Bryn Lennon), 67 (Serge Krouglikoff), 69 (Reza Estakhrian), 71, 78b (AFP), 86br (Clarissa Leahy), 86bl (Mitch Kezar), 92, 94, 96, 98, 100t (BLOOMimage), 100c (Chabruken); **Hollandse Hoogte** p 41b; **Mandy Habermann** p 38b (www.anywayup.com); **Motoring Picture Library** pp 70d, 70e; **Photos.com** p 11b; **Punchstock** pp 6t, 10t (George Doyle), 7t, 11t, 15t, 19l, 29t, 33t, 37t, 41t, 51l, 55t, 59t, 63t, 73, 77, 81t, 85 (Photodisc), 7b (Digital Vision/Panoramic images), 10b (Stuart O'Sullivan), 12cl (John Cumming/Digital Vision), 12b (Studio Peter Frank/Digital Vision), 12cr (Andersen Ross/Digital Vision), 14 (Eric Audras/PhotoAlto), 16br, 32 (Royalty Free/Corbis), 17c (Christoph Wilhelm/Photodisc), 17l, 101 (Nick Clements/ Photodisc), 18t, 26t, 30t, 34t, 38t, 42t, 44t, 72, 76 (Digital Vision), 20b (Eric Audras/PhotoAlto), 42b (Harry Penton/Digital Vision), 57c (Peter Adams/Digital Vision), 61 (Rob Melnychuk/ Digital Vision), 73 (Blend Images/Colin Anderson), 80,84 (Flying Colours Ltd/Digital Vision), 81b (image100), 86c (Vincent Besnault/ Photodisc), 90 (Paul Edmondson/Photodisc); **Rex Features** pp 26cr (Rex), 26cl (Richard Young), 74b (Jonathan Player); **Science and Society Picture Library** p 46cb (Bletchley Park Trust); **Still Pictures** p 19r (Jorgen Schytte); **The Kobal Collection** pp 82b (DAMFX), 83 (Pathe Pictures Ltd); **Topfoto** p 66b (John Balean/Topham Picturepoint)

THOMSON

HEINLE

Best Practice Intermediate Coursebook
Bill Mascull / Jeremy Comfort

Publisher: *Christopher Wenger*
Director of Content Development: *Anita Raducanu*
Director of Product Marketing: *Amy Mabley*
ELT Editorial Manager: *Bryan Fletcher*
Associate Development Editor: *Sarah O'Driscoll*
Production Editor: *Maeve Healy*
Manufacturing Buyer: *Maeve Healy*
Compositor: *Oxford Designers & Illustrators*

Project Manager: *Howard Middle/HM ELT Services*
Development Editor: *Antoinette Meehan*
Contributing Writers: *Gill Francis, Kerry Maxwell*
Photo Researcher: *Suzanne Williams/PictureResearch.co.uk*
Illustrator: *Mark Duffin*
Text Designer: *Oxford Designers & Illustrators*
Cover Designer: *Thomas Manss & Compnay*
Printer: *Canale*

Cover Image: *© Getty Images*

For more information contact Thomson Learning, High
Holborn House, 50/51 Bedford Row, London WC1R 4LR
United Kingdom or Thomson Heinle, 25 Thomson Place,
Boston, Massachusetts 02210 USA. You can visit our web
site at elt.thomson.com

For permission to use material from this text or product,
submit a request online at www.thomsonrights.com

Any additional questions about permissions can be
submitted by email to thomsonrights@thomson.com

ISBN 10: 1-4130-2185-9
ISBN 13: 978-1-4130-2185-1

The publishers and authors are grateful to the following teachers
for their advice during the development of the book:
Silvija Andernovics (Latvia), Martin Goosey (Korea), Manuel
Hidalgo Iglesias (Mexico), Blanka Frydrychova Klimova (Czech
Republic), Angela Lloyd (Germany), Kathryn McNicoll (United
Kingdom), Luisa Panichi (Italy), Tony Penston (Ireland), Andy
Roberts (Switzerland), Linda Marie Salamin (Switzerland), Julio
Valladares (Peru), Julia Waldner (Germany)